ROGERS®

GOLDEN RULES FOR BETTER TASTE

Golden Rules For Better Taste

Published in Canada in 1996 by
Rogers Sugar Ltd.
P.O. Box 2150
Vancouver, B.C.
V6B 3V2

Produced by Creative Solutions Inc.
Distributed by Gordon Soules Book Publishers Ltd.
1354 B Marine Drive
West Vancouver, B.C.
V7T 1B5
Tel: (604) 922-6588 or 688-5466 or 688-5467
Fax: (604) 688-5442
Email: books@gordon.soules.com

Printed in Canada

Canadian Cataloguing in Publication Data
Rogers Golden Rules for Better Taste

Includes bibliographical references and index.
ISBN 0-9681081-0-5

1. Cookery. I. Kibble, Roger W. II. Kirby, Rachel Jane. III. Hennessy, Amy, IV. Rogers Sugar Ltd.
V. Title: Golden rules for better taste
TX714.R63 1996 641.5 C96-910674-2

Design & Production: Creative Solutions Inc., Roger Kibble
Food Editors: Rachel Kirby, Amy Hennessy, Donna Wuest, Aimee Kibble, Cristina Carneiro
Art Directors: Peter Winnett & Roger Mansel
Photography: Colin Goldie, Hans Sipma, Manfred Weber
Copy Editing: West Coast Editorial Associates
Pre Press: Chromatech Inc.
Printing: Teldon Press
Rogers Sugar Ltd.: Robert Copeland, Sandra Dolhaine

For Peter

"Life is a banquet."

Auntie Mame
Rosalind Russell, 1908-1976

ROGERS®

GOLDEN RULES FOR BETTER TASTE

ROGERS Sugar

ROGERS SUGAR LTD.
VANCOUVER TABER WINNIPEG

CONTENTS

"Tell me what you eat,
and I will tell you who you are."

The Physiology of Taste
Anthelme Brillat-Savarin, 1755-1826

INTRODUCTION

"I feel a recipe is only a theme, which an intelligent cook can play each time with a variation."

Madame Benoit

All About Taste

When you get right down to it, food is all about taste - great taste. But too often we end up with dishes that are soon forgotten. In this book, Rogers Sugar presents many of the golden rules of cooking that help to make all the difference.

Anybody can prepare really memorable food. A magnificent meal stems from more than simply following a recipe. It is often a matter of adding the right sugars, herbs, pepper or salt. But taste is also determined by the way ingredients are selected and prepared, how they interact, how they are mixed and how they are cooked.

Hold onto your hat and dive in! You can start anywhere, and we have cross-referenced many of the recipes and cooking hints so you can jump back and forth throughout the book. Our comments and suggestions are simple but timeless. They work hand in hand with any recipe, and give you a springboard for your own experimenting.

Often, simple is best. Some fresh herbs and a grind of pepper, a drizzle of olive oil, an easy marinade: these basic additions can transform a dish. In fact, nearly anything that is in your kitchen can be made into a delicious meal - it is just a matter of taking everyday ingredients and adding a little creative savvy.

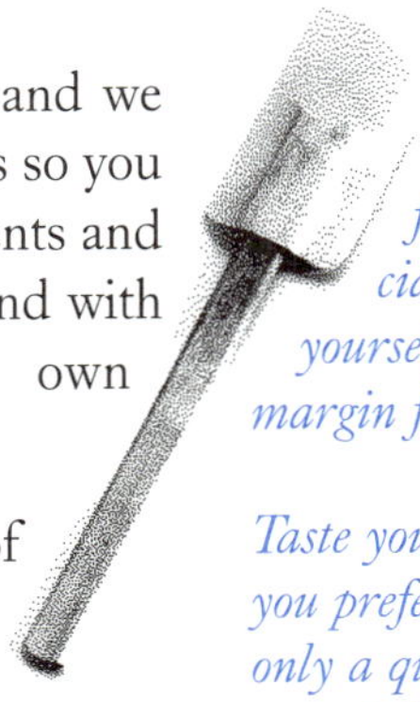

Experiment with different ingredients. If you come up with a combination of flavours that works especially well together, scribble yourself a reminder in the margin for next time.

Taste your cooking at every stage. If you prefer the flavour of a dish with only a quarter of the cream, then stop right there.

Recipes for Everyone

With over 70 different recipes, this book has something for everyone. Rogers has taken classic, much loved dishes and developed them without shortcuts or compromises. The rationale wasn't difficult: we simply decided to show how to get the best taste possible. Whether it is for French Onion Soup or an elegant Christmas cake, each recipe has clear, concise instructions so you can't go wrong.

As Good As It Can Be

We want your cooking to taste as good as it can possibly be. That's why we've packed the book with descriptions of the various sugars, herbs and spices, and explanations on how to use them in your cooking. There is also fascinating food trivia, and sources for free recipes, advice and samples.

At the end of each section you'll find reviews of some recommended cookbooks. We have found them all to be clear and informative with plenty of good recipes.

Food should be a constant treat for your taste buds. Whether it is a plate of delicious creamy pasta, a juicy roast chicken with the tantalizing aroma of herbs and garlic, or even a perfectly boiled egg, every meal deserves to become a wonderful memory. We at Rogers Sugar hope that *Rogers Golden Rules for Better Taste* is a book that will help you make some wonderful memories.

Bon Appetit!

"Life is a series of great meals interrupted by euphoria and disappointment."

Anonymous

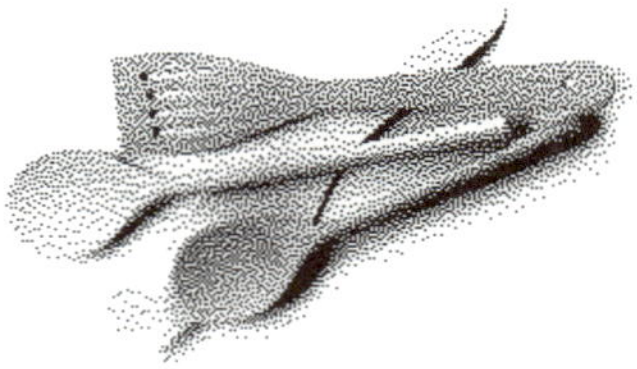

The recipes in *Rogers Golden Rules for Better Taste* are some of the best you will find. Simple, easy to follow and absolutely delicious. However, it is all personal opinion - if you think you have a better version, send it to us. You may just discover it in the pages of the next Rogers cookbook!

Our address is:

ROGERS SUGAR LTD.
P.O. Box 2150
Vancouver, B.C.
Canada V6B 3V2

The name of the oldest known cookbook, written in 350 B.C. by Archestratus, a Greek, survives to this day. It was entitled *Gastrology*, and you still see many cookbooks with "gastronomy" or "gastronomique" on the title page.

WEIGHTS & MEASURES

"To be a good cook means the economy of great-grandmothers and the science of modern chemists. It means English thoroughness, French art and Arabian hospitality."

John Ruskin, 1819-1900

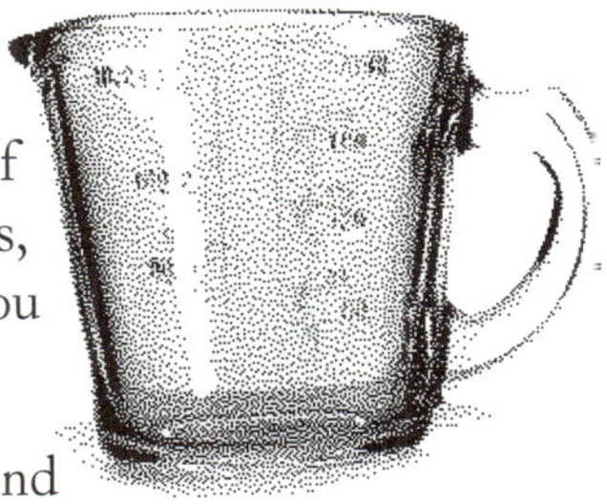

Isn't it infuriating when you have a recipe that has metric measurements but your kitchen scales are in ounces and pounds? Or you have plenty of spoons but not a cup to be found? To help baffled cooks, we have put together an easy-to-use guide to help you convert weights, measures and oven temperatures.

Depending on what cookbook you read, you are bound to find different opinions when it comes to weights and measures. It's impossible to be completely accurate: a pound is actually 454 grams, but invariably you will find it rounded down to 450 grams or rounded up to 500 grams to make things simpler.

Here are some measurement tips and tricks:

- ❒ Never mix metric and imperial measures in one recipe: stick to one system or the other.
- ❒ Always be precise with your measurements and use the dull edge of a knife to level off your measuring spoons.
- ❒ Sift your flour after you have measured it, not before, unless a recipe states otherwise.
- ❒ Try to remember that a "pinch" is less than 1/8 tsp of something dry, while a "dash" is a quick shake or a sprinkle, usually of a liquid. When a dash is mentioned in a recipe, it is usually for additional flavour, so the actual amount is up to you.

If a recipe calls for 1 cup (250 ml) of cake flour, you can use 1 cup minus 2 tbsp (30 ml) of all-purpose, sifted flour instead.

Professional cooks always add herbs or spices to a dish by rubbing them between their thumb and fingers. This helps release the flavour, and makes controlling the amount easier.

❐ To measure sticky liquids such as Rogers Golden Syrup, wipe your measuring cup with oil first and the syrup will slide right out.

Abbreviations and Symbols

Before we get started, here are some common abbreviations and symbols to keep in mind:

tsp is a teaspoon; **tbsp** is a tablespoon.

oz is an ounce; **lb** is a pound.

g stands for gram; **kg** stands for kilogram.

ml stands for millilitre; **L** stands for litre.

1 tsp is **5 ml**
1 tbsp is **15 ml**
1 cup is **250 ml**

Quantity

1 tsp	=	1/3 tbsp	=	5 ml
2 tsp	=	2/3 tbsp	=	10 ml
3 tsp	=	1 tbsp	=	15 ml
6 tsp	=	2 tbsp	=	30 ml

¼ cup	=	60 ml
1/3 cup	=	80 ml
½ cup	=	125 ml
2/3 cup	=	160 ml
¾ cup	=	180 ml
1 cup	=	250 ml
1¼ cups	=	315 ml
1½ cups	=	375 ml
1¾ cups	=	440 ml
2 cups	=	500 ml

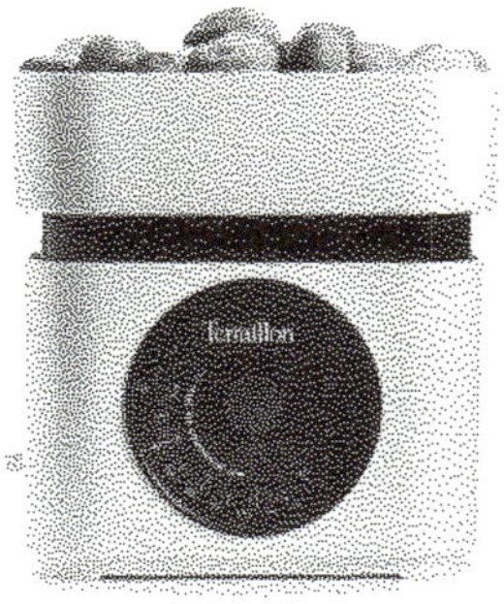

If you would rather not use a cup of heavy cream in a recipe, replace it with 7/8 cup (230 ml) of buttermilk or yogurt and 3 tbsp (45 ml) of butter.

Weight

1 oz	=	28 g	
2 oz	=	55 g	
3 oz	=	85 g	
4 oz	=	110 g	*4 oz is also ¼ lb*
5 oz	=	140 g	
6 oz	=	170 g	
7 oz	=	200 g	
8 oz	=	225 g	*8 oz is also ½ lb*
9 oz	=	250 g	*250 g is ¼ kg*
10 oz	=	280 g	
16 oz	=	450 g	*16 oz is also 1 lb*

1 oz is the same as 28 g.

1 lb is 16 oz. In metric weight, it is 454 g.

1 kg is 1,000 g. In imperial weight, it is 2.25 lbs.

If you need to thicken a sauce with 1 tbsp (15 ml) of cornstarch but you don't have any, replace it with 2 tbsp (30ml) of flour.

Temperature

Getting your oven temperature right is important when baking. Since ovens can vary as much as 25 degrees either way, it's a good idea to use an oven thermometer and to check your temperatures. If your oven temperature is too high or too low, adjust the settings accordingly.

212°F	100°C	*Water Boils*
300°F	150°C	
325°F	160°C	
350°F	180°C	*Baking*
375°F	190°C	
400°F	200°C	
425°F	215°C	
450°F	230°C	*Very Hot*
475°F	245°C	
500°F	260°C	*Broiling*

Getting Heavy

Getting Heavy

- 1 lb is 0.45 kg
- 2 lb is 0.9 kg
- 3 lb is 1.35 kg
- 4 lb is 1.80 kg
- 5 lb is 2.25 kg
- 10 lb is 4.5 kg
- 15 lb is 6.75 kg
- 20 lb is 9 kg

Rogers Golden Syrup can be substituted for honey in any recipe.

When You Have the Weight, But Need the Volume

When you look at the side of a measuring cup, don't be confused by the ounces that are marked on it - these are fluid ounces, which measure volume. You don't usually need to convert volume measurements to weight, but here are the equivalents for sugar, flour and butter. If you want to know the weight of other ingredients, *The Joy of Cooking* is a great reference book. It has 10 pages on volumes and equivalent weights!

If you don't have 1 tsp (5 ml) of baking powder, you can use 1/4 tsp (5 ml) of baking soda plus 5/8 tsp (2 ml) cream of tartar.

Measuring Sugar

Granulated sugar:	8 oz (225 g)	=	1 cup
Icing sugar:	4½ oz (125 g)	=	1 cup
Best Brown sugar:	6 oz (170 g)	=	1 cup
Syrup or molasses:	12 oz (335 g)	=	1 cup

Measuring Butter

4 oz (110 g)	=	½ cup or 1 stick
8 oz (225 g)	=	1 cup or 2 sticks
12 oz (350 g)	=	1½ cups or 3 sticks
1 lb (450 g)	=	2 cups or 4 sticks

Measuring Flour

4 oz (110 g)	=	1 cup
8 oz (225 g)	=	2 cups
12 oz (350 g)	=	3 cups
1 lb (450 g)	=	4 cups

SUGARS

"A spoonful of sugar helps the medicine go down... in the most delightful way."

Mary Poppins

Walt Disney Productions

Sugar, in one form or another, is essential for cooking. Baking wouldn't be the art it is without the unique qualities of sugar. Sugar is a vital ingredient, not only for adding sweetness and flavour, but also because it aids the chemical reactions in baking. It can slow down the setting of a cake and blend with butter to give height and lightness to baked goods.

Not many people realize the importance of sugar. Sugar is a natural preservative and a meat tenderizer. Sugar lowers the freezing point of food - without it, ice cream would freeze so solidly you couldn't eat it. Sugar helps fruit release its natural juices and pectin in jam making, and adds sparkle to vinaigrette dressings. Many of us wouldn't touch our daily bowl of cereal or cup of coffee without a sprinkle of sugar.

Candy making used to be known as "the art of sugar boiling," because the process depends on the dissolving, and re-crystallizing, of sugar. At different temperatures sugar takes on different forms. Beautiful spun sugar, cotton candy, caramel, toffee, brittle, fudge and blown sugar are just some of the magical results obtained from the heating and processing of sugars.

Spun sugar makes a truly unique decoration for desserts, and it's lots of fun to make yourself. Cook sugar syrup to roughly 312°F (155°C). Take the pan off the heat, but put it in a saucepan of hot water to keep it warm. Dip two forks into the syrup and flick them quickly back-wards and forwards over a lightly greased rolling pin. The pretty sugar strands can then be gathered up and used to decorate cakes. But work quickly - they melt after an hour!

Rogers Caramel Almonds

1 tbsp / *15 ml*	butter
3 tbsp / *45 ml*	Rogers Golden Syrup
1/3 cup / *80 ml*	Rogers Granulated Sugar
1 cup / *250 ml*	blanched almonds
¼ tsp / *1 ml*	salt

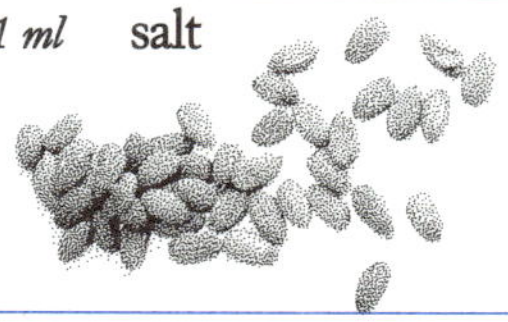

Rogers Caramel Almonds

These are fun, easy and ready to eat in 15 minutes.

COMBINE THE BUTTER, Rogers Golden Syrup and Rogers Granulated Sugar in a heavy frying pan and heat until everything has melted.

ADD THE ALMONDS and cook the mixture over a medium heat for 10 to 15 minutes, stirring constantly. When the almonds are a rich caramel colour, spread the mixture on foil and sprinkle it with the salt.

COOL THOROUGHLY and break into bite-sized pieces.

Rogers Sugar is the only Canadian producer of beet sugar. It operates beet sugar factories in Winnipeg and in Taber, Alberta. Rogers also produces cane sugar at its Vancouver refinery, while an affiliated company - Lantic Sugar - operates cane refineries in Saint John, New Brunswick and Montreal. Together, Rogers and Lantic account for roughly two-thirds of all sugar produced in Canada.

As well as being essential for cooking, sugar gives us the energy to function. In fact, by licking sugar maples in the spring, certain animals indulged in "dessert" long before we did! Fruits and vegetables contain sugars, which is why adding a pinch of granulated sugar actually enhances their existing flavours, but doesn't add sweetness.

FIVE THOUSAND YEARS OLD, BUT STILL FULL OF ENERGY

Sugars have been prized by humans since the early days of civilization. It is believed that Pacific Islanders were adding sugar to their cooking more than 5,000 years ago!

While sucrose is found in almost all plants, it occurs in the greatest concentration in sugar cane and sugar beets. For that reason, sugar cane and sugar beets are the major sources of the world's sugar supply.

Conquerors such as Alexander the Great and the Moors introduced sugar cane to the Mediterranean from India and Asia. Christopher Columbus brought sugar cane to the New World and for a time, during the 17th century, tropical America was the world's largest sugar-producing area.

In the 1800s, sugar production from beets began when Napoleonic France was cut off from its traditional Caribbean cane supplies by a British blockade. Today, France is an important producer of sugar, most of it from beets.

The World's Sugars

Roughly 70 percent of the world's sugar is produced from sugar cane, the other 30 percent from sugar beets. In Canada, approximately 15 percent of our total sugar production is from sugar beets, grown and processed right here in western Canada. The remaining 85 percent of Canadian production is from imported raw cane sugar that is then refined, packaged and marketed by the four cane sugar refineries located across the country.

Nothing is wasted in the sugar production process. Once all the sugar has been extracted from the beet, the remaining liquid molasses is sold for various uses, including yeast fermentation. The leftover protein-rich beet pulp is also used as animal feed. At tropical sugar cane mills, the residual fibre (known as bagasse) is used as fuel and to make paper.

Refining Sugar

While refined cane and beet sugars are virtually identical, the production process for each type differs. However, whether cane or beet, there are no artificial flavourings, colourings or preservatives of any kind used in the production of sugars.

At the Rogers Winnipeg and Taber factories, beets are sliced into thin strips and heated in water to extract their sugar. A three-stage crystallization process is then followed that results in the pure, granulated sugar that you buy at the store.

The process that is used to produce sugar from raw cane is quite different but has the same result. Soft sugars such as Rogers Golden Yellow, Best Brown and Demerara, as well as Rogers Golden Syrup and Rogers Pancake Syrups are all made from cane sugar.

From its Winnipeg, Taber and Vancouver plants, Rogers Sugar produces a full range of quality sugar products that are marketed throughout western Canada.

In the 13th century, sugar was so expensive that people often displayed it as a symbol of great wealth. When King Henry III visited Venice, he was treated to a banquet where the plates, knives, forks, and even the tablecloth and napkins were made from spun sugar.

Sugars in Food

Sugars are important ingredients in cooking and are in many of the things we eat. Sucrose, the kind of sugar in sugar cane and sugar beets, is a vital source of energy for humans and other animals. But there are other sugars besides sucrose that are important to our diets. These sugars are found in foods such as milk, honey and plants of all kinds. Our bodies convert these sugars in basically the same way, whatever the source, to provide the energy so we can function.

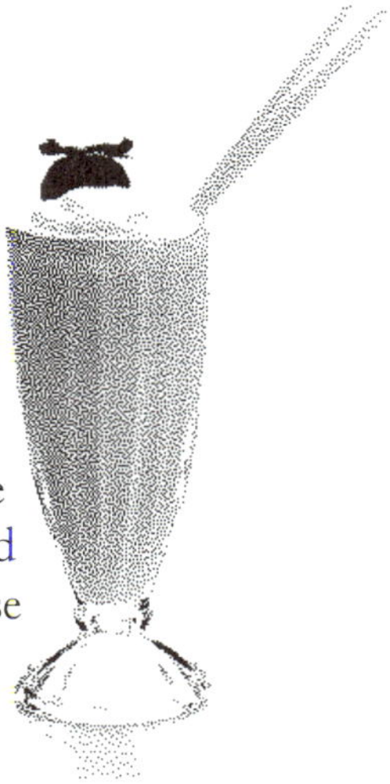

Sweetness is the first taste perceived by a newborn baby.

Sugar	Source of Sugar
sucrose	sugar cane, sugar beets, fruits
glucose	fruits, vegetables, honey
fructose	fruits, honey
maltose	barley
lactose	milk

Everyone needs the right nutrients and calories - and we all like to enjoy what we eat. Sugar is a source of pure carbohydrates. It also enables us to enjoy a wider range of foods for a more balanced diet.

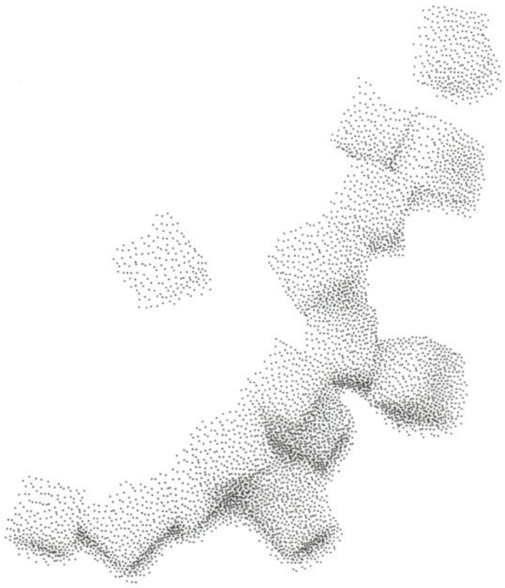

Types of Sugars

Different types of sugars enable you to experiment with new tastes and textures. There are sugars to match every baking or cooking need. Their individual properties can make a big taste - and performance - difference.

Here are descriptions of the main types of sugars available in Canada and the best ways to use them.

Sprinkle Rogers Berry Sugar over cakes and cookies before baking for a delicious decoration.

If Berry Sugar becomes lumpy, roll it in a plastic bag with a rolling pin.

GRANULATED SUGARS

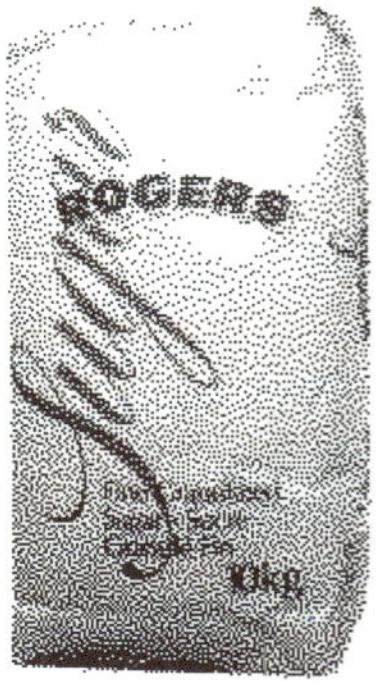

Granulated sugar is the hardest working sugar around. Besides being the usual resident of the sugar bowl, it is the sugar used most often in home cooking. When a recipe calls for "sugar," granulated sugar is what is meant. Granulated sugar is best for baking cookies and breads. It makes dough more tender and gives bread a golden brown crust.

Here are some other ways to use granulated sugar.

- A pinch of sugar gives that just-picked taste to vegetables that are past their peak. In fact, sugar makes most vegetables taste better, and it also keeps them green when they are cooked.

- Every Italian chef will tell you to add granulated sugar to tomato sauce - it produces a better flavour by balancing the natural acidity of the tomatoes.

- Mix a spoonful of sugar with water and brush it over meat before you roast it. It seals in the juices and keeps the meat moist.
- Sugar is also an important ingredient in most stir fries, as it brings out natural flavours.
- When you make jams and jellies, use oven-warmed granulated sugar. It will dissolve faster, which helps the fruit release its natural juices and helps the jam to set.
- Use 1 tbsp (15 ml) of granulated sugar when you cook diced meat. It won't add any sweetness, just a beautiful brown colour. Add the sugar to the heated fat, stir it over medium heat until the mixture browns, then add the meat.

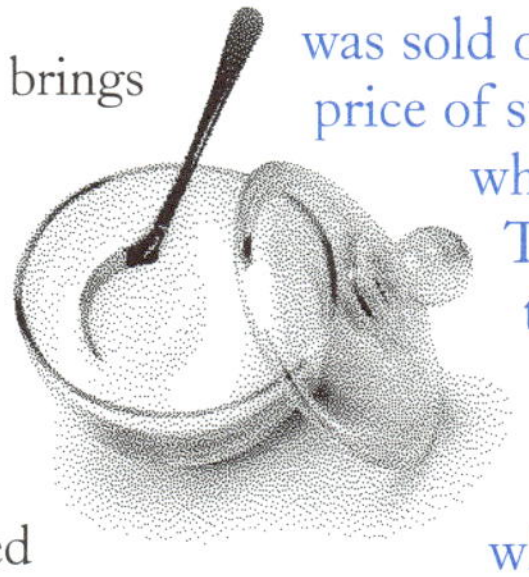

In the late 19th century, most of the world's sugar was sold only in large cones. The price of sugar depended on its whiteness and fineness. The whitest sugar was the most expensive.

Then as today, the whiter the sugar the purer it is since sucrose itself is a pure, white substance.

Strawberry Rhubarb Sorbet

Strawberry Rhubarb Sorbet

Sweet and tart both at once - this sorbet is a real gem and a perfect summertime treat.

3 cups / *750 ml*	chopped rhubarb
¼ cup / *60 ml*	water
1 cup / *250 ml*	Rogers Granulated Sugar
2 cups / *500 ml*	strawberries
	Strips of lemon zest for garnish

IN A SAUCEPAN, cook the rhubarb with the water over low heat for 10 minutes, or until the juices are released.

STIR IN THE ROGERS GRANULATED SUGAR, cover and cook over medium heat for 5 minutes until the rhubarb is tender. Then let the mixture cool.

IN A FOOD PROCESSOR, purée the cooked rhubarb with the strawberries until you have a smooth mixture. Pour it into a shallow metal pan and freeze for 4 hours. The mixture should be almost firm but not solid.

BREAK UP THE MIXTURE into chunks and transfer it back to the food processor. Purée the mixture again until it is smooth. Spoon it into an airtight container and freeze for 1 hour. Use the sorbet immediately - it will keep for a day but not much longer.

ROGERS BERRY SUGAR (also called fruit powdered, superfine or caster sugar)

Berry Sugar has smaller crystals than granulated sugar, which makes it perfect for creaming with butter. It combines more easily with other ingredients and it needs less mixing. It is the "secret ingredient" in the best cakes. Berry Sugar helps to get air into the mixture, which produces a lighter and more delicate texture. Rogers Berry Sugar is the crucial ingredient for delicious high-rising sponges, is the magic in meringues and makes the best shortbread ever.

Rogers Berry Sugar has many uses in the kitchen.

- When a cake recipe calls for a cup of granulated sugar, try a cup of Rogers Berry Sugar instead. The results are definitely worth it.
- Because it dissolves more quickly, Rogers Berry Sugar brings out more of the natural juices of fruit in homemade pies.
- Use a sprinkle of it in your whipped cream. It gives a delicious flavour without changing the texture.
- If you are making your own lemonade or iced tea, quick-dissolving Rogers Berry Sugar is perfect. It adds sweetness and leaves the liquid crystal-clear.

Old-Fashioned Lemonade

Old-Fashioned Lemonade

6 to 9	large lemons
2 cups / *500 ml*	Rogers Berry Sugar
2 cups / *500 ml*	water
	pinch salt
	ice cubes and lemon slices
	fresh mint sprigs

Nothing compares to real lemonade made with fresh lemons and Rogers Berry Sugar. This lemon concentrate is great, because you don't need to start from scratch each time you feel thirsty. This recipe makes 4 cups (1 L) of lemonade concentrate.

FINELY GRATE THE RIND from two lemons. In a small saucepan, combine the lemon rind, Rogers Berry Sugar, water and salt. Bring to a boil over high heat, stirring constantly. Now boil for 5 minutes, stirring occasionally. Remove the syrup from the heat and leave it to cool completely.

MEANWHILE, SQUEEZE THE JUICE from the lemons to yield 2 cups (500 ml) of juice. Stir it into the cooled syrup. Pour the lemonade concentrate into a container with a lid and cover tightly. It can be refrigerated for up to three weeks.

TO MAKE A GLASS OF LEMONADE, combine ¼ cup (60 ml) concentrate and ¾ cup (180 ml) of cold water or soda water. To make lemon iced tea, stir ¼ cup (60 ml) of lemonade concentrate into ¾ cup (180 ml) of iced tea. Serve it in frosty glasses with plenty of ice and fresh mint.

Sugars are always needed to activate dried yeast. Use soft sugars for whole-wheat loaves and granulated sugars for white bread. Rogers Golden Syrup, molasses or honey are sometimes added to give a different flavour.

ROGERS ICING SUGAR (also called confectioner's sugar)

Powdery, white and light as air, icing sugar is the essential ingredient in frostings and glazes. It is powdered granulated sugar, with a touch of starch added to prevent caking that would otherwise occur when icing's very fine particles absorb moisture from the air. Beautifully iced cakes, dusted fruits and glazed desserts all owe their taste and beauty to icing sugar.

Like all sugars, Rogers Icing Sugar is useful as well as beautiful.

- A thin dusting over your cake layers or baked pie shell will stop the filling from soaking in.
- Sifted over cream puffs, fresh fruit and cakes, Rogers Icing Sugar adds a delicious and elegant touch.
- It dissolves quickly without heating, which makes it ideal for glazes.
- Rogers Icing Sugar is the critical ingredient for your frosting and cream icing, but to get the best consistency, let the icing stand over hot water for 10 to 15 minutes.
- Rogers Icing sugar mixes easily and makes the smoothest uncooked desserts and candies.

Maple Syrup is another type of sweetener. It is made from boiling the sap of sugar maple trees and is produced only in Canada and the northeast United States. Maple Syrup adds a distinct flavour to frosting, confectionery and of course, pancakes and waffles. Once you have opened pure maple syrup, keep it in the refrigerator.

SOFT SUGARS

Soft sugars, often referred to as 'brown sugars', add taste, colour and body to everything they meet. It's the unique cane sugar compounds that give Rogers Golden Yellow, Best Brown and Demerara sugars their deeper, richer flavours and colours.

Don't substitute icing sugar for granulated sugar when you are baking.

Sift Rogers Icing Sugar onto a paper doily placed on top of a cake. Carefully remove the doily and you will have created a lovely, lacy decoration.

Rogers Golden Yellow Sugar

Rogers Golden Yellow is a light brown sugar with a subtle buttery flavour. It is ideal for glazes, butterscotch, oatmeal cookies, pecan pie, baked apples, cinnamon buns, peanut brittle and plum pudding.

Golden Brownies

Golden Brownies

The English name for these treasures is Elizabethan Brownies, and they are indeed fit for a queen!

½ cup / *125 ml*	butter
2 cups / *500 ml*	Rogers Golden Yellow Sugar
2	eggs
1 tsp / *5 ml*	vanilla extract
1 cup / *250 ml*	flour
1 cup / *250 ml*	chopped nuts

Preheat your oven to 325°F (160°C).

Combine the butter and Rogers Golden Yellow Sugar into a saucepan and cook over medium heat, stirring constantly, until bubbly. Let the mixture cool to room temperature.

Beat in the eggs and vanilla, then quickly stir in the flour and chopped nuts.

Pour the batter into a greased 9 x 9 in (23 x 23 cm) baking pan and bake for about 35 minutes, or until the edges begin to brown. Cool before cutting.

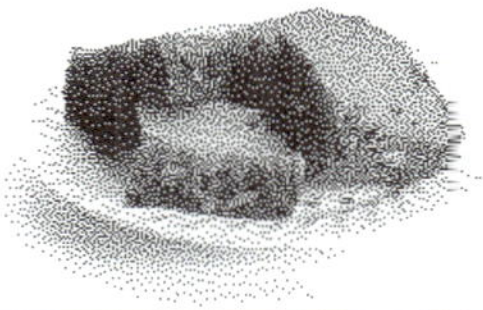

Rogers Best Brown Sugar

Rogers Best Brown is a distinctively dark sugar with a hearty taste and a soft, moist texture. It's perfect for any recipe that calls for a deep, rich taste and colour. Best Brown is the one to use in apple pie, toffee bars, bran muffins, apple crisp, gingerbread, sweet and sour sauce, pumpkin pie and maple fudge.

Best Brown Sugar Cookies

1 cup / *250 ml*	butter
¾ cup / *180 ml*	Rogers Best Brown Sugar
1	egg yolk
2 cups / *500 ml*	flour, sifted
	pecan halves

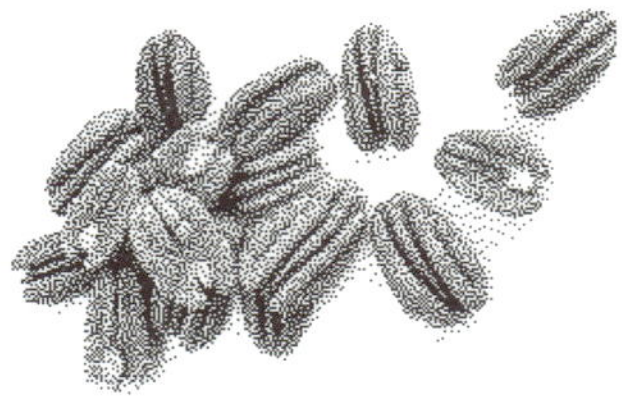

Best Brown Sugar Cookies

Simple little sugar cookies, with a lot of character.

PREHEAT your oven to 375°F (190°C).

CREAM THE BUTTER and add the Rogers Best Brown Sugar gradually, beating until fluffy.

BEAT IN THE EGG YOLK thoroughly. Add one-quarter of the flour at a time, mixing gently until just combined.

SHAPE THE DOUGH into ½ in (1.5 cm) balls and place them 2 in (5 cm) apart on ungreased cookie sheets. Flatten with a lightly floured fork, making a crisscross design on the tops. Press a pecan half onto the centre of each. Bake for about 10 minutes, or until the cookies turn slightly brown around the edges.

The White House Cookbook, *published in 1923, had an unusual remedy for skin cuts and burns: "for a slight cut...press on cobwebs and sugar."*

Rogers Demerara Sugar

Rogers Demerara Sugar is a brown sugar with larger golden crystals and a rich, almost spicy taste. It dissolves slowly and adds a tantalizing crunch. Demerara gives a special taste to cappuccinos, espresso and your favourite herbal tea. It's also the perfect choice for cereals, oatmeal, crunchy granola, candied nuts, streusel topping and brandied peaches. Go wild!

Make your cut flowers last longer by adding granulated sugar to the water in the vase. When flowers are growing, sugars are collected and used by the petals. For cut flowers, sugar can be absorbed through the stem and transported to the petals where it is metabolized.

Rogers Plantation Raw

Easy-pour Rogers Plantation Raw Sugar crystals incorporate some of the other non sucrose compounds occuring naturally in the sugar cane. Plantation Raw adds a new dimension to your favourite hot beverages. It makes cappuccinos marvellous and adds variety and taste to fresh fruit, cereals, desserts and barbeque sauce. It is unique among the soft sugars in that it is conveniently free-flowing.

Get Sprinkling

You don't need a recipe to enjoy soft sugars:

- Sprinkle them over your cereal or porridge.
- Spread them on half a grapefruit.
- Stir soft sugars into your coffee or tea.
- Mix equal quantities of plain yogurt and chopped fruit - strawberries, blueberries, blackberries or cranberries are all good - then add enough soft sugar to sweeten.

During the Great Depression, a big pail of Rogers Golden Syrup was a common sight in Prairie kitchens. When the last of the syrup had been ladled out of the bottom, the pail was washed clean and passed on to the children to use as a lunch pail.

Storing Soft Sugars

Always store soft sugar in a tightly sealed plastic bag. It will go lumpy if it's not stored properly. If hardening occurs, put the sugar in an air-tight container with one of the following:

- half an apple
- an orange slice
- a crisp lettuce leaf

If you are following an American recipe that calls for "brown sugar," use Rogers Golden Yellow Sugar rather than Best Brown. American soft sugars are generally lighter than Canadian. Rogers Best Brown sugar is a uniquely dark, flavourful sugar available primarily in western Canada.

Sprinkle crunchy Rogers Demerara over cornflakes or muesli and slice up some banana.

Rogers Golden Syrup

Full bodied, delicious and easy to use, Rogers Golden Syrup is made only from natural sugar cane compounds. Its smooth blending qualities make it a pleasure to cook with. It adds extra flavour in the same way as soft sugars but is easier to blend. Golden Syrup is an essential ingredient in many classic cake and dessert recipes.

You can substitute Rogers Golden Syrup for sugar, cup for cup, in a recipe. Just remember to reduce the total amount of liquid by ¼ cup (60 ml).

Here are some ways you can use Rogers Golden Syrup in your cooking:

- Golden Syrup makes a delicious glaze when you pour it over roasting meat.
- It heightens the flavour of sauces and stews without adding extra sweetness.

Besides Rogers Golden Syrup, try Rogers delicious pancake syrups in original, Canadian maple and butter flavours.

The darker the colour of the sugar, the stronger the molasses flavour.

When you measure soft sugars, pack them down tightly so there is no air trapped between the crystals.

- Rogers Golden Syrup adds a wonderful taste and texture to muffins and cakes.
- Chili just wouldn't be the same without a spoonful of Rogers Golden Syrup to bring out the flavour.
- It makes a delicious topping over pancakes, waffles, porridge, French toast and ice cream.
- The best Christmas cake you will ever taste is made with Rogers Golden Syrup (turn to page 122 for the recipe).

Brandy Snaps

Brandy Snaps

¼ cup / *60 ml*	butter
¼ cup / *60 ml*	Rogers Berry Sugar
¼ cup / *60 ml*	Rogers Golden Syrup
¼ cup / *60 ml*	flour
¼ tsp / *1 ml*	ground cinnamon
¼ tsp / *1 ml*	ground ginger
2 tsp / *10 ml*	brandy
1 cup / *250 ml*	whipping cream
	Few pieces crystallized ginger, finely chopped

All you need to make perfect, crunchy, brandy snaps is a bit of practice. They taste divine filled with whipped cream and ginger pieces. This recipe makes 12 to 16 brandy snaps.

IT IS ESSENTIAL to bake these biscuits in batches and, if possible, to put the mixture onto cold baking sheets for the best results.

PREHEAT YOUR OVEN to 325°F (170°C). Line three or four baking sheets with wax paper before you begin. Also, lightly grease four wooden spoon handles.

MELT THE BUTTER in a saucepan with the Rogers Berry Sugar and Rogers Golden Syrup over a gentle heat, then remove from the element.

SIFT THE FLOUR, cinnamon and ginger together and combine them into the melted mixture with the brandy. Put 4 tsp (20 ml) of the mixture onto a lined baking sheet, making sure the spoonfuls are well separated because the snaps spread out as they bake.

BAKE FOR ABOUT 10 minutes, or until an even golden brown. Take the baking sheet out of the oven and let it cool briefly, pushing the edges of the snaps into shape with a small knife. Carefully ease the snaps off the paper, one at a time, and immediately wind each one around a greased wooden spoon handle, lacy side out, so you end up with long tubes. You need to do this quickly, before they set. If the snaps become too hard to bend around the spoons, put them back in the oven for a minute or so and then try again.

COOL THE HOLLOW TUBES on a wire rack until firm, then slide them off the handles. Cook and shape the remaining mixture in the same way.

TO SERVE THE BRANDY SNAPS, whip the cream until stiff and add a few pieces of ginger, then fill the snaps using a piping bag.

BRANDY SNAPS (without the cream!) will keep for up to two weeks if stored in an airtight container.

Blackstrap Molasses

Blackstrap molasses is residual to the sugar-refining process; once all sugars have been economically recovered, the remaining compounds and sugars are referred to as molasses. Rich in iron, molasses improves the shelf life of breads and cakes, as well as providing a strong, sweet flavour.

- Blackstrap molasses is very dark and thick, with a strong, unique flavour that is ideal for commercial bakeries.
- Unsulphured molasses is a lighter colour and has a milder flavour.
- If you bake with molasses, use "fancy molasses." It is the most suitable and doesn't have an overwhelmingly strong taste.
- Drizzle molasses over cornbread, muffins or oatmeal.

Honey is an age-old sweetener, composed of fructose and glucose. It varies greatly in flavour and colour depending on the seasons, the source of nectar and its age. Some of the most sought-after honey in the world is the rare fairweed honey found in the Peace River Valley of British Columbia. Its pale, clear colour gives it the name "white-water" honey.

Beekeeping is the oldest form of farming. There are pictures on Egyptian tombs of "candy," made from dried fruit, nut meats, sesame or poppy seeds and spices mixed together with honey.

Syllabub

This is the definitive cream dessert that always inspires, yet is so easy to prepare.
This recipe serves 4 to 6 people.

1	large lemon
1 cup / *250 ml*	sherry (dry or medium)
2 tbsp / *30 ml*	Cognac
2 cups / *500 ml*	whipping cream
1	egg white
2 tbsp / *30 ml*	Rogers Berry Sugar
1 tbsp / *15 ml*	Rogers Granulated Sugar
½ tsp / *5ml*	Ground nutmeg

Peel a lemon very thinly so no white pith shows under the peel.

In a porcelain bowl cover the lemon with the sherry and leave to soak overnight.

Remove the peel by straining through a sieve. Add the cognac, whipping cream, egg white and Rogers Berry Sugar to the sherry and beat the mixture until stiff.

Be careful not to over beat.

Pour into tall parfait glasses and refrigerate for at least 5 hours.

Combine the grated nutmeg and Rogers Granulated Sugar and sprinkle on before serving. A little lemon zest is also an attractive garnish.

Serve with small, plain, sponge fingers.

You can do some amazing things with sugars - and this book proves it!

First Steps in Cake Decorating
by Janice Murfitt
New York:
Sterling Pub. Co., 1993

Everything you ever might want to know about sugar is probably explained in this definitive collection of feature articles.

Sucrose: A User's Guide to Sugar
Edited by N.L. Pennington and C.W. Baker
New York:
Van Nostrand Reinhold, 1990

Other interesting books on the history and special uses of sugar can be obtained from your local library.

Refining sugar is a complicated and fascinating process, but it is something that we tend to take for granted. If you would like to find out more, contact the Canadian Sugar Institute. It also has information on health and nutrition, the role of sugars in cooking and many recipes:

Canadian Sugar Institute
c/o Nutrition Information Program
10 Bay Street, Suite 620
Toronto, Ontario
M5J 2R8
(416) 368-8091
Fax: (416) 368-6426

BC Sugar Refinery, Limited, parent company of Rogers Sugar, operates a sugar museum that you can visit free. It is open from Monday through Friday
9 am - 4 pm and is located at:
123 Rogers Street
Vancouver, British Columbia
V6B 3V2
(604) 253-1131

Other Uses for Sugar

Here is something that most people don't know: sugar helps heal serious wounds and burns. So the next time you burn your tongue and someone suggests sprinkling sugar on it, give it a try!

Here are some other interesting things that sugars are used for:

- A teaspoon of sugar is a great home remedy for hiccups.
- Sugar, in solid form, is used to make the harmless stunt glass people fall through in movies.
- You will find sucrose in detergents, paint and plastics.
- The glue industry uses sugar to slow down the setting process.
- Sugar plays an important role in leather tanning and in the manufacturing of paper ink and dyes.

"How sweet it is..."

James Taylor, 1979

HERBS & SPICES

"Variety's the very spice of life,
That gives it all its flavour."

The Task
William Cowper, 1731-1800

How dull food would be if there were no herbs, spice and all things nice! Can you imagine an apple pie with no pinch of cinnamon? A sauce without fresh herbs to bring out its delicious flavours? Impossible. One of our most important golden rules is, without a doubt, to use herbs, spices, salt and pepper in your cooking. These tastemakers can open up the world of flavour and expand your cooking horizons. We are not talking about throwing anything and everything together and hoping for the best. Experiment with a variety of flavours and be inspired to add a little magic to all your meals.

Cooking With Herbs

Herbs have been described as the soul of cooking and the praise of cooks. The aromatic leaves of rosemary and thyme add a delicate flavour to cooked dishes. The seeds of dill, fennel and coriander bring out the best in fish, salads and vegetables. Not only do herbs turn a meal into a sensuous experience, but you can preserve their flavours in oils and vinegars, add them to butters, and use them to flavour jams and jellies.

Don't use too many kinds of herbs in the same dish. You can often use two and sometimes three, but make sure the combination is not overpowering.

A salad that was made for King Henry VIII included over 50 different herbs - including their leaves, buds, flowers and roots!

Basil is very easy to grow at home, either in pots or in the garden. Cutting off the leaves actually encourages growth, so don't feel bad about using lots in your cooking.

Fresh herbs always give the best flavour. If you can't get hold of fresh ones, dried herbs are better than none, but remember these points:

- One teaspoon of dried herbs generally equals one tablespoon of fresh ones.
- Dried herbs will last for about six to nine months before they completely lose their flavour.
- Store herbs in a dark place, away from sunlight.
- Always buy whole herb leaves not ground, they have more flavour.

- Rub dried herbs through your fingers before you add them to food. This releases their oils, which contain all the flavour.

Pesto Sauce

2 cups / *250 ml*	fresh basil leaves
2	garlic cloves, peeled and chopped
2 tbsp / *30 ml*	toasted pine nuts
1 cup / *250 ml*	olive oil
2 tbsp / *30 ml*	freshly grated Parmesan
2 tbsp / *30 ml*	freshly grated Pecorino
	freshly ground black pepper

Pesto Sauce

Originally from Genoa, this rich sauce contains all the flavours of summer. This recipe makes 2 cups of pesto.

PUT THE BASIL LEAVES, garlic and pine nuts in a blender and blend at top speed. The mixture will become a thick paste (if you can't find pine nuts, use walnuts instead).

WITH THE MOTOR RUNNING, add the olive oil in a slow, steady stream. Add the cheeses and pepper, and continue to process until blended.

PESTO WILL KEEP for up to two weeks in the refrigerator.

TYPES OF HERBS

Here is a selection of our favourite herbs, with guidelines on how to use them in your cooking:

BASIL

Basil is an Italian herb with a sweet taste and a warm, pungent scent. Its taste increases with cooking, and the leaves will add their flavour when stored in oil or vinegar.

- Basil is indispensable for many Mediterranean and Italian dishes.
- Anything that has tomato in it will be improved with a sprinkle of basil. Fresh tomatoes taste superb with basil and a drizzle of olive oil.

- Pesto sauce, made from basil leaves, pine nuts, garlic, oil and cheese is perfect for tossing with pasta (see page 20 for recipe).

- Basil is a favourite addition to rice salads and green salads.

Bay

This is one herb that is better dried than fresh. Bay is best known as an ingredient in the traditional *bouquet garni*, along with parsley and thyme.

- When you cook with bay, add it at the beginning and remove it before serving.

- Use a bay leaf or two to make marinades, stock, pâtés, stuffings and curries.

- Add a bay leaf when you are poaching, boiling, baking or steaming a fish.

- If you keep a bay leaf in a jar of uncooked rice, it will give the rice a lovely flavour.

Chives

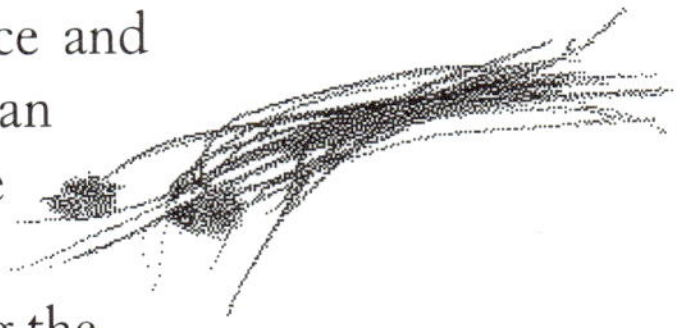

Chives have a pretty appearance and will suit any dish that calls for an onion flavour. Chives are destroyed if they are cooked for too long, so add them during the last 5 to 10 minutes.

- Garnish soups, salads, chicken, potatoes, cooked vegetables and egg dishes with chives.

- The flavour of chives marries well with tomato.

- Chop some chives and blend them with butter to garnish broiled meats and fish.

- Use chives instead of raw onions in hamburgers for a milder flavour.

- Mix chives into cream cheese or yogurt and add to baked potatoes.

A bouquet garni *is simply a collection of fresh herbs bound together to make a "bouquet". Add one to your cooking to enhance the flavour, but make sure you take it out before serving.*

Fines herbes, *the traditional flavouring for classic omelettes, is a finely chopped mixture of fresh chives, parsley, tarragon and chervil.*

Chive buds and flowers are delicious in salads, soups and herb vinegars.

In Chengdu, China, there's a pharmacy with a difference. It has a restaurant attached to it, and the walls of the restaurant are lined with hundreds of large wooden drawers containing dried herbs. If you eat there, you don't order from the menu, but simply tell the waiter how you feel. Your meal is then carefully designed to improve your condition!

"The herbs were springing
in the vale:
Green ginger plants and
liquorice pale
And cloves their sweetness offer,
With nutmegs too, to put in ale
No matter whether fresh or stale,
Or else to keep in coffer."

The Canterbury Tales
Geoffrey Chaucer, 1340-1400

CILANTRO (also known as Chinese parsley or coriander)

The lacy, feathery foliage of cilantro has a distinctly earthy flavour. The seeds are warmly aromatic and are often used to flavour pickled vegetables, oils and vinegars.

- Cilantro is indispensable in tomato chutney, salsa and curries.
- It makes an excellent flavouring for stir-fried vegetables, soups and sauces.
- Add chopped cilantro leaves (sparingly!) to chicken, poultry, lamb and vegetable dishes.
- Cilantro teams well with Asian-style salads and with fruits such as pears and mangoes.
- A pinch of ground cilantro seeds sprinkled over cooked, buttered vegetables gives them an interesting taste.

DILL

Dill has a totally unique, spicy green taste. It can be used to replace parsley, mint, basil or tarragon in a recipe.

- Add whole dill seeds to potato salads, pickles, bean soups, salmon dishes and apple pies.
- Use ground dill seeds to flavour herb butter, mayonnaise and mustard (there is a great recipe for potato and dill salad on page 49).
- Add finely chopped dill leaves to seafood, lamb or chicken dishes.
- Dill soup is unusual and tasty.

Planting dill in your garden is said to help corn, lettuce, cucumbers and cabbages grow. The flowers also attract honey bees.

When you are barbequing fish outdoors, put some fennel seeds or stalks directly onto the coals. The smoke will infuse the dish with wonderful flavour.

FENNEL

Traditionally served with fish, fennel is also a delicious tastemaker for other dishes. Fennel seeds, like dill and caraway, are good for the digestion. They can be used whole or ground and have a strong anise flavour (similar to licorice).

- Scatter finely chopped fennel over salads.
- Fennel adds great flavour to cooked, buttered vegetables.
- Stir fennel into a spaghetti sauce or cooked rice.
- The swollen base of fennel is an Italian delicacy, traditionally served as a salad with oil and vinegar.

Marjoram

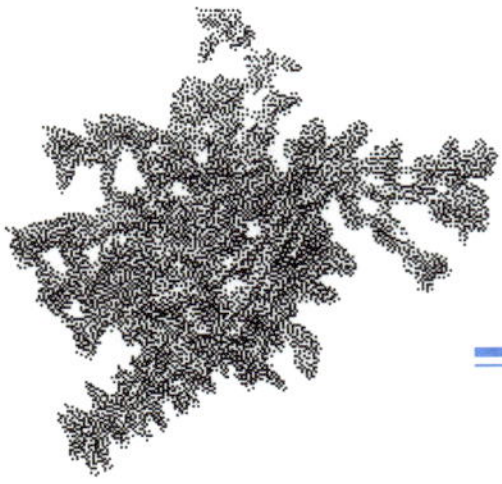

Marjoram and oregano are closely related - oregano is really a wild form of marjoram - but they have distinctly different flavours. Marjoram has a soft, gentle taste and combines well with other herbs.

If you strip marjoram leaves carefully from their stalks they don't need to be chopped.

- Marjoram is one of the ingredients in traditional mixed herbs, along with thyme and sage.
- Add freshly chopped marjoram to dumplings (see recipe on page 40) and scones.
- Use marjoram with fish, beef, chicken, sausages and meat loaf.
- The taste of marjoram enhances tomatoes, zucchini, potatoes and peppers.
- Marjoram is ideal for omelettes and cheese dishes.
- Fresh marjoram leaves are delicious torn into green salads.

"May I ask you to bring up some herbs from the farm-garden to make a savoury omelette? Sage and thyme, and mint and two onions, and some parsley."

The Tale of Jemima Puddle-Duck
Beatrix Potter, 1866-1943

Mint

Mint has a clean, sharp flavour and helps the digestion. There are many varieties of mint on the market, each with its own scent and flavour.

- Mint is a vital ingredient of mint jelly and mint julep. It is also excellent in iced tea.
- Add a sprig of mint to new potatoes, green peas and tomatoes.
- Use it in cream-cheese dips and yogurt dressings.

- Mix chopped mint leaves into chocolate cakes, rich desserts and raisins or currants in pastry. Mint also tastes great in fruit salads.

- Crystallize mint leaves for a sweet decoration.

Oregano can replace basil or parsley in a recipe.

To store fresh parsley: cut the stems and place the whole bundle in a jar of water. Put a small plastic bag over the leaves and keep it in the fridge.

OREGANO (also known as wild marjoram)

Oregano is sharper than marjoram, with a pungent, dominating flavour. It is used in the regional dishes of many countries, especially around the Mediterranean.

- Oregano is perfect in Italian food such as pizza toppings, pasta dishes and tomato sauces.

- Use chopped oregano for chicken, meat loaf, hamburgers, stews and chili sauce.

- Oregano sparks up zucchini, bell pepper and eggplant.

- Try sprinkling some dried oregano on lamb or pork next time you roast it.

PARSLEY

The mild flavour and bright green leaves of parsley make it a useful and popular kitchen herb. It is often served as a garnish in restaurants because of its breath-freshening qualities. Always use fresh parsley, never dried.

- Parsley enhances the flavours of other herbs and food when it is cooked with them.

- For a stronger parsley flavour, use generous amounts and include the stems.

- Use chopped parsley in salads, soups, sauces, mayonnaise and egg dishes.

- Wash sprigs of parsley, dry them thoroughly, then fry quickly in butter until crisp. This is a traditional accompaniment to fried or grilled fish.

Rosemary

Rosemary is one of the most pungent herbs and has a warm, resinous scent. It aids the digestion of rich and starchy food, and is perfect to eat with meat. Strip the stiff leaves from the stem and chop the leaves well before you use them.

- Rosemary is traditionally sprinkled on roast lamb and pork, but also try it in sausage meats, pâtés and stuffings.
- Flavour bottles of oil or vinegar with a sprig of rosemary.
- Sprinkle finely chopped rosemary on cooked, buttered vegetables.
- It gives a delicious flavour to bread and dumplings.

Sage

Sage is a robust, pungent herb that complements strongly flavoured foods. The leaves, whether fresh or dry, also help to digest rich food. You can use sage on its own or with other herbs.

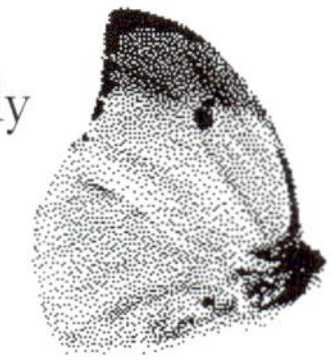

In the garden, sage will improve the flavour of cabbages if it is grown nearby. Sage also helps to repel the cabbage butterfly.

- Sage is a great tastemaker for cheese and cream-cheese dips.
- Use sage leaves in onion soup, with stewed tomatoes and in omelettes.

Apple, Sage and Onion Stuffing

This stuffing is a wonderful accompaniment to more than simply roast chicken. Try sautéing balls of it to serve with your favourite fish, pork or game dish.

4 oz / *110 g*	fresh white bread, crusts removed
1 tbsp / *15 ml*	freshly chopped parsley
1½ tbsp / *22 ml*	freshly chopped sage
1	dessert apple, cored and quartered
1	small onion, peeled and quartered
	liver from 1 chicken
8 oz / *225 g*	pork or pork sausage meat, minced
¼ tsp / *1 ml*	powdered mace
	salt and freshly ground black pepper

IN A FOOD PROCESSOR, process the pieces of bread until they are crumbs, then add the parsley, sage leaves, apple and onion quarters. Process until everything is finely chopped.

TRIM THE CHICKEN LIVER, rinse it under cold water and pat dry. Add it to the bread crumbs, together with the meat, mace, salt and pepper.

GIVE A FEW PULSES in the processor until everything is thoroughly blended. Remove the stuffing with a spatula, then put it in a freezer bag and store in the refrigerator until you are ready to use it.

Apple, Sage and Onion Stuffing

If you add fresh herbs to a sauce such as mayonnaise, first put them in boiling water for a minute or two, then strain and pat dry with a dishtowel. The leaves will be greener and have more flavour.

- Add chopped sage to herb scones, dumplings and bread.
- Sage is especially delicious chopped into a rich cream sauce for leeks or onions.
- Sage and onion stuffing for roast chicken or duck is perfect (see the recipe on page 25).

In Roman times, tarragon was believed to have the power to heal snakebites.

Tarragon

Tarragon has a uniquely spicy, licorice flavour and is one of the most popular herbs. Fresh or dried, heat intensifies the taste of tarragon, so use less in your cooking.

- Tarragon is an essential ingredient in Béarnaise and Hollandaise sauces.
- Use it in soups, salads and fish and chicken dishes.
- Add chopped tarragon to any delicate vegetables, or splash on a little tarragon vinegar.
- Tarragon tastes particularly good in chicken stuffing, or as an addition to egg dishes.

Thyme

The special flavour of thyme improves many dishes and blends well with other herbs such as sage and marjoram. Thyme is very pungent when it is fresh, so use it with discretion.

- Thyme is tasty with meat, shellfish and game.
- Add thyme to herb bread for a delicious savoury taste.
- Thyme adds flavour to cooked, buttered vegetables.
- Lemon thyme is perfect for fish and poultry dishes, because it's milder and never overpowers the more delicate flavours.

The ancient Romans stored their peppercorns in giant warehouses built in the "spice quarter". In AD 408, they paid the Visigoth King Alaric 1,200 kilograms of pepper not to destroy their city. Unfortunately the payment didn't work; he took the pepper and attacked Rome anyway.

Pepper

Whenever pepper is mentioned in this book, we mean whole black peppercorns, freshly ground. It would be hard to survive without the pepper grinder - no other kitchen tool can improve your food so easily, or so dramatically. If you have white pepper in your cupboard, save it for light-coloured dishes, like cream sauces, mashed potatoes or chicken consommé.

Garlic

Since ancient times, the Chinese, Egyptians and Hebrews have cooked with garlic. Countless dishes rely on this magic tastemaker, and it is hard to imagine life without it.

- Always use fresh garlic when you're cooking at home. Buy fat, firm cloves with no green sprouts.
- Garlic crushed through a press tastes stronger than when it is chopped up.
- The longer garlic is cooked, the milder it becomes. For a stronger flavour, add garlic to a dish just before serving.
- Rub a clove around a salad bowl to subtly flavour your salads.
- Add one or two garlic cloves to dressings and marinades.

"There is no such thing as a little garlic."

Arthur Baer

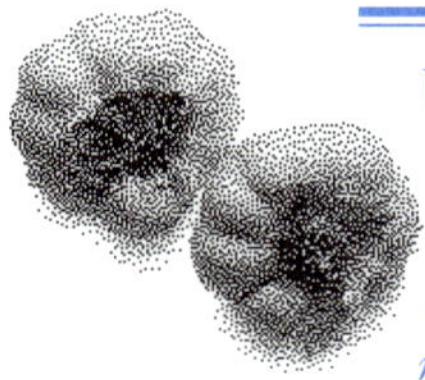

Whole garlic cloves, roasted in their skins, are deliciously sweet and buttery. They are a perfect side dish for roasted meats and vegetables.

Garlic juice is a powerful antiseptic and was widely used during both World Wars.

Garlic Mushrooms

These marinated mushrooms are loaded with the wonderful flavour of garlic. They are perfect on their own, on top of pizza or served with salads and entrées. This recipe makes 4 servings.

4 tbsp / *60 ml*	olive oil
6 slices	bacon, chopped small
8 oz / *225 g*	mushrooms, wiped and sliced
4 cloves	garlic, very finely chopped
8 fl oz / *225 ml*	red wine
	salt and freshly ground black pepper

HEAT THE OLIVE OIL in a large frying pan, add the chopped bacon and fry just until it begins to brown.

ADD THE SLICED MUSHROOMS along with the garlic and cook for a couple of minutes - shaking the pan and stirring the mushrooms around constantly.

POUR IN THE RED WINE, turn the heat up high and let it all bubble for 2 minutes until reduced a little.

TURN THE HEAT DOWN and cook for another 4 minutes. Season the mushrooms with the salt and pepper, and spoon them into a serving dish. Allow the mushrooms to cool before putting the dish into the refrigerator to chill.

SERVE THE MUSHROOMS on crisp lettuce leaves with freshly chopped parsley sprinkled on top and some garlic mayonnaise.

Saffron is expensive, and it is not difficult to see why. It comes from the stigmas of the saffron crocus, and the only way to pick the strands is by hand. It takes thousands of flowers to make even several grams of saffron. The flowers must be picked as soon as they bloom, and they only bloom for two weeks in the autumn. Just a few yellow saffron strands represent an enormous amount of tedious, backbreaking work. It's ideal for Bouillabaisse, risotto and gives colour to rice, cakes and breads. Use just a little because it is very strong.

- Mash garlic with butter and spread it inside a French loaf before you bake it. Garlic butter also tastes wonderful on grilled meat or fish.

- Insert sliced cloves of garlic into meat before roasting.

Salt

Salt is the most basic seasoning used in cooking all over the world. It's amazing the difference salt can make to food, almost magically bringing out the flavour of a soup or sauce that had originally seemed quite bland. Salt preserves foods, heightens flavours and provides that distinctive salty taste.

- Consider using sea salt in your cooking. It has a stronger, purer taste which means you actually use less.

- Temperature affects salt. The cooler the food, the saltier it will taste, so it's best to under salt hot foods that you are then going to chill. You can always add more salt later.

- If you think you have over salted a liquid dish, add a couple of peeled potatoes to absorb the flavour.

Cooking with Spices

Spices have been used for thousands of years and for many different purposes. The Romans used spices as perfumes, medicines and preservatives. Spices were extremely expensive, however, and only the wealthiest citizens were privileged enough to flavour their food with them. These days, we are lucky to have spices easily available in our supermarkets. They enhance the aromas of food and provide a wealth of flavour to nearly any dish.

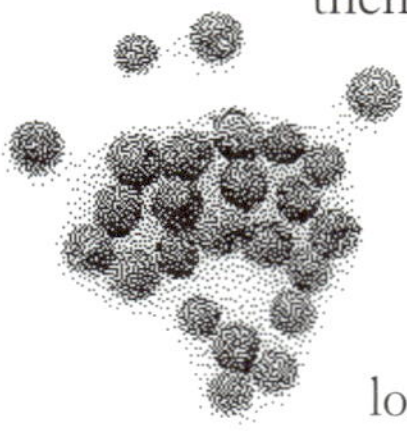

- Grind whole spices in a spice mill or coffee grinder for the freshest taste. You can also use a blender, although it does take longer.

- If you buy spices already ground, they begin to lose their flavour after about three months.

- Spices stay fresher longer if they are stored away from heat and light.

Allspice

Allspice is only one spice, but it tastes like a blend of cloves, nutmeg and cinnamon. Its berries resemble oversized peppercorns and are used both whole and ground.

- Whole allspice is often used in pickles and preserves.
- The flavour is perfect for all kinds of fish and shellfish - use three allspice berries for each pound (450 g) of fish when poaching.
- Ground allspice is used in cakes, cookies and fruit pies.
- Allspice also adds a depth of flavour to meatloaf and chili sauce.

Cardamon

Cardamon is an Eastern spice with a highly aromatic seed. It is one of the most expensive spices, apart from saffron, and should never be bought ground. Use it sparingly as it is sharply aromatic.

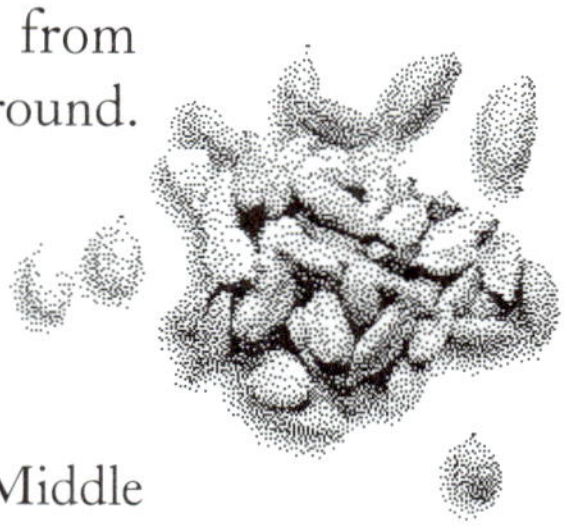

- Add both cardamon pods and seeds to rice for a delicious flavour.
- Cardamon is widely used in Indian and Middle Eastern dishes, and is indispensible in curry dishes.
- In Scandinavia, cardamon is used to flavour breads and pastries.
- Add a pinch of ground cardamon to a sweet recipe for an interesting change.

Cayenne

Cayenne, sometimes labelled "red pepper," is a fiery spice. It's ground from a blend of several hot types of dried chile peppers and has a finer texture than chilli powder, which makes it more suitable for sprinkling on food. Use cayenne carefully, adding a little at a time.

- Cayenne adds zesty flavour to smoked fish pâtés, cheese dishes and cheese scones.
- Mix cayenne with some grated cheese and breadcrumbs for a delicious baked-dish topping.

North Indian Spice Mix

Garam Masala

2	cinnamon sticks
¼ cup / *60 ml*	coriander seeds
2 tbsp / *30 ml*	cumin seeds
2 tbsp / *30 ml*	black peppercorns
2 tsp / *10 ml*	cardamon seeds
2 tsp / *10 ml*	whole cloves
1 tsp / *5 ml*	fennel seeds

PREHEAT YOUR OVEN to 200°F (90°C). Using a rolling pin, crush the cinnamon sticks into small pieces. Put all the spices in a roasting pan and heat for 30 minutes, stirring once or twice.

LET THE SPICES COOL, then grind them together in a spice mill. Store in a container and use to season meat, fish and vegetable dishes.

Just to confuse you, chile is spelt three different ways! Chile refers to the plant, chili refers to the meat stew that contains chiles, and chilli is the commercial spice powder.

Microwave Baked Apple

Microwave Baked Apple

1	apple, cored and peeled on the upper half
2 tbsp / *30 ml*	Rogers Best Brown Sugar
1 tsp / *5 ml*	ground cinnamon
½ tsp / *2 ml*	ground nutmeg
1 tsp / *5 ml*	finely chopped or grated lemon zest
1 tbsp / *15 ml*	chopped toasted walnuts

A simple little recipe that is ready in minutes.

PLACE THE APPLE in a serving bowl. Mix together the sugar, cinnamon, nutmeg and lemon zest and fill the centre of the apple.

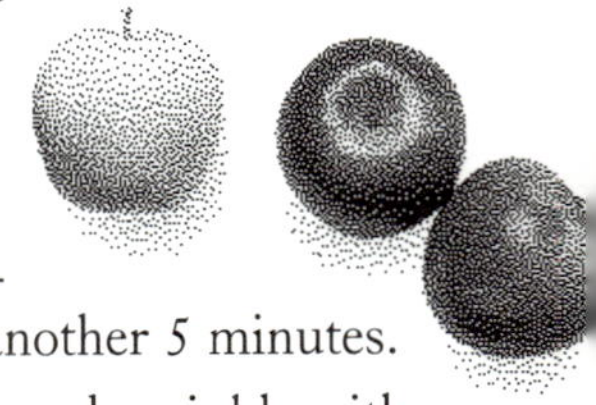

COVER WITH PLASTIC WRAP and pierce two holes in it to let the steam escape.

MICROWAVE AT HIGH POWER for 5 minutes, then remove the bowl and let stand for another 5 minutes.

SPOON THE SUGAR SYRUP over the apple and sprinkle with the chopped toasted walnuts.

In the 1500s, the Portuguese had such a craving for cinnamon that as soon as they reached India, they decided to invade Sri Lanka. In 1536, they occupied the island and demanded a tribute of 110,000 kilograms of cinnamon each year from the king.

CINNAMON

Cinnamon is a familiarly fragrant spice. It's usually bought ground because it is difficult to grind it yourself. Try adding a stick or two to stews and curries. Cinnamon sticks can be used again and again.

- Cinnamon is the favourite tastemaker for fruit pies, especially apple.
- It is most often associated with desserts, but cinnamon also tastes wonderful with lamb and spicy Middle Eastern dishes.
- Use whole cinnamon sticks in rice and curry dishes.
- Add cinnamon to moussaka to give an authentically Greek flavour.
- Enjoy cinnamon in mulled wine, cookies and sweet breads.

CLOVES

Cloves have a strong, pungent and sweet aroma. They are usually used whole, but their taste intensifies when ground.

- Nail-shaped whole cloves are widely used to stud hams.
- They are ideal for flavouring apple dishes.
- The flavour of ground cloves enhances Christmas cake, curry, chili sauce and mincemeat.

Cajun Spice Blend

Cajun Spice Blend

1 tbsp / *15 ml*	garlic powder
1 tbsp / *15 ml*	onion powder
2 tsp / *10 ml*	white pepper
2 tsp / *10 ml*	cracked black pepper
1½ tsp / *7 ml*	cayenne pepper
2 tsp / *10 ml*	dried thyme
½ tsp / *2 ml*	dried oregano

Mix the spices together and store in a jar.

Cumin

Cumin is the seed of a small, delicate plant in the parsley family. It has a powerful earthy flavour and tends to dominate a dish when it is added.

- Cumin, whole or ground, is essential in Indian cooking, especially in curry dishes.
- Try adding cumin powder to sausage meat for an interesting flavour.
- It is ideal for Mexican dishes.

If you have room, keep your paprika and chilli powder in the refrigerator. It will make their colours and flavours last longer.

Rogers Pumpkin Chutney

Here is a delicious, simple chutney that will use up all your pumpkins at the end of Halloween.
This recipe makes about 3 lbs (1½ kg) of chutney.

2 lbs / *1 kg*	cubes of pumpkin, coarsely chopped
4	tomatoes, skinned and chopped
8 oz / *225 g*	onions, chopped
¼ cup / *60 ml*	golden raisins
1 lb / *½ kg*	Rogers Best Brown Sugar
2 tsp / *10 ml*	salt
2 tsp / *10 ml*	finely chopped fresh ginger
1 tsp / *5 ml*	ground black pepper
2 tsp / *10 ml*	grated fresh nutmeg
2	garlic cloves chopped
2 cups / *500 ml*	apple cider vinegar

PUT ALL THE INGREDIENTS into a large pan, bring slowly to the boil and simmer for about 1 hour. As the chutney thickens, stir it constantly to keep it from sticking to the bottom.

WHEN IT IS READY, pour the chutney into jars, cover and seal (read the Jams, Jellies & Chutneys section to find out more about making your own chutneys).

Ginger

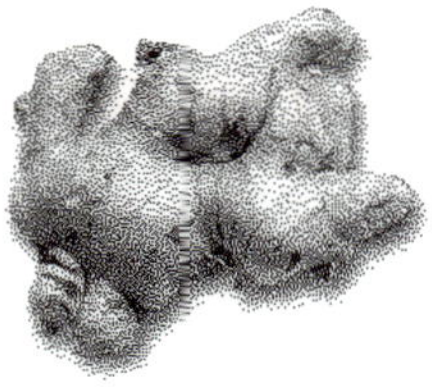

While ginger can be used fresh, dried or powdered, raw ginger definitely has the best taste. Peel the root, then grate or chop it finely.

- Ginger adds a clean, fresh taste and spiciness to curries and stir-fries.
- When dried, ginger is ideal for chutneys and pickles.
- Ginger is indispensible in gingerbread, cakes and puddings.
- Ginger is delicious sprinkled over fruits and vegetables such as squash, carrots and sweet potatoes.

The spice market in Delhi, India, is one of the largest in the world. Spices are usually bought whole and then ground by professional grinders. They visit homes in the city and prepare whichever fresh spices are needed by the household.

Find out more about Herbs & Spices and how they can make meals marvelous. More and more people are discovering the delight of ethnic cooking and these books are highly recommended.

Red, Hot and Green: 50 Spicy Vegetarian Recipes
Janet Horzen
San Francisco:
Chronicle Books, 1995

A new taste experience for all vegetable lovers. Spice up your life. Live on the edge!

Madhur Jaffrey's Spice Kitchen
Madhur Jaffrey
New York:
Carol Southern Books, 1993

Madhur Jaffrey makes authentic Indian cooking really understandable. There's a whole new world of intense taste and flavours waiting for you in this book.

The Instant Ethnic Cook: A Herb and Spice Blend Cookbook
Mara R. Rogers
New York:
Lake Isle Press, 1993

This is for people who like to travel the world in their kitchen. You'll find easy ideas for a wide range of ethnic cuisine.

Also recommended:

Herbs: a Country Garden Cookbook
by Rosalind Creasy
San Francisco:
Collins Publishers, 1995

Here's a web site with over 2000 recipes from all over the world!

http://www.accessnow.com/herbshop/recipes.html

NUTMEG

Nutmeg is a dark brown fruit encased in an outer shell called mace. Buy nutmeg whole and grate as you need it, so it is always fresh.

- Nutmeg enhances rum and eggnogs.
- It is an essential ingredient for many cakes and puddings.
- For an attractive appearance, grate nutmeg over the top of custard.
- Add a pinch of nutmeg to cheese dishes, vegetables, granulated sauces and tomato-meat sauces.

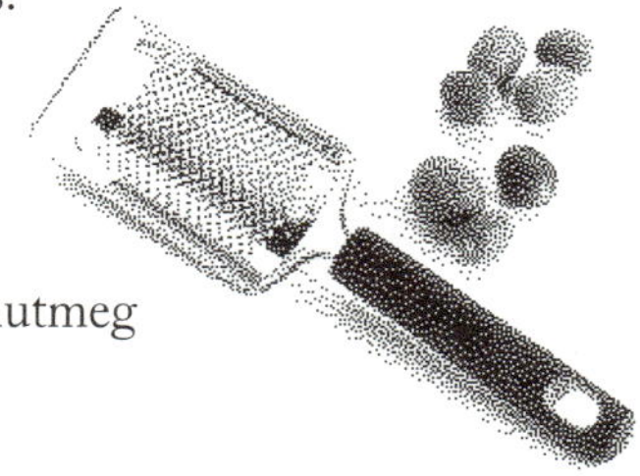

PAPRIKA (also known as Hungarian pepper)

Paprika comes from the ground seeds of sweet chile peppers, but it lacks the heat of chilli powder. The flavour of paprika ranges from sweet to pungent; the scent is distinctive and strong.

- Paprika is essential for many Spanish and eastern European dishes.
- Paprika makes an appealing garnish on soups and egg dishes.
- It is tasty in mustards, dressings, sausages and fish dishes.

"The only real stumbling block is fear of failure. In cooking you've got to have a what-the-hell attitude."

Julia Child

SOUPS

"Only the pure of heart can make a good soup."

Ludwig van Beethoven, 1770-1827

Nothing beats the taste of homemade soup. Packaged and canned soups don't come close, no matter how expensive they may be. Soup making has been elevated to the level of haute cuisine, capturing the flavours and colours of the freshest vegetables and meats. It is also the very essence of comfort food: hot, nourishing and satisfying.

Delicious soup can be made quickly and from nearly anything. As always, the better the ingredients are to begin with the better the final taste will be.

To make the best soup:

- Use homemade stock and fresh, quality ingredients.
- Be generous with herbs, spices, salt and sugar to accentuate the soup's flavours.
- Balance the flavour of the soup with the rest of the meal, particularly if you are serving it as a starter.
- Always serve soup piping hot or nicely chilled. There is nothing worse than a bowl of lukewarm soup.
- Flavours need time to blend and grow used to each other. Make soup a few hours before you plan to serve it, then reheat.

If the soup is being served as a starter, dish it up in small bowls. You want to encourage appetites rather than spoil them.

Stock: The Foundation of Soup

When it comes to flavour, homemade stock is the secret behind the best soup. It adds a full, rich taste and body you can't get from anything else. And it is so easy! Stock is simply the liquid that comes from simmering fresh meat bones, fish, chicken or vegetables. Although stocks need to simmer for an hour or more to get the best flavour, you can leave them and do something else - all they need is a stir and a skim now and then. Stock also freezes beautifully, so make a big pot of it.

Always start with cold water when you boil stock. The amount of water depends on how many bones you have. Make sure they are covered by at least 1 in (2.5 cm) of water before boiling.

- The best vegetables to use in any stock are onions, carrots and celery.
- Add parsnips to stock for a sweeter taste.
- Fresh meat will always give a better flavour than cooked leftovers.
- Use peppercorns, not ground pepper, to avoid clouding the liquid.
- Don't use any salt in stock - add it when you make the soup.
- Reducing stock gives it a more intense flavour.

Freezing Stock

To freeze stock, store it in several small containers. Alternatively, simmer it uncovered until it has reduced by three-quarters, then freeze the concentrated stock in ice cube trays. One or two stock cubes can then be diluted with water as a base for your soup, or added to a sauce to enrich it.

Beef Stock

Make your beef stock from marrow bones, chopped carrots, onions and celery. Before you simmer the stock, roast the ingredients for about 45 minutes, basting now and then. This brings out the juices and creates a richer stock. Gently simmer beef stock for about 4 hours.

Marrow bones are available at very low cost. Either get your butcher to chop some up for you, or buy them pre-packed at the supermarket.

Chicken Stock

Make your chicken stock from uncooked chicken bones and trimmings. Save them in the freezer until you have about 2 lbs (1 kg), or buy them fresh and cheap – chicken necks and backs are often on sale. You can use leftovers from last night's meal, but the stock will be a darker colour and unsuitable for clear soups. Simmer chicken stock for an hour or two.

The 1800s were the golden age of cooking in Britain. Legs of prime veal, pounds of lean ham and several of the best roasting chickens were often used just to make the stock for a soup.

Fish Stock

Get bones from non-oily fish at a fish market. A fish head will give the stock even more flavour - as long as you don't mind looking at it! Don't simmer fish stock longer than 20 minutes or it will become bitter.

Vegetable Stock

You can use combinations of almost any vegetables - carrots, onions, parsnips and leeks are all good. Avoid cabbage, broccoli or cauliflower, however; they give stock an unpleasantly strong flavour. Simmer vegetable stock for 2 hours.

Not all soups are based on stock. Some vegetable soups have their own distinct flavour, and you can spoil them with a strong stock. Try adding flavour in other ways. Apple juice is fabulous in squash soup, for example, especially if you heighten the flavour with a teaspoon of Rogers Best Brown Sugar and a sprinkle of cinnamon.

Only use one stalk of celery if you are adding it to vegetable stock, as it can easily overpower the other vegetables.

Keep a plastic container in the freezer for leftover raw vegetables. A few mushrooms here, half an onion there – they soon add up. When the container is full, add them to your stock.

Mexican Fish Soup

A favourite with the crew! All the flavours of the sea are captured in this spicy concoction.
This recipe makes 10 bowls.

2 tbsp / *30 ml*	olive oil
2	medium onions, chopped
4	garlic cloves, chopped
14 oz / *398 ml*	canned plum tomatoes, chopped
4	celery stalks, diced
1	green bell pepper, seeded and chopped
8 cups / *2 L*	fish stock
	salt and freshly ground black pepper
2	potatoes, peeled and diced
13 lb / *6 kg*	snapper, filleted and cut into chunks
20	medium shrimps, cleaned and deveined
24	oysters, shucked
1	jalapeño pepper, seeded and minced

Heat the olive oil in a large, heavy-based frying pan over medium heat. Add the onions and garlic and sauté until they are soft (about 5 minutes).

Add the tomatoes, celery, green pepper, stock and salt and pepper. Bring to a boil, then reduce the heat to medium-low and cook the soup, uncovered, for 15 minutes.

Add the potatoes and cook for another 20 minutes, or until tender. Now add the fish to the soup and let it quickly simmer for about 2 minutes. Do all this ahead of time - preferably 5 hours before you want to serve the meal - and leave the soup covered in the refrigerator. This gives the flavours time to develop.

When you are ready to serve the soup, bring it to the boil and add the shrimp and oysters.

As soon as it begins boiling again, take the soup off the heat and leave it to stand for a minute so all the seafood finishes cooking. Add the minced jalapeño pepper.

Spoon the soup into shallow bowls. Garnish each one with slices of avocado, and serve with lime wedges and Tabasco sauce.

Troubleshooting

If your soup is too thin:

- ❒ Add a beaten egg yolk for each cup of soup just before serving. Make sure the soup is not too hot and don't boil it.
- ❒ Don't use flour or cornstarch - your soup will taste like it has been poured straight from a can.
- ❒ Add 3 tbsp (45 ml) of grated raw potato for each cup of soup, then leave it to cook for 15 minutes.

If your soup is too weak:

- ❒ Take the lid off and let it reduce by simmering gently.
- ❒ Add more herbs, spices, sugar or salt, according to taste.
- ❒ Add more stock.

If your soup is too thick:

- ❒ Add milk or stock to thin it down, but be careful not to dilute the flavour.

If your soup is too salty:

- ❒ Add a piece of raw, peeled potato for 15 minutes. Remove it when it has absorbed enough salt.

Vegetable Soups

Got some vegetables in your refrigerator? An onion? A clove of garlic? Then you have the makings of a delicious vegetable soup! In summer, simmer chopped zucchini and potatoes in a chicken or vegetable stock. In winter, you can use parsnips, carrots, potatoes - or all three.

Always taste your soup as you go and make sure that it has plenty of flavour. Don't just throw in anything; think about the various vegetables and how they will suit each other. If the flavour is weak, add some more herbs or spices and let the soup simmer for a while, reducing it to a richer soup.

Here are some tips for the best tasting vegetable soup:

- ❒ Cut all the vegetables the same size so they cook evenly.
- ❒ Sauté the vegetables gently in butter before adding the stock. It brings out the flavour of the natural sugars.
- ❒ Add cream, if you like, but don't boil the soup or it will curdle.
- ❒ Add a teaspoon of granulated sugar to enhance the flavour.

Herbs and Spices for Vegetable Soups

Vegetable soups have subtle flavours that are brought out with the careful use of herbs and spices. Some seasonings will taste better than others, however. Here are a few that work particularly well:

- **Asparagus:** chives, mint, sweet marjoram, oregano, thyme, tarragon
- **Bean**: basil, parsley, cumin
- **Minestrone:** basil, rosemary, thyme
- **Parsnip:** allspice, parsley, paprika
- **Pea:** basil, dill, marjoram, parsley, rosemary
- **Potato:** bay, caraway, parsley
- **Pumpkin or squash:** curry powder, cinnamon, ginger, coriander
- **Tomato:** basil, dill, oregano, tarragon, thyme

Vegetable Variations

The joy of soup is that it is so easy to create your own flavours. See what you have in the cupboard and don't be afraid to experiment with combinations of ingredients. Soup won't work if you throw in anything and everything, but simply by putting a little thought into the ingredients you use, you can make a soup to be proud of.

Some flavours go particularly well together:

- **Potato:** leek; bell pepper; garlic; celery
- **Bean:** ham; bacon; corn; tomato; bell pepper
- **Corn:** chicken; crab; zucchini; potato; onion; celery
- **Mushroom:** clam; broccoli; asparagus; carrot; barley
- **Tomato:** sweet potato; bell pepper; chick pea; green bean; pumpkin

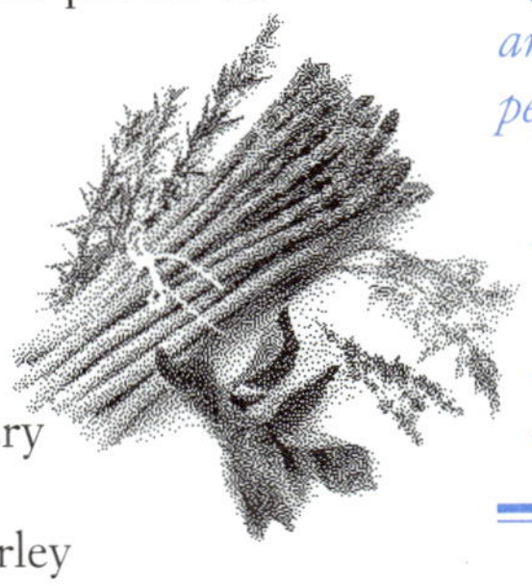

When you add spices to your soup, sauté them with vegetables and butter to bring out the flavours. Add herbs to the stock, right at the beginning, and keep the salt and pepper until the end.

Adding a pinch of Rogers Granulated Sugar to classic tomato soup balances the acidity and brings out the natural flavours of the soup.

Minestrone

To be worthy of its Italian heritage, this soup should be strong, rich and have the wonderful combination of ingredients that makes this recipe so special.
This recipe makes 6 to 8 bowls.

4 oz / *110 g*	cannellini beans
1	large onion, sliced
2	leeks, white parts only, sliced
4 tbsp / *60 ml*	olive oil
2	stalks celery, chopped
2	carrots, chopped
2 oz / *50 g*	fennel, chopped
2	unpeeled zucchinis, chopped ½ in *(1.5 cm)* thick
6 oz / *170 g*	spinach or cabbage, cut across in 1 in *(2.5 cm)* lengths
4 oz / *110 g*	string beans, cut in 1 in *(2.5 cm)* lengths
8 oz / *225 g*	tomatoes, skinned and chopped
3 pints / *1.7 L*	light chicken stock, heated
	salt and black pepper
2 oz / *50 g*	elbow macaroni, plain or wholemeal

Soak the dried beans for 3 to 4 hours, then drain. Cover them with fresh cold water, bring slowly to the boil, and let them simmer until they are soft. This will take about 25 to 45 minutes, depending on how old the beans are. When they are cooked, turn off the heat and leave them sitting in the water.

In the olive oil, cook the onion and leeks in a large, heavy-based saucepan for about 8 minutes. They should be soft and shiny, but don't let them change colour.

Add the celery, carrots and fennel and cook for another 8 minutes. Now add the zucchinis and the spinach or cabbage. Finally, put in the string beans and the tomatoes.

Cook for 5 minutes longer, then add the heated chicken stock, salt and pepper. Bring to a boil. Simmer, half covered, for 50 minutes.

Add the drained beans and the macaroni elbows, bring back to the boil and cook until the macaroni is soft (about 15 minutes).

Stir in some parsley and 2 tbsp (30 ml) of olive oil, and have a bowl of freshly grated Parmesan cheese waiting on the table.

"Beautiful soup, so rich and green
Waiting in a hot tureen!
Who for such dainties would
not stoop?
Soup of the evening,
beautiful soup!"

Alice in Wonderland
Lewis Carroll, 1832-1898

A consommé is simply double-strength broth that has been clarified. Clarifying is the process of simmering stock, with eggshells and egg white, that makes it sparklingly clear and full of flavour. Many cookbooks explain the process well and for those willing to take the time, consommés are well worth the extra effort.

French onion soup has had a chequered history. It began magnificently enough in the 14th century, when it was created. By the 17th century, however, it was ignored in the royal court and considered to be a soup for peasants. This all changed when the former king of Poland stopped at an inn on his way to Versailles. He was so taken by the onion soup that he insisted on staying so he could learn to prepare it himself.

Chowders

Chowders are a meal in a bowl, more like a stew than a soup. They are normally made from seafood or corn. Potato adds substance, and bacon or salty pork chunks provide a wonderful flavour.

When you make a chowder, keep these points in mind:

- ❒ Don't liquefy chowder - it's supposed to be chunky!
- ❒ Serve chowder in shallow bowls with knives and forks, as well as spoons.
- ❒ Season chowder carefully. Taste it often and don't add more than one seasoning at a time.
- ❒ Sprinkle finely minced raw garlic on top of seafood chowder - it tastes wonderful!

Broths and Consommés

Broth (also called clear soup) is based on fish, meat, chicken or vegetable stock. Soups in this category are thinner and clearer than vegetable soups and chowders, but are much richer. Easy to digest, broths have a great depth of flavour and make a wonderful change of pace for any meal.

- ❒ Begin by applying the same method used for stock, but make both with meat, fish or poultry rather than just bones.
- ❒ The traditionally cheaper cuts of beef, like neck or shank, will produce a tastier broth.
- ❒ Broths are the base for many meat and vegetable classics like Scotch Broth or Chicken Noodle Soup. Unlike soup, broths of this kind are often served as a main course.

Herbs and Spices for Clear Soups

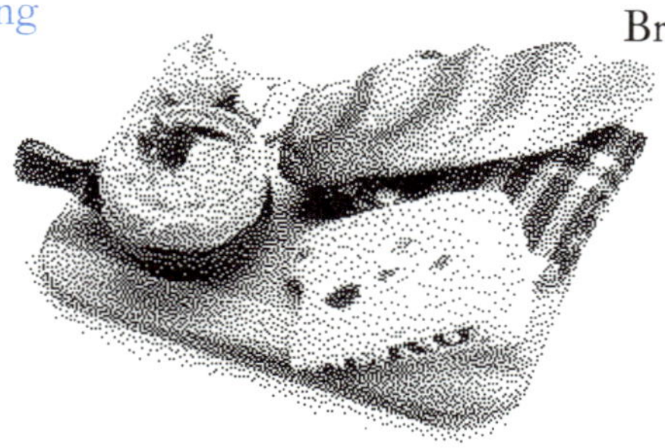

Broths and consommés don't look as good if there are all sorts of herbs floating in them. Instead, use a *bouquet garni* to season them. This is simply a collection of fresh herbs bound together to make a "bouquet."

French Onion Soup

One of the great and glorious meals of the world. The French invented it, and know to sauté their onions slowly to make the real thing. The sugar helps the onions to caramelize and liberates the deep, golden flavour. This recipe makes 6 bowls.

2 tbsp / *30 ml*	olive oil
2 oz / *50 g*	butter
1½ lbs / *700 g*	onions, thinly sliced
2	garlic cloves, crushed
1 tsp / *5 ml*	Rogers Granulated Sugar
2 pints / *1.25 L*	beef stock
10 fl oz / *275 ml*	dry white wine
	salt and black pepper
2 tbsp / *30 ml*	cognac
8 oz / *225 g*	freshly grated Gruyère cheese

MAKE THE CROÛTONS first (see the recipe below), so they can bake while you are preparing the soup.

MELT THE OLIVE OIL and butter together in a large, heavy-based saucepan over high heat, add the onions, garlic and sugar, and keep turning them until the edges of the onions are dark. This will take about 6 minutes.

REDUCE THE HEAT to its lowest setting and let the onions continue cooking, very slowly, for about 30 minutes. This caramelizes them and leaves the base of the pan covered with a rich, brown film.

POUR IN THE STOCK and the white wine and season with the salt and pepper. Stir with a wooden spoon, scraping up all the mixture on the base of the pan.

WHEN THE SOUP reaches the simmering point, turn down the heat to its lowest setting and leave the soup to cook very gently, without a lid, for about 1 hour.

ALL THIS CAN BE DONE in advance. When you are ready to serve the soup, bring it back to the simmering point, add the cognac and check if it needs more salt and pepper.

POUR THE SOUP into 6 ovenproof bowls and add the croûtons, so they float on the top. Now sprinkle the grated Gruyère thickly over the croûtons and put the bowls of soup under a hot broiler. When the cheese is golden brown and bubbling, serve immediately.

Croûtons

1 tbsp / *15 ml*	olive oil
2	garlic cloves, crushed
	French bread, cut into 1 in *(2.5 cm)* diagonal slices

PREHEAT YOUR OVEN to 350°F (180°C).

DRIZZLE THE OLIVE OIL on a large, solid baking sheet and add the crushed garlic. With your hands, spread the oil and garlic all over it.

NOW PLACE the bread slices on top of the oil, turning them over so both sides are lightly coated. Bake for 20 to 25 minutes until crisp and crunchy.

MAKING A MEAL FROM CLEAR SOUPS

All over the world, and for centuries, people have been adding food to clear soup to give it extra substance. This is a deliciously easy way to make soup into a meal.

Here are some additions from around the world that are simple to make yourself:

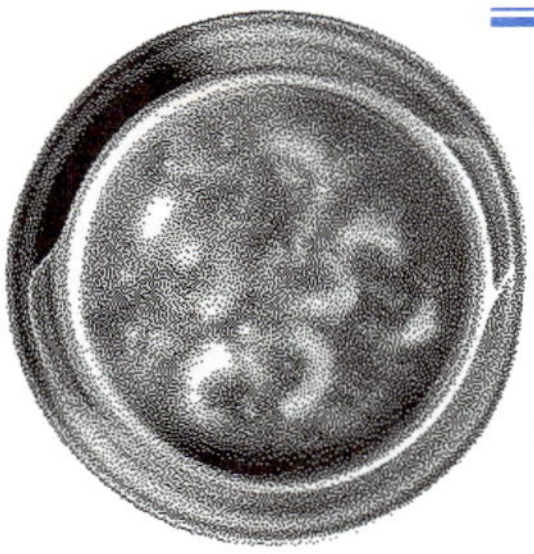

Broth is perfect for convalescents, as it is nourishing and full of flavour but very easy to digest.

Only cook with wine that you would be happy to drink.

- **Dumplings:** doughy balls, often flavoured with herbs or onion
- **Pasta:** cooked in the soup - thinner, lighter noodles work best
- **Gnocchi:** Italian potato balls, often made with cheese
- **Meatballs:** ground meat cooked separately with herbs and spices, then added to the soup
- **Egg drop:** beaten egg, simmered in the soup for 1 minute

Bread Dumplings

Bread Dumplings

2	eggs, beaten
¾ cup / *180 ml*	fine breadcrumbs
½ tsp / *2 ml*	cornstarch
1 tsp / *5 ml*	milk
2 tsp / *10 ml*	freshly minced parsley
¼ tsp / *1 ml*	salt
¼ tsp / *1 ml*	grated lemon peel
1 tsp / *5 ml*	grated onion

Small dumplings add delicious taste and texture to soups and stews. Make them extra appetizing with bacon, chives and cheese. This recipe makes 24 dumplings.

MIX ALL THE INGREDIENTS together until they form a dough (use more breadcrumbs if you need to).

CHILL THE DOUGH for at least 1 hour, then roll it into small balls. Throw them into the soup while it is still simmering, about 5 minutes before serving. The dumplings will rise to the surface and puff up when they are ready.

If you don't have any fresh herbs, you can make a bouquet garni *from dried ones. Use a square of cheesecloth and tie it tightly to make a small bundle of herbs.*

Add chopped fresh herbs or spices to frozen soup as you reheat it. They provide a lovely, fresh flavour.

Keeping Soup Fresh

Store your soup in the refrigerator for three to four days, or three months in the freezer. Cream soup will separate after freezing, but it becomes smooth again if you stir it as it reheats. Undercook the vegetables in soup that is going to be frozen; they will finish cooking when you reheat it. To save on freezer space, use only half the liquid that is called for in the recipe. You can add the rest when you prepare the soup later.

Great Garnishes

Adding a garnish to your soup makes it extra special:

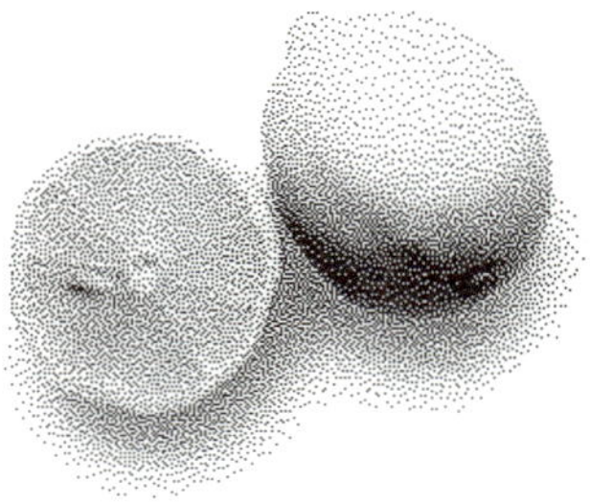

- Float homemade croûtons.
- Add thin slices of lemon.
- Decorate with a handful of chopped chives.

- Add a spoonful of sour cream.
- Dust with freshly grated Parmesan.
- Bring a blush to pale soups with a powdering of paprika.
- Sprinkle finely chopped parsley.
- Scatter cooked, crumbled bacon just before serving.

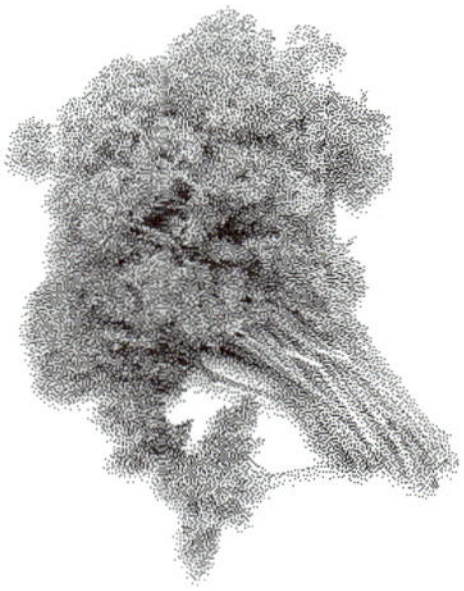

Thick, hearty soups were often served in Canadian settlers' homes, as they made a little food go a long way. In the early 1830s, John Langdon wrote that his potato soup was so good it was "the ordinary dish at breakfast."

Pumpkin and Ginger Soup

Pumpkin and ginger are two flavours that seem made for each other - this soup is a perfect example. This recipe makes 4 bowls.

5 cups / *1.25 L*	pumpkin, peeled, seeded and cubed
2 cups / *500 ml*	chicken stock
4½ cups / *1.125 L*	water
2 tsp / *10 ml*	fresh gingerroot, grated and peeled
¼ tsp / *1 ml*	cumin
¼ tsp / *1 ml*	cinnamon
¼ tsp / *1 ml*	allspice
1 tbsp / *15 ml*	honey
½ tsp / *2 ml*	orange zest, chopped or grated
½ cup / *125 ml*	fresh orange juice
1 cup / *250 ml*	cream
¼ cup / *110 g*	unsalted butter, cut into chunks
	salt to taste

SIMMER THE PUMPKIN cubes, chicken stock and water in a large saucepan until the pumpkin is soft. This will take about 25 minutes.

IN A BLENDER, purée the mixture in two batches, then force each batch through a fine sieve into a bowl.

BRING THE PURÉE TO A SIMMER in a saucepan and add the gingerroot, spices, honey, orange zest, orange juice, cream, butter and salt to taste, stirring until the butter is melted. Remove the pan from the heat and leave it to stand, covered, for an hour or two. This gives the flavours time to develop.

WHEN YOU ARE READY TO SERVE, reheat the soup until it is hot, but do not let it boil or the cream will curdle. Garnish with a dab of sour cream and a powdering of paprika.

Famous Soups of the World

There are some soups that are so delicious, they have become "classics" - not just in their country of origin but around the world. Any good cookbook will have the recipes, and it is definitely worth adding them to your repertoire:

- **Bouillabaisse**: The ultimate fish stew made with at least six varieties of fish, tomatoes and olive oil. Traditionally cooked in France over an open fire and served on slices of toasted bread.

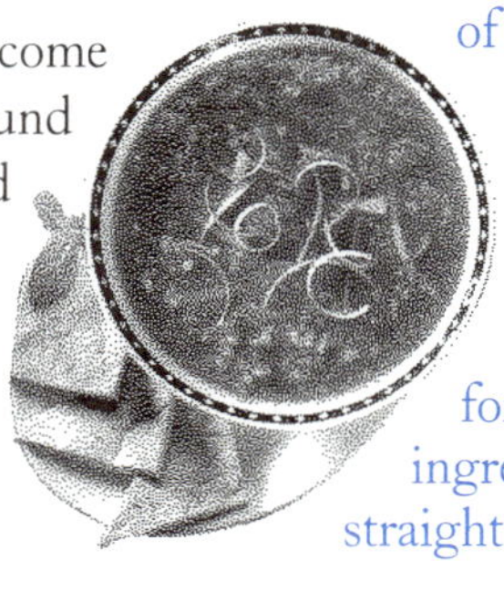

The essence of a good bouillabaisse is freshness of the seafood. In earlier days, fishermen's wives would be waiting on the beach with a roaring fire and a cauldron of bouillon and vegetables, ready for the freshly caught ingredients to be thrown straight into the pot.

Most cookbooks will tell you how to make soups, but when you want something extra special we recommend the following:

Soups
by James McNair
San Francisco:
Chronicle Books, c1990

Easy-to-follow directions and glorious photographs show you exactly how each delicious bowl should look. This is only one of McNair's many books; we recommend them all.

New Recipes from Moosewood Restaurant
by The Moosewood Collective
California:
Ten Speed Press, 1987

The Moosewood crew runs a restaurant, so you can bet their vegetarian soups are good. The Armenian Lentil Soup with eggplant and dried apricots is one of the best you'll find.

Chicken Soup
by Marcie Ver Ploeg
New York:
Scribner, 1995

This little book offers "75 world-class recipes to warm your heart." Worthy of mention is the Garlic Chicken Soup with Lemon and Sage and the Fiery African Chicken Soup.

Also recommended:

Splendid Soups: Look and Cook
by Anne Willan
Don Mills, Ontario:
Stoddart, 1994

If you are looking for interesting soup recipes, check out this web site:

http://www.cs.cmu.edu/~mjw/recipes/soup/soup.htm

- **Borscht**: There are lots of variations on this Russian soup, but it is normally made with beets. Both tart and refreshing, there is nothing quite like it on a hot day, especially with a dab of sour cream and chopped onion.

- **Gazpacho**: A refreshing Spanish soup that is delicious on a hot summer day, chilled and served with avocados and salsa.

- **Mulligatawny**: This Indian curried chowder, rich and spicy, was originally developed by Indian cooks to suit British taste. It has the perfect blend of spices, vegetables and coconut milk to serve before the main meal of curry.

- **Vichyssoise**: This leek and potato soup is equally delicious served hot or very cold. Serve it sprinkled with chopped chives and a swirl of cream.

"Of soup and love the first is the best."

Spanish Proverb

SALADS

"My salad days, when I was green in judgement."

Antony and Cleopatra
William Shakespeare, 1564-1616

In today's world of fresh food and widely available produce, salads have taken on a new importance. No longer limited to summer time and relegated to the side plate, a salad tossed with grilled chicken or spicy prawns becomes the perfect evening meal. Soft textures are offset by crisp raw ones, and strong flavours by mild. Experimenting with taste, colour and texture has transformed ordinary ingredients into works of art that delight our palates and excite the eye.

For the best tasting salads:

- Always use fresh produce and ingredients.
- Don't break up lettuce leaves too soon or they will quickly become limp. Leave them whole until you are ready to toss the salad.
- Never cut lettuce with a knife, it browns the edges of the leaves.
- Balance the tastes. A salad should be like a partnership, with no single flavour overpowering the others.
- Taste the salad as you make it to be sure you've got it right.
- Keep the salad simple if it is accompanying a cooked dish.
- Go easy on the dressing! All you need is a light drizzle.

Don't limit yourself to greens – some of the tastiest salads don't have a leaf in them! Try a salad made from zucchini and avocado, onion and bell pepper or fresh fruits.

"It's oil and vinegar dears,

No need to tiddle and toil;

Just salt and pepper and mustard,

And vinegar, and oil."

"It's Too Hard To Do It Easy"
Ogden Nash, 1902-71

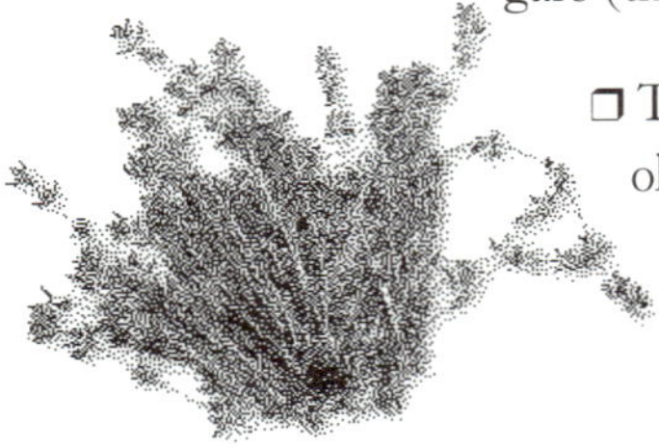

Dressing Up

It is the job of a good dressing to complement a salad rather than disguise it. That is why the right ingredients are so important. There is no mystery to French dressing or vinaigrette, just be sure to use olive oil for great flavour, and a good vinegar or some fresh lemon juice.

- ❒ To add variety, experiment with herb-flavoured oils and fruit vinegars (the recipe for raspberry vinegar is on page 48).
- ❒ To make your olive oil even "fruitier," soak a few plump black olives in the oil bottle. Leave them in the bottle for a week or so.
- ❒ Never use malt vinegar for your dressing; the strong taste is too overpowering. Wine, fruit or herb vinegar is a better alternative.
- ❒ Balsamic vinegar, from Italy, has a strong, pungent flavour, which makes a wonderful vinaigrette.
- ❒ For a refreshing change, splash in some lemon juice or sour wine instead of vinegar.
- ❒ Try adding a little garlic, curry powder, parsley, chives, Worcestershire sauce or thyme to your dressing for extra flavour.

There is nothing like real, homemade mayonnaise to use in coleslaws, potato salads and sandwiches. It can seem quite daunting if you haven't made it before, but with a good recipe, homemade mayonaise really is foolproof. The key to success lies in adding the oil one drop at a time. Whisk each drop in before you add the next, and you are guaranteed thick, creamy mayonnaise. There is nothing like it in the supermarkets. See our potato salad recipe on page 49.

Take Your Pick

Salad greens vary dramatically in taste, texture and colour. In Canada, we are lucky to have plenty of choice, so make the most of it. A good way to try the more exotic lettuces is to buy a bag of the mixed kinds that are sold by the kilo. There is no waste, and the colours look wonderful all tossed together in a big salad bowl.

Classic French Vinaigrette

The best flavours are often the most simple ones. This red wine and mustard vinaigrette is from a timeless French recipe, and is perfect to drizzle on any leaf salad.

½ cup / *125 ml*	red wine vinegar
2 tsp / *10 ml*	Rogers Granulated Sugar
1 tbsp / *15 ml*	Dijon mustard
1 tsp / *5 ml*	salt
1½ tsp / *7 ml*	ground black pepper
1 tsp / *5 ml*	dried tarragon
1 cup / *250 ml*	olive oil

In a small bowl, whisk the vinegar, sugar and seasonings together. Drizzle in the olive oil and continue whisking until the mixture thickens slightly. If you refrigerate the dressing, bring it to room temperature and whisk (or shake well) before serving.

The more common kinds of lettuce are:

- **Arugula** has an intense colour and a pungent flavour. It makes an ideal companion for softer, sweeter leaves and can stand up to a strong vinaigrette.
- **Butter Lettuce** is a pale green, fragile lettuce. Lovely and tender, it has a pleasing flavour. The outer leaves are dark green, while the inner ones are light green with a buttery flavour.
- **Curly Endive or Chicory** has tart and crunchy leaves. Its flavour is rather bitter and it has a prickly texture, but endive combines well with other greens for a salad.
- **Iceberg or Crisphead Lettuce** adds crunch and doesn't wilt quickly. The leaves are pale and watery, but iceberg is available year-round.
- **Leaf Lettuce** has curly, green- or red-tipped leaves. It's tasty and tender, and delicious when young.
- **Radicchio** is ruby-red with a slightly bitter flavour. Radicchio adds colour and flavour to other greens and goes well with a strong vinaigrette.
- **Romaine** is the foundation of Caesar Salad. It has firm, tight leaves with a robust nutty flavour. Romaine can be dressed with a strong vinaigrette and tastes good in nearly any salad.
- **Spinach** has dense, small, rounded leaves. Its flavour blends well with many salad combinations.
- **Watercress** is a good addition to any tossed salad. The leaves and tender parts of the stem are spicy and peppery and make a good taste balancer.

"The cherry tomato is a marvelous invention, producing as it does a satisfactorily explosive squish when bitten."

Miss Manners

Preparing Your Greens

There is nothing worse than preparing a salad and realizing your lettuce is past performing. Unfortunately, even the freshest greens won't last long in your refrigerator. They soon begin to wilt and soften, especially if they are wet.

The tradition at 18th-century French dinner parties was for the salad to be tossed in the hands of the most beautiful woman present. Hence, the French used to say admiringly of an attractive woman, *"elle retourne la salade avec les doigts"* (she turns the salad with her fingers).

We all know that salad dressings are great on salads, but how about using them as marinades? Any dressing made with oil, vinegar and lemon or lime juice will do. Pour it over mushrooms, olives, meat or fish and leave for an hour or two. Easy!

To avoid a case of the droops, buy your greens as close as possible to the time you want to use them. Have a look at the stalks where they have been cut from the root. If they are brown, they are not as fresh as they should be. One last thing: before you put greens in the refrigerator, try to have the leaves as dry as possible so they last longer.

When it comes to preparing salad, treat your greens gently:

- ❐ Separate the leaves and wash them thoroughly.
- ❐ Use a salad spinner, cotton tea towels or paper towels to dry the leaves. They need to be completely dry when you make a salad, so the flavours don't become diluted.

Spinach Salad With Prosciutto Dressing

Dressing:	
6 tbsp / *90 ml*	olive oil
1½ oz / *42 g*	prosciutto ham, chopped
2 tbsp / *30 ml*	minced garlic
6 tbsp / *90 ml*	dry white wine
6 tbsp / *90 ml*	fresh lemon juice
2 tbsp / *30 ml*	Rogers Granulated Sugar
	salt and freshly ground black pepper
Salad:	
10 oz / *280 g*	bag fresh spinach leaves
2½ cups / *625 ml*	sliced mushrooms
½ cup / *125 ml*	chopped walnuts
½ cup / *125 ml*	freshly grated Parmesan cheese

We couldn't resist including this tasty version of a classic salad. The unusual combination of flavours makes this salad an ideal starter, but serve it with the dressing warmed.
This recipe serves 4 as a side salad, 2 as a main course.

HEAT THE OIL in a heavy, small skillet over medium heat. Add the prosciutto and garlic and sauté them together for 3 minutes.

ADD THE WINE, lemon juice and sugar and simmer for 5 minutes.

POUR THE DRESSING into a bowl and leave it to cool slightly. When you serve it, it should be warm but not hot. Season with salt and pepper to taste.

CUT THE STEMS OFF the spinach leaves. Tiny spinach leaves are the best to use (avoid the very large leaves as they can be tough). Combine with the mushrooms, walnuts and cheese in a large bowl.

Toss with enough dressing to lightly coat the leaves.

After the French Revolution, several refugees went to America and made their fortunes as salad-dressers. They stunned the New World with exotic dressings that included perfumed vinegars, oils tasting of fruit, truffles - even caviar.

In Praise of Olive Oil

Everyone is talking about olive oil, and for good reason. It may well be one of the reasons that people in Corsica live to an impressive age. Olive oil adds a wonderful flavour to your food and we prefer it in our salad dressing.

Don't use cheap olive oil. You get the quality you pay for, and although extra virgin is more expensive than the other types, it is definitely worth it. Virgin olive oil is made from the first pressing of the olives and is the best quality.

Take good care of your oil. Once it has been opened for two weeks, you should keep it in the refrigerator. Don't worry if the oil turns cloudy, it soon returns to its natural state at room temperature.

Hail Caesar Salad

Hail to the chef! All the freshest ingredients, in just the right proportions, make this the best Caesar Salad of them all. But maybe we should have a competition? Send us your favourite recipe to the address on page 02. This recipe serves 4 as a side salad, 2 as a main course.

1	garlic clove
¼ cup / *60 ml*	olive oil
½ tsp / *2 ml*	Dijon mustard
½ tsp / *2 ml*	ground black pepper
	A dash of Worcestershire sauce
2 tbsp / *30 ml*	red wine vinegar
1	egg yolk
	juice of 1 lemon
3	anchovy fillets, finely chopped
1	head romaine lettuce
¼ cup / *60 ml*	freshly grated Parmesan

SOAK THE GARLIC in the olive oil for an hour or so, then remove it.

WHISK TOGETHER all the ingredients to make the dressing. Don't be tempted to leave the anchovies out; they give it a lovely, salty flavour and hardly any fishy taste. If you really don't like them, substitute 2 tbsp (30 ml) of crumbled blue cheese instead.

TEAR THE LETTUCE into pieces and arrange in a salad bowl.

ADD THE CROÛTONS and freshly grated Parmesan cheese. Drizzle on the dressing and toss well.

Croûtons

1	garlic clove
¼ cup / *60 ml*	olive oil
1 cup / *250 ml*	bread, cut into small cubes

THE NIGHT BEFORE, place the garlic in the olive oil. The next day, remove it and sauté the bread cubes in the oil. Use a frying pan over medium heat and cook the cubes until they are golden brown on all sides. Drain well on a paper towel.

ALTERNATIVELY, there is a recipe for baked croûtons on page 39.

MEDITERRANEAN TOMATO SALAD

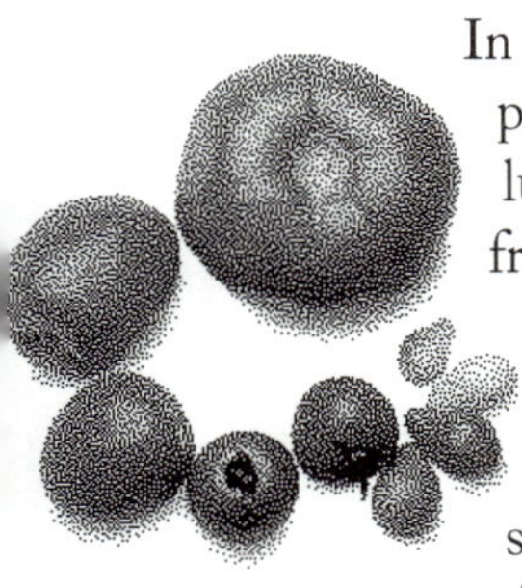

In the summertime, when tomatoes are at their prime, a fresh tomato salad makes the perfect lunch served with crusty French bread and fresh butter. Choose ripe but firm tomatoes and arrange slices on a large, flat plate. Scatter some finely chopped spring onions on top, as well as lots of freshly chopped parsley and some fresh basil leaves torn into small pieces. A sprinkling of granulated sugar will bring out the wonderful flavour of the tomatoes. Now all the salad needs is a

Caesar Salad is named after Caesar Cardini, a restaurant owner in Tijuana, Mexico. The salad came into existence when Mr. Cardini had nothing left to sell in his restaurant. In desperation, he gathered up all the ingredients in the kitchen and tossed them together in a large bowl for his customers.

Don't prepare this salad too far in advance - tomatoes quickly lose their freshness once they have been cut.

Raspberry Vinegar

Flavoured vinegars add a subtle zest to any salad. With bright ribbons and handmade labels, they also make great gifts for friends.

8 cups / *2 L* raspberries

4 cups / *1 L* apple cider vinegar

CRUSH THE BERRIES in a pan and add the vinegar. Bring the mixture to the boil, remove it from the heat and let it stand for an hour.

STRAIN THE VINEGAR into a clean pan, bring to the boil again and remove any skins that rise to the surface.

POUR THE VINEGAR into sterilized bottles and store in the fridge.

drizzle of olive oil, and some salt and pepper to taste. If the tomatoes aren't at their best, use a vinaigrette rather than oil (see the recipe on page 44). Slices of fresh Mozzarella also make a tasty addition.

Make Your Salad Into an Entrée

These days, we are rethinking salads. Not only are they served as accompaniments to the entrée, they often are the entrée! For a hearty, healthy meal, cook up one of these tasty additions to toss with a salad. Keep the flavour combinations simple. If there are too many ingredients, they will spoil the effect. Prepare the salad slightly ahead of the hot ingredients so everything can be served immediately.

Turn a salad into a meal with these delicious additions:

- Pan-fried chicken breasts with tarragon and black pepper, cut into strips. This is especially good with romaine lettuce and a Caesar dressing.
- Thinly sliced roast lamb and roasted eggplant, with pine nuts, on a bed of butter lettuce and a fruit vinaigrette.
- Peeled, spicy shrimps with bean sprouts and water chestnuts. Try this with watercress and a combination of lettuce leaves.
- Crab or lobster meat is especially good in salads made with hardboiled eggs.

Herbs for Salad

Herbs add a wonderful flavour to salads. Sprinkle on one or two kinds before serving, or add them to the dressing. Either way, use a small amount as they can taste quite sharp:

Bean: marjoram, tarragon, parsley

Tomato: basil, tarragon, parsley

Potato: mint, dill, parsley, chives

Egg: garlic, paprika, pepper, chilli powder

Green: cilantro, dill, thyme

Take a look at the Herbs & Spices section for more advice on individual salad herbs.

Potato Salad

Not all salads are green! Potato salad, with a light cream dressing or a vinaigrette, is the perfect side dish for any time of year.

Baby potatoes are best for salad, but if you have older ones cook them in their skins, then peel while they are still hot. Dress them immediately so that the dressing seeps into the warm flesh.

Some other points to remember:

- ❐ Always make salad from fresh potatoes. Save yesterday's cold boiled potatoes to use as a soup base or to make hash browns.
- ❐ If you are making a bowl of potato salad for a picnic, use an eggless dressing so it doesn't spoil in the heat.
- ❐ Present potato salad on a bed of lettuce leaves for extra colour, with some hard-boiled eggs scattered over the top.

"Four people are needed to make salad dressing. A spendthrift for oil, a miser for vinegar, a counsellor for salt, and a madman to stir it all up."

Spanish Proverb

Lettuce is an appetizer, but it also clears the palate. The ancient Greeks believed lettuce should be eaten "after the dinner, the toasts and the smearing of perfumes." In other words, after the meal but before the serious drinking began!

Potato and Dill Salad

Potato salad is the perfect excuse to experiment with unusual flavours. In this recipe, we have complemented the creamy new potatoes with an exciting dill and mustard dressing.
This recipe serves 6.

8 cups / *2 L*	chicken stock
2¼ lbs / *1 kg*	new baby potatoes, unpeeled
¾ cup / *180 ml*	vegetable oil
1	egg, at room temperature
3 tbsp / *45 ml*	Dijon mustard
2 tbsp / *30 ml*	finely chopped fresh dill or 2 tsp *(10 ml)* dried
1 tsp / *5 ml*	red wine vinegar
½ cup / *125 ml*	sour cream
1 tsp / *5 ml*	lemon juice
	freshly ground black pepper
3	celery stalks, thinly sliced
1	onion, thinly sliced
½	bunch fresh chives, snipped

PUT THE STOCK and potatoes in a saucepan and bring to a boil over high heat. Reduce the heat and cook the potatoes just until tender. Drain them immediately and keep them warm.

MEANWHILE, IN A FOOD PROCESSOR or blender, combine the oil, egg, mustard, dill, vinegar, sour cream, lemon juice and pepper. Blend until the mixture is smooth.

CUT THE POTATOES into bite-sized chunks, add the dressing, toss in remaining ingredients and serve.

Potato and Dill Salad

Buy unripe avocados and put them in a brown paper bag to soften. Once they are sliced, eat them as soon as possible. Lemon juice stops sliced avocados from going brown, but only for a short time.

Avocados

The less you do with an avocado the better. Treat it gently - a dash of lemon juice, some crisp bacon or a dribble of olive oil is all you need for the best flavour.

- Slice avocado into a tossed salad for a creamy contrast.
- Make an avocado and ham salad with chunks of leftover baked ham, avocado, tomato, onion and a lemon vinaigrette.
- Guacamole, an avocado dip, tastes wonderful eaten with corn chips or spread on French bread. To make guacamole, mash two avocados with a fork. Stir in chopped onion, one or two fresh green chile peppers, very finely chopped, a clove of crushed garlic and a squeeze of lime juice.

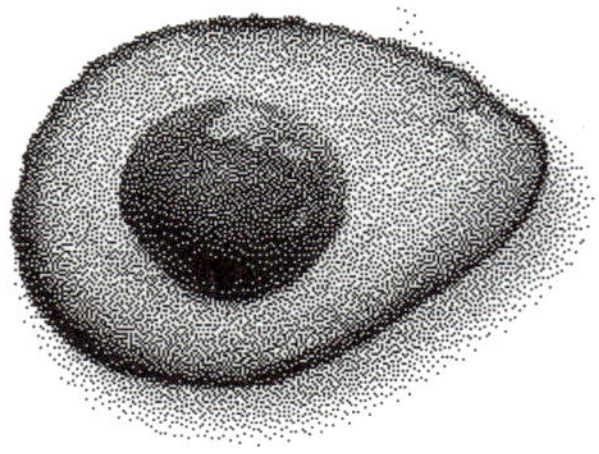

Thanksgiving Turkey Salad

1	Golden Delicious apple, cut into strips
1	Granny Smith apple, cut into strips
1 tbsp / *15 ml*	lemon juice
1 lb / *500 g*	cooked turkey breast, cut into strips
½ lb / *250 g*	Roquefort cheese
1 cup / *250 ml*	seedless grapes
1 cup / *250 ml*	chopped celery
½ cup / *125 ml*	raisins or cranberries
1 cup / *250 ml*	plain yogurt
2 tbsp / *30 ml*	cider vinegar
1 tbsp / *15 ml*	liquid honey
	salt and freshly ground black pepper
½ cup / *125 ml*	coarsely chopped cashew nuts
	lettuce leaves
6	strips smoked bacon

Thanksgiving Turkey Salad

Here is a salad that is completely different. Blow your guests away with this unbelievably tasty meal, concocted from cold turkey and Roquefort cheese.

TOSS THE APPLE STRIPS with the lemon juice to keep them from darkening.

MIX THE APPLE with the turkey, crumbled cheese, grapes, celery and raisins or cranberries.

WHISK TOGETHER the yogurt, vinegar, honey, salt and pepper to taste. Pour the dressing over the salad and toss. Add the cashew nuts.

CHILL THE SALAD, covered, for 3 hours in the refrigerator before serving. To serve, mound the salad on a bed of crisp greens. Fry the bacon slices until crisp and golden, then crumble them over the top.

Customized Green Salad

To a bed of the crispest, freshest lettuce you can find, experiment with adding different ingredients to create an original masterpiece. Have some fun creating your own signature green salad.

Make up your own or give one of the following combinations a try:

- Shreds of sun-dried tomato, marinated artichoke hearts and a sprinkling of freshly grated Parmesan cheese

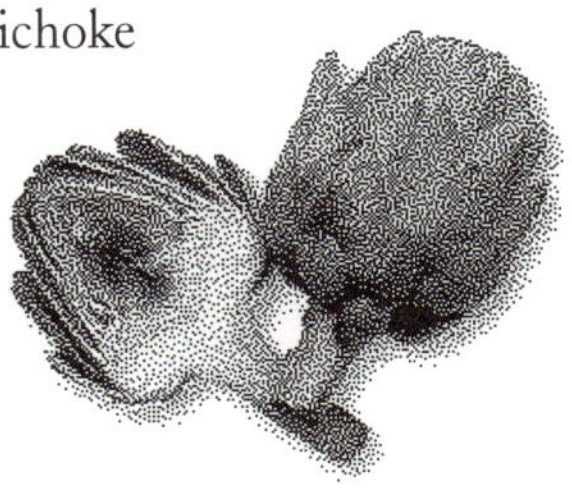

- Minced red onion and mandarin orange segments
- A handful of bean sprouts, some Chinese greens and a dash of sesame oil added to the dressing
- Chopped fresh thyme, basil, lemon balm or chives, berries of the season and a raspberry vinaigrette
- Toasted walnut halves and small chunks of goat cheese or crumbled blue cheese
- Chopped apples, peanuts and a mango chutney dressing
- Freshly cooked shrimps and scallops with a tarragon vinaigrette

Brighten up a bean salad with some simple additions. Chopped fresh parsley, diced onion, finely chopped tomatoes, mustard or paprika are all perfect accompaniments for beans.

Famous Salads of the World

Even in colder countries, where lettuce and tomatoes are not as easily available, salads are a popular part of the meal. People concoct wonderful salads from all kinds of other ingredients.

Try these yourself, as a delicious change from green salads:

- **Salade Niçoise**: This salty, zesty salad from the south of France is a garlicky treat made with tomatoes, anchovies, olives and lettuce.
- **Greek Salad**: Originally from Greece, this salad is popular all over the world. The tomatoes, olives, feta cheese, onions and cucumber are simple ingredients that taste wonderful.

Two of the greatest complements to salad are cheese and cream. Try some different kinds: freshly grated Parmesan, feta cheese or cottage cheese all give extra flavour and texture to a tossed green salad, while cream cheese and sour cream are perfect for adding to the dressing.

For a taste of some favourite salad books, have a "leaf" through these:

Healthy Home Cooking
by Margaret Howard & Ellie Topp
Toronto:
Macmillan Canada, 1993

This book has low-fat recipes galore, including some temptingly unusual salads. Lentil and Brown Rice Salad with Mustard Dressing and Peach, Basil and Chicken Salad are just two mouth-watering examples.

The Greens Cook Book
by Deborah Madison
Toronto:
New York, Bantam Books, 1987

Filled with recipes from the famous restaurant in San Francisco, this vegetarian cookbook is teeming with salad ideas.

Rose Reisman Brings Home Light Cooking
by Rose Reisman
Toronto:
Macmillan Canada, 1993

Rose Reisman is one of our favourite cooks. Her glorious collection includes recipes such as Mushroom and Snow Pea Salad, and a Japanese Salad with Peanut Dressing.

The B.C. Vegetable Marketing Commission has some excellent free salad recipes:

B.C. Vegetable Marketing Commission

201-7560 Vantage Way
Delta, British Columbia
V4G 1H1
1-800-663-1461

- **Italian Salad**: It is no surprise that an Italian salad is made from pasta shells, but the zucchini and sweet corn add great flavour.
- **Waldorf Salad**: This is a famous salad created by the maître d'hôtel of the Waldorf in 1896. Made with celery, apples, grapes, walnuts and a creamy dressing, it is a delicious summertime salad.

"To make a good salad is to be a brilliant diplomatist - the problem is entirely the same in both cases. To know exactly how much oil one must put with one's vinegar."

Oscar Wilde, 1856-1900

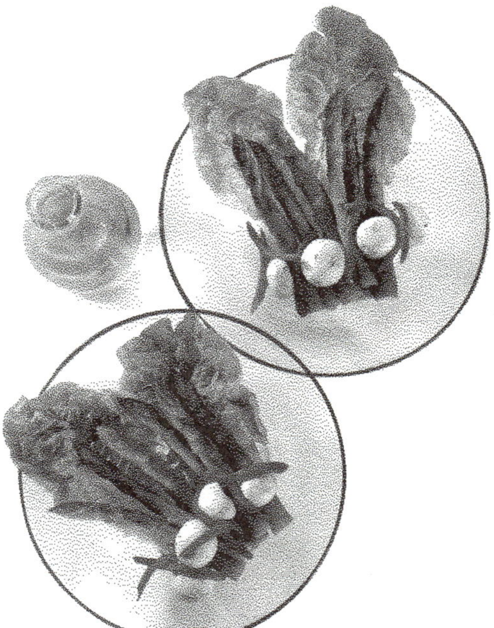

VEGETABLES

"Only two things in this world are too serious to be jested on - potatoes and matrimony."

Irish Proverb

Changing ideas about healthy eating have nudged vegetables from a supporting role to a starring one in our meals and diets. No longer a last-minute addition to the evening meal, vegetables are now found centre stage. Shiny, smooth eggplant, brightly coloured peppers or melt-in-your-mouth corn on the cob, the possibilities are endless and ripe. Bursting with flavour and colour, vegetables have been stars all along.

Buy vegetables as fresh as possible. The less processed they are, the better they taste. Follow our tips when cooking vegetables:

- ❒ Use vegetables as soon as possible – the most vulnerable, thin-skinned ones first.
- ❒ Don't soak your vegetables in water. This is the quickest way to lose their nutritious vitamins, minerals and sugars.
- ❒ Trim and wash vegetables at the last possible moment to retain their natural moisture.
- ❒ Put green vegetables straight into a small amount of boiling water; they only need a minimum of cooking.
- ❒ Boil root vegetables thoroughly, starting with plenty of cold water and a pinch of salt.

Young vegetables contain sugars, that's why fresh-from-the-garden ones are so sweet. Add a pinch of granulated sugar, and all your cooked vegetables will taste equally young and fresh.

The younger the vegetable, the less seasoning it needs. Older vegetables can always use a little more help.

In the English court of the 1700s and early 1800s, carrots were an exciting novelty. All the well-dressed ladies wore them like feathers in their hats.

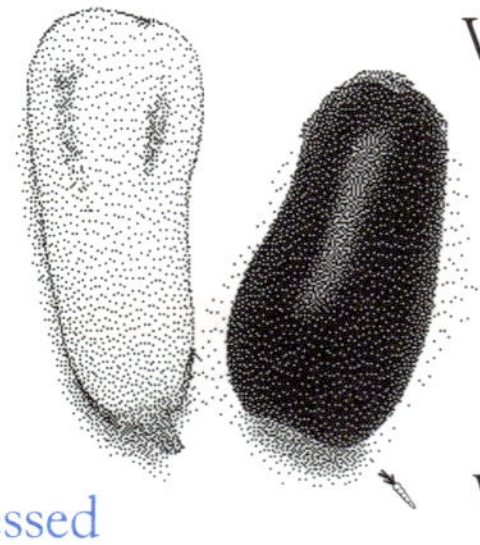

Wake Up to Vegetarian Cooking

Even if you are a committed meat lover, serve up a tasty vegetarian meal for a change. For many cultures, vegetarian eating is the norm. Whether as a way of life or simply as a change of pace, vegetarian cooking offers delicious, satisfying and economical alternatives.

- Eggplant is "meaty" and delicious, especially when served in a ratatouille or baked with tomato sauce and topped with cheese.
- Vegetarian pasta dishes will satisfy even the biggest appetites.
- Robust soups made from lentils and beans offer tasty, filling meals.
- Throw together an Asian stir fry with lots of fresh vegetables, ginger and rice.
- See the Salads section (page 48) for ideas on how to turn a salad into a complete evening meal.

Orange-Cinnamon Carrots

½ cup / *125 ml*	orange juice
1 tbsp / *15 ml*	Rogers Golden Syrup
1 tbsp / *15 ml*	oil
½ tsp / *2 ml*	each of grated orange and lemon peel
	pinch of salt
	pinch of cinnamon
8	medium carrots, peeled and cut into julienne strips

In a heavy skillet, bring the orange juice, Golden Syrup, oil, peels, salt and cinnamon to the boil.

Add the carrots, bring back to the boil and cover the pan. Turning occasionally, simmer carrots 3 to 5 minutes or until just tender. Chill.

Spotlight on Carrots

Fresh carrots, pulled straight from the ground and rinsed, are pure pleasure. If you aren't lucky enough to have a vegetable garden, look out for sweet "baby" carrots in your local supermarket and try one of these ideas:

- Toss steamed carrots with butter, a sprinkling of granulated sugar and chopped fresh dill or mint.
- Stir steamed carrots with butter, honey and cinnamon.
- Mix with orange juice and ginger and cook carrots in the microwave.
- Sauté carrots in butter, then simmer with 2 tbsp (30 ml) of white wine to glaze them.
- Marinate in French vinaigrette and fresh parsley for two hours.
- Season cooked carrots with sage.

Herbs for Vegetables

These herbs add a wonderful flavour to vegetables:

Asparagus: chives, dill, lemon balm, tarragon

Avocado: dill, marjoram, tarragon, garlic

Mushrooms: basil, dill, lemon balm, marjoram, parsley, rosemary, tarragon, thyme

Onions: basil, marjoram (in soup), oregano, sage

Potatoes: mint, basil, chives, dill, marjoram, oregano, parsley, rosemary, thyme

Tomatoes: basil, bay, chives, dill seed, garlic, mint, oregano, parsley, sage, tarragon

Zucchini: basil, dill, marjoram, rosemary, tarragon

Cooking With Chiles

There seems to be an infinite variety of chile peppers, ranging from fiery to mild. If you or your guests are not fans of spicy food, it's best to make a chile salsa and have it on the table. Then people can help themselves and adjust the dish to their taste. To lessen the heat of chiles, remove the ribs and the white tissue inside the pepper.
If you get a bite that is too hot, don't drink water - it spreads the heat around your mouth! Instead, take a bite of rice, bread, banana or potato.

Mediterranean Vegetables

One look at the ingredients in this recipe is all you need to be convinced of the flavour promise of this classic Mediterranean dish.

4 tbsp / *60 ml*	olive oil
1	medium onion, finely chopped
1	garlic clove, crushed
2 tbsp / *30 ml*	red wine vinegar
1	14 oz *(398 ml)* can tomatoes
1 tsp / *5 ml*	dried oregano
1 tsp / *5 ml*	whole coriander seeds, crushed
8	black peppercorns, lightly crushed
	juice of 1 lemon
¼ cup / *60 ml*	water, mixed with 1 tsp tomato purée
	Salt and pepper
1	tin kidney beans
4 oz / *110 g*	cauliflower, broken into 1 in *(2.5 cm)* pieces
4 oz / *110 g*	mushrooms, halved
2 tbsp / *30 ml*	chopped parsley

HEAT 2 tbsp (30 ml) of the olive oil in a heavy-based pan and soften the onion for 5 minutes.

ADD THE GARLIC, wine vinegar, tomatoes, oregano, coriander, peppercorns, lemon juice, water and tomato purée, and some salt. Bring to the boil, cover the pan and simmer for 20 minutes.

ADD THE KIDNEY BEANS, cauliflower and mushrooms, cover the pan again and simmer for another 20 minutes, stirring once or twice. After 20 minutes test the vegetables: they should be tender, but still firm. Taste and add more seasoning, if you like.

POUR THE CONTENTS of the pan into a shallow dish and leave it to cool. If possible, leave overnight, but a few hours will do.

TO SERVE, SPRINKLE THE VEGETABLES with the rest of the olive oil, then scatter the chopped parsley over the top.

Mediterranean Vegetables

You can now buy eggplants year-round, but go for two of the smallest, firmest ones you can find rather than a single large one.

When you refrigerate ratatouille, leave the accumulated olive oil on top. It helps to keep the ratatouille fresh.

Onions have been cultivated since prehistoric times, and were particularly prized by the Babylonians and the ancient Egyptians.

Onions

Onions are the most versatile and economical vegetable you can find, and they add a wonderful flavour to nearly any savoury dish. But as Benjamin Franklin once commented, "Onions can make ev'n heirs and widows weep." To stop the tears, use a very sharp knife so it cuts without crushing the onion and releasing its juice (which stings your eyes). Remove the tip of the onion, peel it, then cut off the base last.

- **Large golden onions** are best for general cooking as they are sweeter than the other varieties. For a tasty change, try baking onions in the oven until they are tender (poke them with a sharp fork or a toothpick to test). Take them out of the oven and let them rest for a moment and the skins will slip off easily. Serve hot with butter, salt, pepper and a small pinch of cinnamon or nutmeg.

- **Purple (Spanish) onions** have a lighter flavour and aren't as tear-inducing as golden onions. Always use them raw, as they become bitter and turn a strange colour if cooked. Serve purple onions in salads and on top of hamburgers.

- **White onions** have a softer flavour and are more delicate; use them in dishes such as creamed onions. They are also more likely to go bad, so store them in the refrigerator and keep them dry.

Roasted Ratatouille

Roasted Ratatouille

Ratatouille is a classic eggplant dish from the south of France. Try this recipe for roasting it, and we guarantee you will never do it another way. This recipe makes 4 to 6 servings.

2 cups / *500 ml*	unpeeled yellow summer squash, in 2 cm cubes
1½ tsp / *7 ml*	salt
3	large garlic cloves, minced
1/3 cup / *80 ml*	olive oil
2 cups / *500 ml*	peeled eggplant, in 2 cm cubes
½ tsp / *2 ml*	dried oregano
3	onions, thinly sliced
2	green peppers, cut into thin strips
½ tsp / *2 ml*	dried marjoram
4	firm-ripe peeled tomatoes, sliced
¼ tsp / *1 ml*	dill seeds

PREHEAT your oven to 350°F (180°C).

BUTTER A LARGE CASSEROLE DISH and cover the bottom with cubes of unpeeled squash.

SPRINKLE with a third of the salt, garlic and oil.

MAKE A SECOND LAYER with the eggplant cubes. Repeat the salt, garlic and oil and add the oregano. Make a third layer of onion slices, then a fourth layer with the green pepper strips.

SPRINKLE WITH THE REST of the salt, garlic and oil. Add the marjoram. Cover the casserole dish and bake for about 45 minutes.

NOW TAKE THE LID OFF and add another layer, this time of tomato slices sprinkled with dill seeds. Put it back in the oven, uncovered, for 10 minutes.

The Magic of Mushrooms

Next time you go to the store to buy mushrooms, why not try a fresh, wild variety, or some Japanese *shiitake* mushrooms? There are also varieties that you can buy dried. All they need is to be soaked in liquid (port or chicken stock give the best flavour), then sautéed in butter. Combine them with cultivated mushrooms to make them go further (see our Garlic Mushrooms recipe on page 27).

- The secret to mushrooms is never to overcook them. All they need is a few minutes for perfect flavour.

- Little white button mushrooms are best eaten raw. Toss them with a squeeze of lemon and some chopped fresh parsley.
- Huge flat mushrooms are as juicy and tender as a piece of steak. Brush them with olive oil and a squeeze of lemon, then broil them and serve with the juices that collect in the pan.

The ancient Greeks used to call mushrooms "food for the gods."

"Whether found in shop or field,
Your mushrooms can
remain unpeeled,
Although they should be
washed and dried
Before in butter they are fried."

The Rhyming Irish Cookbook
Gorden Snell

Potatoes: Apples of the Earth

How can we discuss vegetables and not mention potatoes? They are a staple food in many countries, and ways of cooking potatoes are nearly limitless.

Boiled: New potatoes need nothing more than a quick boil with a sprig of mint added to the water. Add butter to the dish just before you serve them. For older potatoes start with plenty of cold water, and leave the lid off the saucepan to cook.

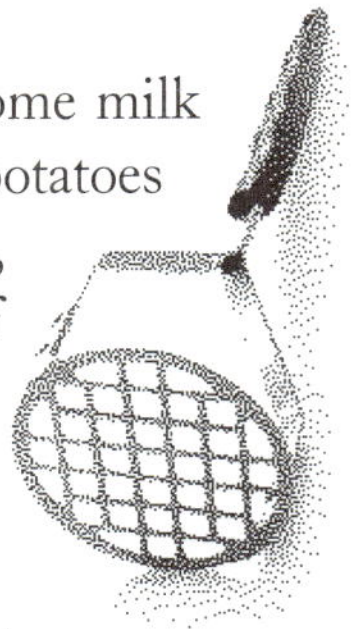

Mashed: Add salt, pepper, a knob of butter and some milk to boiled potatoes. Whisk, beat or mash until the potatoes are creamy and free of lumps. By themselves, mashed potatoes are true comfort food. Add any of the following ingredients and they become luxurious:

- Simmer one or two peeled cloves of garlic in the same water as the potatoes, then mash them all together.
- Blend in chopped chives or green onion and sour cream.

When the potato was first brought to Europe in the 16th century, from its native Peru, it was not well liked. It only became accepted when King Louis XVI of France was persuaded to eat one. He and his courtiers liked the taste so much they even began wearing potato blossoms in their buttonholes!

The potato is far more nutritious than is often imagined. It is high in complex carbohydrates and fibre, and is an important source of vitamin C and several minerals.

"Brave King Edwards, rough-backed in your dry scrubbed excellence, or with butter, salty. Sweet potatoes! Dear new knobbly ones, beside the oiled sides of meaty carrots."

Collected Poems, 1932-92
George Macbeth

Never cook with sprouted potatoes that have turned green from exposure to light. The green portions, and also the sprouts, are mildly poisonous.

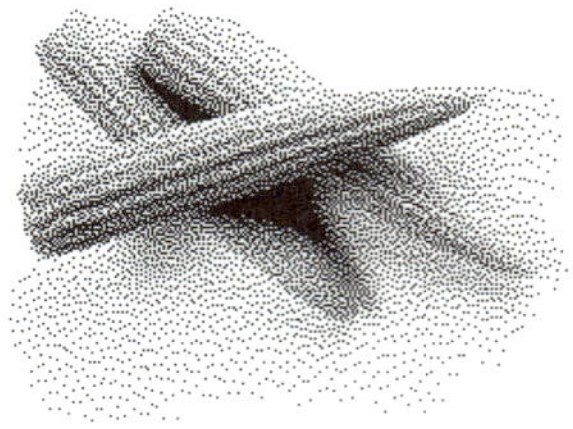

Corn has been a staple of Central American diets for at least 5,000 years. When Columbus first took corn back to Europe, it was named "Turkish wheat." But the Turks called it "foreign grain"!

- Add a dash of hot mustard or a pinch of nutmeg.

Roasted: Leave the nutritious skins on. Scrub the potatoes well, then dry them and put them straight into the pan with the roasting meat juice for 45 to 55 minutes. Make sure the juice is really hot when you put the potatoes in, or they will stick and become greasy.

Fried: For a tasty alternative to French fries, cut potatoes into wedges and brush them with a little olive oil mixed with salt, pepper and herbs or spices. Try seasoning them with oregano for a nice accompaniment to barbequed chicken. Paprika, crushed garlic or curry powder also taste great. Place the wedges on a non-stick cookie sheet and bake at 400°F (200°C) for 10 minutes. Turn the potatoes over and brush with a little more of the seasoned oil mixture, then bake for another 5 to 10 minutes or until they are done.

Baked: Preheat your oven to 400°F (200°C). Boil the potatoes first for 10 minutes in water with 1 tsp (5 ml) of Rogers Granulated Sugar. Dry them and rub the skins with olive oil and a bit of salt. Prick the potatoes a couple of times (to keep them from going soggy), then bake for about 1 hour.

When you stuff baked potatoes with tasty fillings, you have a complete, nutritious meal at your fingertips. Slice off a "lid" and scoop out the flesh. Mash it with one of the following, then stuff it all back into the potato shell:

- Cottage cheese, freshly chopped tomatoes and garlic
- Small cubes of ham, sweet corn and chopped parsley
- Crumbled goat cheese and shredded baby spinach leaves
- Olives, fresh green finely chopped chile peppers and sour cream
- Thinly sliced Mozzarella cheese and chopped fresh oregano
- Pesto sauce (see page 20 for the recipe) and a little grated Parmesan cheese
- Crumbled bacon with toasted pumpkin seeds and melted butter

Put the potatoes back in the oven for 5 minutes after you have filled them, and give them a good grinding of black pepper.

Scalloped Potatoes

There are a hundred and one different ways to prepare potatoes for the evening meal. We heartily recommend this recipe for creamy scalloped potatoes, seasoned with salt, pepper and paprika.
This recipe makes 6 servings.

3 lbs / *1.5 kg*	potatoes
2	medium onions
5 tbsp / *75 ml*	butter
2 tbsp / *30 ml*	flour
1 tsp / *5 ml*	salt
	freshly ground black pepper
2 cups / *500 ml*	milk or cream
¼ tsp / *1 ml*	paprika

PREHEAT your oven to 375°F (190°C). Butter a 10 in (25 cm), ovenproof casserole dish.

PEEL AND SLICE the potatoes. Cut up the onions.

BOIL THE POTATOES and onion pieces in salted water for about 8 minutes, then drain them thoroughly.

ARRANGE A LAYER of potato slices in the casserole, top with a layer of onion slices, then dot with part of the butter. Sprinkle with some flour, salt and pepper.

REPEAT THIS LAYERING until all the potatos and onion are used up, finishing with a layer of onions on the top. Don't fill the dish more than three-quarters full or it's likely to boil over in the oven.

HEAT THE MILK or cream and season it with a pinch of salt and the paprika. Carefully pour this mixture over the onions and potatoes, then top with the rest of the butter and a grind of pepper.

BAKE, UNCOVERED, in the oven for about 35 minutes. The scalloped potatoes should be nicely browned and tender when you prick them with a fork.

STIR FRIES FROM HEAVEN

Want a meal that is ready in the time it takes to set the table? Get out your wok or frying pan and discover the fun of stir frying. This is a quick cooking technique that uses a small amount of oil, a high heat and much stirring and tossing of food. Flavours, juices, nutrients and the natural colours of the vegetables are all preserved when you stir fry them.

Never add acidic ingredients such as wine, tomatoes, vinegar or lemon juice to green vegetables when you cook them. They will quickly lose their colour.

Enhance the nutty flavour of parsnips with a scattering of Rogers Golden Yellow Sugar, spices, butter, and olive oil or cream.

To improve the flavour of corn, add a little milk and Rogers Granulated Sugar to the water when you are cooking it.

For the best stir fries, remember these points:

- Thinly slice vegetables that take longer to cook. Quick cooking ones can be cut into chunks. Your goal is to have everything ready at the same time.
- Have all the ingredients cut and ready before you begin, because once you start to cook, there won't be time.
- Add vegetables in order of their cooking time - the firmer ones first.
- Cook on high heat, but be careful with onions and ginger. If you brown them too quickly, they will become sticky and crispy and you will have to start again.

Royal Stir Fry

This recipe combines some of our favourite ingredients. It has a wonderful ginger flavour and looks beautiful served over rice.
This recipe serves 4.

2 tbsp / *30 ml*	sesame oil
1	clove garlic, chopped
2 tbsp / *30 ml*	sliced ginger root, cut in matchstick-sized slices
2	shallots, cut in 1 in *(2.5 cm)* pieces
1	onion, sliced
½	red bell pepper, cut in strips
4 tbsp / *60 ml*	mushrooms
1 tbsp / *15 ml*	oyster sauce
1 tbsp / *15 ml*	fish sauce
½ tsp / *2 ml*	Rogers Granulated Sugar
	pinch of white pepper
2 tsp / *10 ml*	finely chopped fresh cilantro leaves for garnish

HEAT THE SESAME OIL in a hot wok or frying pan and fry the garlic and ginger until they are golden.

NOW THROW IN THE SHALLOTS, onion, red bell pepper and mushrooms. Stir fry furiously for several minutes until everything is half-cooked, then add the oyster and fish sauces, sugar and pepper.

PUT THE LID ON and let everything soften in the steam. When you have tender but still crunchy vegetables, it's ready to eat. Remove the stir fry from the heat, sprinkle with the chopped cilantro leaves and serve immediately.

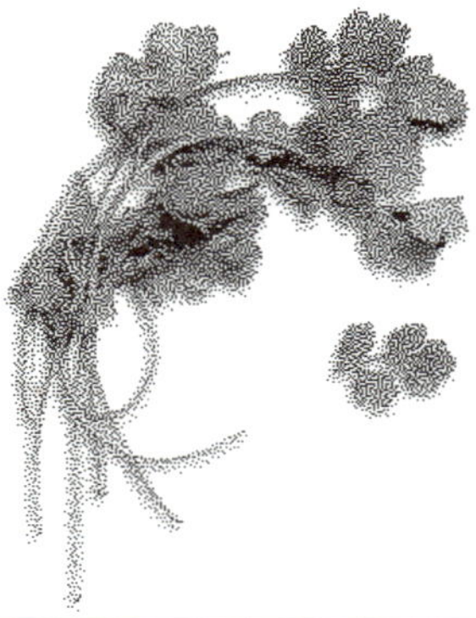

Rice

Rice, with more than 7,000 varieties in the world, is a valuable form of starch. Use it as a stuffing in tomatoes, peppers, vine leaves, poultry or pancakes. It's a fine garnish for soups, and it can also be tossed with an oil and vinegar dressing and served cold. Try rice with vegetables, shrimps or fish.

- Cooking rice in chicken or vegetable stock will give it extra flavour (see pages 34, 35 for how to make stock).
- Long-grain rice is best for general dishes like curries, while short- and medium-grain rice is the best choice for risottos and puddings.
- For something different, try wild or Basmati rice. Both are absolutely delicious with an exotic nutty flavour. Mixed with normal rice they will go further, but cook them separately.

Good Things to Stir Into Rice

There are times when a bowl of steaming rice, pure and comforting, is all you want for dinner. When this is the case, try combining it with one of the following ideas for added flavour:

- Lots of butter and Parmesan cheese
- Sliced mushrooms, sautéed in butter with a teaspoon of coriander
- Thin shreds of hot bacon or cubes of ham
- Finely chopped chile peppers
- A handful of freshly chopped mint and half a cucumber, peeled and diced
- A spoonful of black olive paste and a couple of finely sliced sun-dried tomatoes
- A spoonful of pesto sauce (see page 20 for the recipe)

Most rice doubles or triples in size during cooking, so make sure your cooking pan is big enough.

"One cannot think well, love well, sleep well, if one has not dined well."

A Room of One's Own
Virginia Woolf, 1882-1941

Know Your Vegetarians

The term "vegetarian" was coined in 1847. Before that, people who didn't eat meat were called "Pythagoreans," after the ancient Greek mathematician Pythagoras - who was a vegetarian.

- **Ovo vegetarians** don't eat meat or fish, but they do eat eggs.
- **Lacto vegetarians** don't eat meat or fish, but they do eat milk and dairy products.
- **Lacto-ovo vegetarians** don't eat meat or fish, but they do eat eggs and dairy products.
- **Vegans** don't eat any foods of animal origin, including honey or gelatin.
- **Pescatarians** don't eat meat, but they do eat fish.

Vegging out with a good cookbook can give you all kinds of terrific food ideas. We particularly like these ones:

Vegetarian World of the East
by Madhur Jaffrey
New York:
Knopf, 1981

Pick up a few exotic spices at your nearest ethnic market and you'll soon be exploring the wonderful recipes in this book. Discover how simple and delicious Eastern cooking can be. Try a curry of eggplant and potatoes, and zucchini "meatballs" from India.

The Vegetarian Table: France
by Georgeanne Brennan
San Francisco:
Chronicle Books, 1995

Vegetarian or not, you'll find some exceptional dishes here. Our favourites? The Sautéed Baby Spinach and the Winter Vegetable Ragoût with Caramelized Whole Shallots.

Additional Sources:

The Onion Book
Jan Roberts-Dominguez
New York:
Doubleday, 1996

There are many web sites that cover vegetarian cooking and recipes, but here's one that's particularly good:

http://www.foodservice.ca/cuisine/recipes.htm

This marketing board has free vegetable recipes for the asking:

B.C. Vegetable Marketing Commission
201-7560 Vantage Way
Delta, British Columbia
V4G 1H1
1-800-663-1461

Grilling Vegetables

Grilled vegetables are great, especially eggplant, zucchini, bell pepper, mushroom, red onion and tomato. Cut each vegetable into ½ in (1.5 cm) slices, and marinate for 30 minutes in a little olive oil with some freshly chopped oregano and the juice of half a lemon. Now grill them over a medium heat. Perfect.

"I do not like broccoli. I did not like broccoli when I was a kid and my mother made me eat it. Now I am the President of the United States and I do not have to eat broccoli if I don't want to."

George Bush, 1990

P A S T A

"No man is lonely while eating spaghetti - it requires so much attention."

Christopher Morley, 1890-1957

No one knows for sure where pasta originated, but the Chinese were eating it as far back as the Ming dynasty. Pasta is now eaten all over the world, but particularly in Italy where it is practically the national dish. A glorious monument to the Italian love of good food, pasta is delicious, nourishing and quick. The endless variety of shapes, combination of ingredients and different sauces means that pasta could be served every day and we would never tire of it.

To make your pasta in true Italian style:

- ❒ Always cook pasta with plenty of boiling water.
- ❒ Use the best, freshest ingredients you can find for the sauce.
- ❒ Serve short pasta with thicker sauces, thin pastas with thinner sauces.
- ❒ Dried pasta can stand up to robust flavours, but fresh pasta is more delicate so its sauce should be too.
- ❒ If you are serving pasta as a starter, go easy on the quantities - it is very filling!

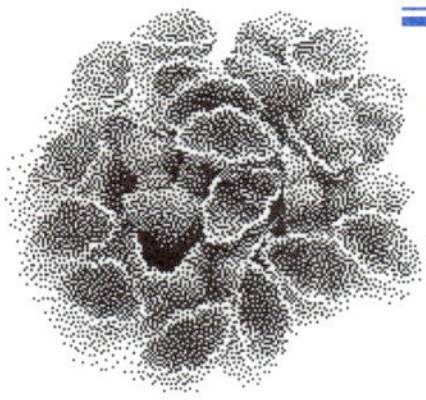

In an Italian meal, each of the four or five courses is equally important. It may take a long time, but as the old Italian proverb says, "A tavola non s'in vecchia" (at the table one never gets old).

Choosing Pasta

Unless you make your own, there are two ways of buying pasta: dried and fresh. You will find that imported Italian dried pasta has the best flavour, although it does cost a little more. In Italy, the government has strict standards for pasta-making companies. They must use pure durum flour without artificial additives. Coloured pasta must be made with natural vegetables. And egg pasta has to contain fresh eggs. Dry pasta keeps almost indefinitely, but store it in a glass jar once the package has been opened.

Use fresh pasta if you are in a hurry. It only takes a few minutes to cook, but be careful not to over boil it. If the pasta has been made with fresh eggs, it will be good. You should use fresh pasta within a few days, or freeze it and use within a month.

Preparing Pasta

Al dente is the beginning point of softness, when your pasta is just tender and a little resistant to the bite. This is the moment when your pasta is perfectly cooked.

To cook perfect pasta every time, follow our seven steps:

- ❒ Use about 4½ quarts (4 L) of water to every 1 lb (450 g) of pasta.
- ❒ Bring the water to a rolling boil before the pasta goes in.
- ❒ Add a pinch of salt to the boiling water.
- ❒ Add the pasta gradually so the water continues to boil.
- ❒ Boil the pasta uncovered, stirring it occasionally with a fork.
- ❒ When you cook dried pasta, start testing to see if it is ready after 8 minutes. Fresh or homemade pasta takes less time – often just a minute or two.
- ❒ Drain the pasta in a large colander as soon as it is cooked. Transfer it to a serving bowl and toss it with just enough sauce to coat.

Pasta Portions

Pasta shapes are so variable, we like to give the weight rather than the volume in all our recipes. The usual pasta serving is 4 oz (110 g) for each person as a main course, and half that amount for an appetizer, but the cooked yield depends on the shape of the pasta:

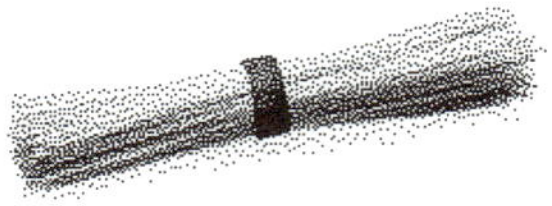

Chinese people traditionally serve long noodles at birthday celebrations to symbolize a happy, long life.

"Everything you see I owe to spaghetti."

Sophia Loren

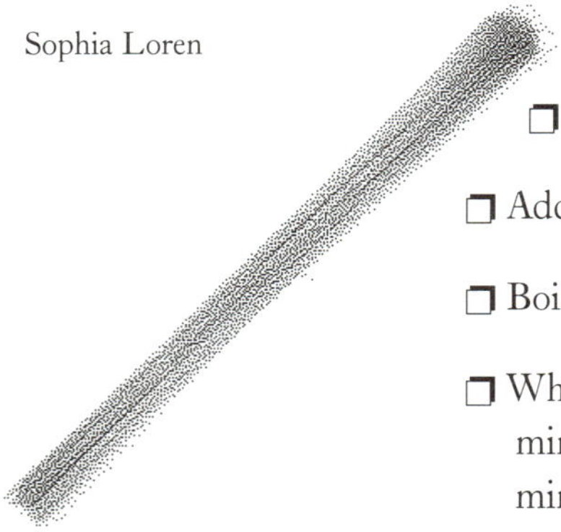

The longer you cook pasta, the fewer nutrients are left in it.

If you use good quality pasta, the sauce should simply enhance it rather than disguise or overpower the flavour.

- Flat, long pastas (spaghetti, vermicelli, linguini, capellini)
  4 oz (110 g) per person = 2 cups (500 ml) cooked

- Shaped pastas (rotini, penne, ziti, elbow macaroni)
  4 oz (110 g) per person = 2½ cups (625 ml) cooked

Making Your Own Pasta

If you love fresh pasta, but have not been swept off your feet by store-bought varieties, consider making your own. Be warned though - it's hard work! You have to knead the pasta dough until it is elastic, then roll it and stretch it to a transparent thinness. If you are really serious about your pasta, it is probably a good idea to invest in a pasta machine (a manual machine will cost around $70, while electric ones can cost as much as $500). You can then have great fun with various flavours and shapes, and create your own delicious fillings.

What's in the Cupboard?

If you keep a supply of tasty ingredients to toss with pasta, you can have dinner ready in less time than it takes for a pizza to be delivered!

Any of these simple ingredients turns pasta into a treat:

Canned tuna

Block of Parmesan cheese

Fresh basil, parsley and oregano

Garlic

Jar of roasted red peppers

Olives

Onions

Sun-dried tomatoes

Fettucine With Basil Alfredo Sauce

This is the creamiest, tastiest version ever. We have added basil to our favourite Alfredo sauce and the results are fresh and delicious. This recipe makes 4 servings.

2 cups / *500 ml*	whipping cream
1 cup / *250 ml*	coarsely chopped fresh basil leaves
9 oz / *250 g*	fresh spinach fettucine or 8 oz / *225 g* dry
8 oz / *225 g*	Parmesan cheese, grated
½ cup / *125 ml*	fresh plum tomatoes, diced and seeded
½ cup / *125 ml*	fresh basil leaves, slivered, as a garnish
	freshly ground black pepper

In a heavy saucepan, bring the cream almost to a boil. Reduce the heat and simmer, uncovered, until thick. It will take about 20 to 30 minutes. Be very careful not to boil the cream, or it will curdle.

Add the chopped basil and cook for 3 more minutes. Remove the pan from the heat.

Bring a large pot of water to a rolling boil. Add the fettucine and cook until just tender. While the pasta is cooking, add three-quarters of the Parmesan to the basil sauce. Let the cheese melt slowly. Return the pan to low heat and stir it to heat through. Transfer the sauce to a warmed serving bowl.

Drain the pasta, add it to the sauce and toss lightly. Don't forget the garnishes – tomato, slivered basil, grated Parmesan cheese and fresh ground pepper really brighten this dish up. Serve immediately!

"Spaghetti can be eaten successfully if you inhale it like a vacuum cleaner."

Sophia Loren

Italian Mozzarella was traditionally made from buffalo milk. In fact, mozzarella di bufala *can still be bought in cheese shops in Italy - and occasionally here in Canada.*

Making a Meal from Pasta

The joy of choosing an accompaniment for your pasta is that there are no rules to follow. Use your imagination - just about anything can be tossed in to make a delicious sauce.

Here are some inspirational ideas for a quick, gratifying meal:

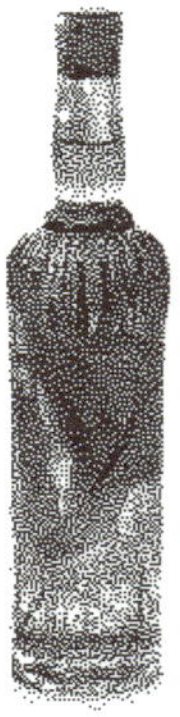

- **Garlic and Oil** - Chop some garlic and heat it in oil until soft. Pour the scented oil over pasta and grind lots of fresh pepper on top.
- **Parsley and Cheese** - Put these two in a processor and chop them up well. Melt some butter with chopped garlic and stir it all into the pasta.
- **Ham and Peas** - Heat a cup of heavy cream, let it thicken slightly, then add some peas and chopped ham. Toss it with the pasta and sprinkle with grated Parmesan.

- **Mushrooms** - Sauté lots of sliced mushrooms in butter with a hint of garlic. Toss with pasta and add chopped chives.
- **Tuna and Parsley** - Warm some olive oil and garlic with a tin of tuna and some chopped parsley. Toss with pasta and add olives if you have them.
- **Yogurt and Herbs** - Mix cooked noodles with a cup of yogurt, some chopped chives and chopped tarragon. Eat it cold.

There are over 300 types of pasta!

Spicy Chinese Noodles

Spicy Chinese Noodles

8 oz / *225 g*	linguine or other thin pasta
2 tbsp / *30 ml*	dark sesame oil
2	garlic cloves, minced
2 tbsp / *30 ml*	sesame paste
3 tbsp / *45 ml*	soy sauce
1½ tbsp / *22ml*	rice vinegar
1 tbsp / *15 ml*	honey
2	scallions, chopped
2 tbsp / *30 ml*	freshly chopped cilantro
	hot chili oil

This recipe serves 4 as a side dish or appetizer.

Boil the linguine with plenty of salt until it is *al dente* (check out page 64 if you are unsure).

Drain the pasta, toss in a mixing bowl with the sesame oil, then leave it to cool while you prepare the sauce.

Purée the rest of the ingredients, except the chili oil, in a blender. Now add the oil a little at a time to the sauce, tasting it constantly, until it has enough spiciness. Don't be afraid to make it quite hot, as the noodles will absorb a lot of the flavour.

Toss the sauce with the noodles and garnish with bean sprouts, peanuts and snow peas to add colour and texture.

Lasagne di Spinnachio

All the wonderful, freshest flavours of Italy come together in this sophisticated dish. Even meat lovers will appreciate this moist vegetarian version. This recipe makes 8 servings.

1 tbsp / *15 ml*	olive oil
½ cup / *125 ml*	chopped onion
1	garlic clove, minced
1½ cups / *375 ml*	mushrooms, sliced
2	cans (28 oz / *796 ml*) crushed tomatoes
¼ cup / *50 ml*	fresh basil
¼ cup / *50 ml*	fresh parsley
¼ tsp / *1 ml*	salt
¼ tsp / *1 ml*	ground black pepper
10 oz / *300 g*	fresh spinach, chopped
1½ cups / *375 ml*	Ricotta cheese
½ cup / *125 ml*	grated Parmesan cheese
1	egg
¼ cup / *50 ml*	chopped sweet red pepper or pimento
2 tbsp / *25 ml*	milk
¼ tsp / *1 ml*	nutmeg
6	oven ready or no-boil lasagna noodles
2 cups / *500 ml*	sliced zucchini
1½ cups / *375 ml*	grated Mozzarella cheese

PREHEAT your oven to 325°F (160°C).

IN A LARGE NON-STICK SAUCEPAN, heat the olive oil over medium heat. Add the onion and garlic and sauté for 2 to 3 minutes until softened.

ADD THE MUSHROOMS and sauté for another 2 minutes. Stir in both cans of tomatoes, basil, parsley, salt and pepper.

BRING TO A BOIL, then reduce the heat and simmer, uncovered, for 20 minutes.

MEANWHILE, squeeze all the moisture from the spinach and combine it with the Ricotta cheese, 1/3 cup (75 ml) of Parmesan cheese, egg, red pepper, milk and nutmeg.

SPREAD A THIN LAYER of tomato sauce in a lightly greased 9 x 13 in (3.5 L) baking dish. Arrange 3 lasagna noodles in a single layer over the tomato sauce. Spread half of the Ricotta mixture over the noodles, cover with half the zucchini and sprinkle with ½ cup (125 ml) of the Mozzarella cheese.

SPOON A LAYER of tomato sauce over the cheese then repeat the layers, ending with a layer of tomato sauce.

COVER AND BAKE for 50 minutes so the noodles are almost tender. Uncover and sprinkle with the remaining Parmesan and Mozzarella cheese. Put the lasagne back in the oven and bake for another 10 to 15 minutes, or until the cheese has melted.

LET THE lasagne stand for 10 minutes before cutting it and serving.

PESTO SAUCE

Pesto sauce is a wonderful way to eat basil and Parmesan cheese. The powerful taste of basil and garlic is only just tamed by the cheese and oil. Lightly cooked pasta tossed with warm pesto sauce is one of the great joys of life. Turn to the Herbs & Spices section, page 20, for the recipe.

Pesto is worth making in large batches, so there is always a jar of it handy in the fridge. Don't limit pesto sauce to pasta:

- Mix pesto with sour cream and add it to soup as a garnish.
- Use it to season mayonnaise for extra flavour.

"The trouble with eating Italian food is that five or six days later you're hungry again."

George Miller

Penne with Crab Meat and Capers

¼ cup / *60 ml*	olive oil
1	medium onion, minced
2	finely chopped garlic cloves
3 tbsp / *45 ml*	fresh, minced parsley
1 28 oz / *796 ml*	can Italian plum tomatoes, chopped coarsley after reserving the juice
¼ cup / *60 ml*	dry white wine
½ lb / *225 g*	crab meat
1 tbsp / *15 ml*	capers
	salt and black pepper
12 oz / *340 g*	penne pasta
	grated Parmesan cheese

This Italian delight is wonderful, yet prepared in less than half an hour. Just serve with fresh crusty bread, a tossed, butter lettuce salad and a little Pavarotti in the background. This recipe serves 4.

Heat the olive oil in a medium skillet. Add the onions, garlic and parsley, and sauté until onions soften. Add the reserved juices from the canned tomatoes and simmer for about 10 minutes.

Add the chopped tomatoes and wine, then simmer for about 5 minutes.

Add the crab and capers and simmer until heated through. Salt and pepper to taste.

For the penne, bring the water to a boil. Add 1 tbsp (15ml) salt and the penne. Cook until just tender, about 9 minutes.

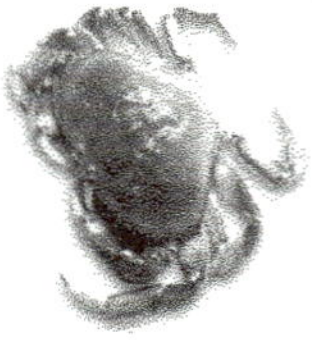

Drain and place penne in a warmed serving dish. Add the sauce and toss with the penne. Sprinkle with Parmesan cheese and serve immediately.

Resist the urge to line fresh tomatoes up along the window sill. They ripen more evenly sitting on the kitchen counter, sheltered from the sun.

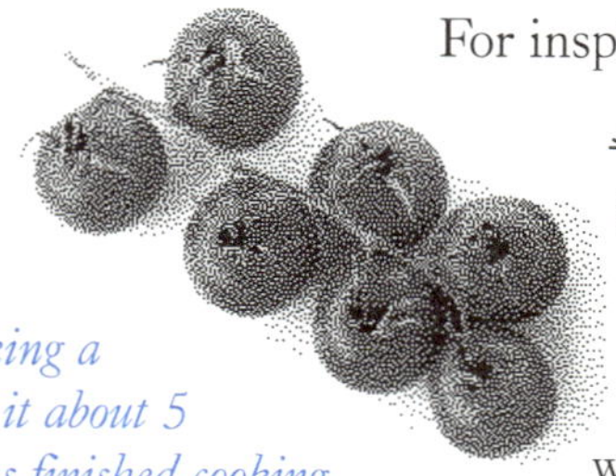

Canned tomatoes vary in sweetness. When you are making a tomato sauce, taste it about 5 minutes before it has finished cooking and add a little Rogers Granulated Sugar if it is needed.

Good Things to Add to Tomato Sauce

Everyone makes tomato sauce to eat with pasta, but why not try some new ways of eating it? There are some wonderful things you can do to a basic tomato sauce, seasoned with plenty of freshly chopped basil and oregano, that will elevate it from the ordinary.

For inspiration, try some of these ideas:

- Pan-fry thick slices of hot Italian sausage. Stir the sausage into the sauce, and simmer for 10 minutes.
- Season ½ lb (225 g) ground beef with oregano and basil. Roll it into small balls and brown in hot oil. Combine with the sauce and simmer gently for 15 minutes.
- Fire up your tomato sauce with a pinch or more of crushed dried chile peppers.
- Add a can of baby clams, drained, to the sauce.

- Slice mushrooms, sauté them in butter and add to your tomato sauce.
- Coarsely chop one red pepper and one red onion. Sauté in olive oil until slightly softened and stir them into the sauce.

Add 1 tsp (5 ml) of butter to the saucepan when you cook pasta to stop it from boiling over.

Get Twisting

When people eat spaghetti, they usually try to wind too much onto their forks at once. The secret is to select just two or three strands with your fork and coax them over to an empty part of the plate. Holding the fork at a right angle, simply wind the fork round and round so that those few strands are twisted into a little bite-sized bundle. Practice makes perfect!

A century ago, making dried pasta was an important way of preserving the wheat crop in Italy. English tourists reported seeing pasta everywhere in Naples, hung out to dry like laundry.

Will the Real Macaroni and Cheese Please Stand Up

No more bland macaroni! Infused with two kinds of cheese and baked slowly, every mouthful is a pleasure. This traditional favourite is definitely worth preparing properly.
This recipe makes 2 servings.

8 oz / 225 g	short macaroni
3 tbsp / 45 ml	butter
1	large onion, chopped
8 oz / 225 g	fresh mushrooms, sliced
1	medium green pepper, chopped
2	medium tomatoes, chopped
2 tbsp / 30 ml	flour
1 tsp / 5 ml	dry mustard
½ tsp / 2 ml	salt
½ tsp / 2 ml	dried oregano
2½ cups / 525 ml	milk
	pinch of cayenne pepper or 2 pinches of chili powder
8 oz / 225 g	cheddar cheese, grated
	handful of bread-crumbs

PREHEAT your oven to 350°F (180°C).

BOIL THE MACARONI until it is just tender. Strain it and put it on one side of a well-buttered casserole dish.

IN A LARGE FRYING PAN, melt the butter over medium heat. Toss the vegetables in the melted butter, cooking until just tender, then stir in the flour, mustard, salt and oregano. Add the milk slowly, stirring continuously.

WHEN THE SAUCE HAS THICKENED, stir in the cayenne pepper and 6 oz (170 g) of cheese. Keep stirring until everything is melted.

POUR THE SAUCE over the macaroni and mix lightly together. Combine the breadcrumbs and the rest of the cheese and sprinkle on top.

COOK for 45 minutes or until the top is bubbling and crispy. Serve immediately.

Choosing Your Cheese

There are dozens of types of cheese to use with pasta, so use your taste as a guide. If you think your tomato sauce is lacking zest, try melting a strong tasting Gruyère, goat or Gorgonzola cheese over the top of it.

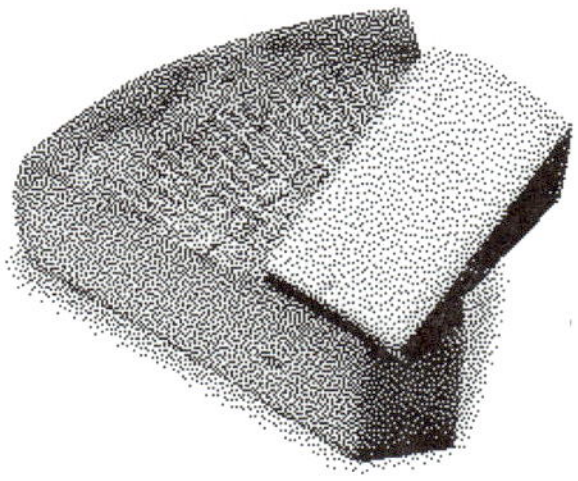

Parmesan cheese makes a good accompaniment for most pastas, but forget the packaged, ready-grated kind. Buy a block of Parmesan instead and grate it as you need it. It's like grinding pepper: if you do it at the last minute, it adds a wonderful flavour to the dish.

Famous Pasta Dishes of the World

Pasta or noodles, kreplach or wontons; no matter what the name, the whole world loves to eat them. Here are a few of the more well-known pasta dishes from various countries:

- **Wonton Soup**: Wontons in a thin chicken broth. What exactly is a wonton? A twist of noodle dough, filled with meat, seafood or vegetables.
- **Pasta Carbonara**: A rich Italian dish that consists of spaghetti or linguine in a creamy bacon sauce.
- **Chow Mein**: A Chinese-inspired dish of fried noodles, accompanied by pork, chicken or seafood. Although you can find this dish in any Chinese restaurant in Canada, it is not actually eaten in China!
- **Kreplach**: These Jewish treats are very similar to wontons, but are filled with beef and onion and shaped like small triangles. They are often added to clear broth to make kreplach soup.

"The definitive recipe for any Italian dish has not yet appeared. We're still creating."

Luigi Barzini

Judging from all the cookbooks published each year, Canada's passion for pasta is insatiable. For the best sauces, check out these sources:

Pasta Classica
by Julia della Croce
San Francisco:
Chronicle Books, 1987

A book for the true pasta fanatic. With gorgeous illustrations and tasty traditional recipes, it's as much fun to read as it is to cook from.

Rose Reisman Brings Home Light Pasta
by Rose Reisman
Toronto:
Macmillan Canada, 1994

Hundreds of delicious low-fat recipes from this Toronto-based cook. You'll find everything from Thai Linguine to a creamy seafood pasta salad.

Umberto's Pasta Book,
by Umberto Menghi
Vancouver:
Whitecap Books, 1985

If you've been to one of Umberto Menghi's wonderful restaurants, you can imagine how good this book is. Umberto's beautiful recipes are classified by type of noodle.

The World's Finest Pasta and Grain
by Anne E. Marshall
New York:
Stewart, Tabori and Chang, 1996

The next time you're "cruising the net," check out this great web site for pasta recipes:

http://web.mit.edu/wchuang/www/cooking/pasta.htm

SEAFOOD

"Fish, in the hands of a skilled cook, can become an inexhaustible source of great pleasures."

The Physiology of Taste

Anthelme Brillat-Savarin, 1755-1826

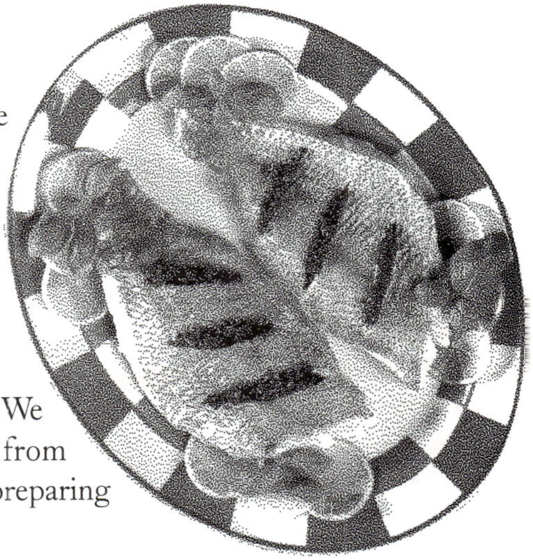

Canadians are eating fish and seafood now more than ever. It's healthy, light and easy to turn into a delicious meal. We have broadened our horizons with a huge variety of fish and new flavours. Garlic, ginger and Asian seasonings marry perfectly with seafood, and there are recipes from all over the world to try.

Seafood offers a spectrum of flavours and styles. We encourage you to experiment with everything from sturgeon to rollmops to fresh lobster! When you are preparing fish and seafood, keep these points in mind:

- The fresher the seafood, the better it will taste.
- So-called "fresh" fish is sometimes frozen fish that has simply been thawed - so beware!
- Sauces should complement or accentuate seafood, not overpower it.
- The best fish and seafood are tender, moist and sweet. Always keep this in mind and never overcook them.

Shopping for Fish and Shellfish

Buying the seafood is the most important step in your recipe. If you start with good, fresh ingredients, you will get good results. Most fish is never inspected, so be sure you are dealing with a quality fish market or supermarket. Seafood should never be out of the water for longer than two or three days.

Research shows that eating as little as one serving of fish per week can significantly reduce your risk of heart disease.

"A loaf of bread,"

the Walrus said,

"Is what we chiefly need:

Pepper and vinegar besides

Are very good indeed -

Now, if you're ready,

Oysters dear,

We can begin to feed."

Through the Looking Glass

Lewis Carroll, 1832-1898

- ❐ Fish should look as though it has just been caught, while shellfish should be tightly closed.
- ❐ Whole fish are more perishable, so they are usually fresher to buy than fillets.
- ❐ Take your fish home immediately. Rinse it under cold, running water, put it in a plastic bag and store in a bowl of ice water.

- ❐ Plan to use the fish on the day you buy it, particularly if it is whole.
- ❐ Sniff shellfish. A clean, fresh smell means they haven't been out of the sea for very long. The same applies to fish - if there is even a hint of a fishy odour, leave it at the store.
- ❐ Mussels, clams and oysters should be tightly closed when you buy them. Touch any open ones with a fork: if they snap shut, they are still alive. Throw out any that remain open.

Manitoba, known as "Land of 10,000 Lakes," is home to Canada's famous goldeye. This freshwater fish got its name because of the way it turns a beautiful golden colour after being smoked.

How to Check for Freshness

Check fish carefully when you buy it. If you are at all doubtful about the freshness of a fish, put it in cold water when you get home. A newly caught fish will always float.

Apart from sniffing it, you can tell if a fish is fresh by looking for the following signs:

- The scales are bright and shiny and adhere firmly to the flesh.
- The gills are reddish and moist but not slimy.
- The eyes are clear, bright and bulging. If they are cloudy and sunken, don't buy it.
- Prepared fillets are firm and moist and their smell is sweet. Avoid fillets that are discoloured around the edges.

"There are as many good fish in the sea as ever came out of it."

Sir Walter Scott, 1771-1832

The "Canadian Method"

To cook your fish, use the world-recognized "Canadian Method," invented by Canada's Department of the Environment. Measure the fish at the thickest part, then allow about 8 minutes* of cooking for each inch (2.5 cm) of thickness. This is a good rule of thumb and works for every fish, cooked every way. The fish is done when its translucent flesh becomes opaque at the thickest part. Test it by inserting a knife, but don't wait for the flesh to flake. By that time it is too late.

* Actually, the "Canadian Method" recommends 10 minutes, but we think that is too long.

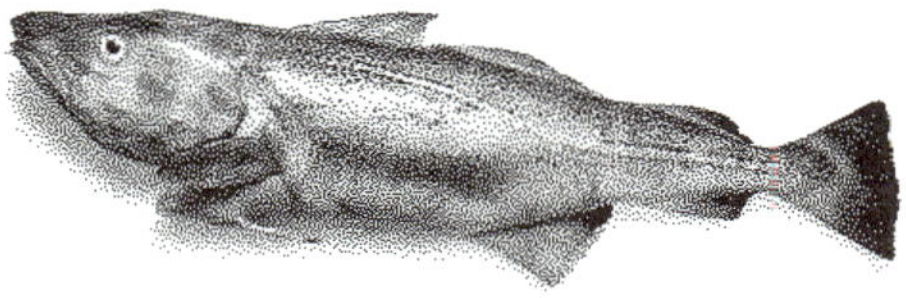

Cod, available off the Newfoundland coast, attracted fishermen from Europe as early as the 16th century. The Europeans would land to preserve their catch, either by salting or drying the cod, then sail back across the Atlantic Ocean to sell it. These days you can still find the remains of abandoned cod-drying racks, called "flakes."

Tuna Steaks With Lemon Soy Sauce

Although canned tuna is a favourite for lots of Canadians, you owe it to yourself and your family or friends to try fresh tuna steaks. Done this way, with a herb crust and a light sauce, they will be the hit of the show. This recipe makes 6 servings.

Sesame Mixture:

1 cup / *250 ml*	sesame seeds
2 tbsp / *30 ml*	minced fresh chives
2 tsp / *10 ml*	minced garlic
2 tsp / *10 ml*	minced gingerroot
½ tsp / *2 ml*	dark sesame oil
¼ cup / *60 ml*	extra-virgin olive oil
2 tbsp / *30 ml*	fresh lemon juice
2 tbsp / *30 ml*	soy sauce

Sauce:

1 cup / *250 ml*	dry white wine
2 tbsp / *30 ml*	fresh lemon juice
¼ cup / *60 ml*	cream
2 tbsp / *30 ml*	soy sauce
2/3 cup / *160 ml*	unsalted butter, cut into pieces
6	tuna steaks, 1 in *(2.5 cm)* thick

PREHEAT your oven to 375°F (190°C).

ON A BAKING SHEET in the oven, toast the sesame seeds until golden. This will take about 10 minutes. Now, in a small bowl, stir together the sesame seeds and the rest of the ingredients for the sesame mixture.

PREPARE THE BARBEQUE, then make the sauce while it is heating.

IN A SAUCEPAN, boil the wine and lemon juice over high heat until the liquid has reduced to about a third of a cup.

ADD THE CREAM and simmer very gently, stirring occasionally, until the sauce has reduced by half. Add the soy sauce and turn the heat right down to low.

WHISK IN THE BUTTER, just a little bit at a time, lifting the pan off the heat every now and then to cool the mixture down. Add each piece of butter just before the previous one melts completely (you can't let the sauce get hot enough to liquefy). Take the saucepan off the heat, but put on the lid to keep the sauce warm while you grill the tuna steaks.

COAT BOTH SIDES of each tuna steak with the sesame mixture. Grill on an oiled rack, about 6 inches (14.5 cm) over glowing coals, for 3 to 4 minutes on each side. Serve the tuna steaks with the warm cream sauce.

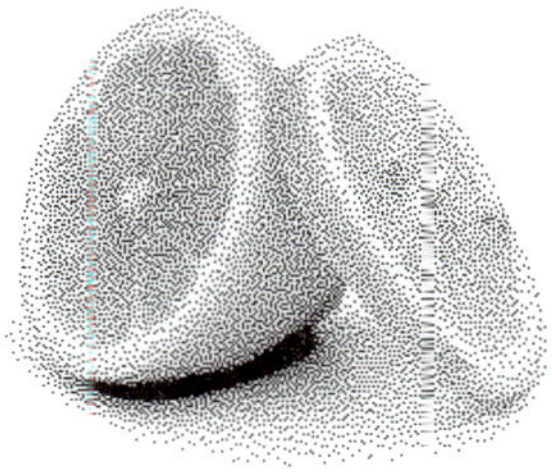

Worldwide, over 90 million pounds of oysters are eaten each year. If you haven't discovered the joy of fresh oysters yet, maybe it's time to get started!

Cooking With Clarified Butter

There is no mystery to clarified butter (also called drawn butter, or ghee). It is simply melted butter with the sediment removed. By clarifying butter, it becomes much lighter than normal butter. Clarified butter is delicious for cooking seafood and makes an especially tasty sauce for drizzling over lobster. You can buy clarified butter, but it is just as easy to make your own. Simply warm some butter in a saucepan. Skim the butter fat from the surface and strain the clear yellow liquid that is left behind into a container. Store your clarified butter in the refrigerator.

Several centuries ago, in England, apprentices petitioned that they should not be forced to eat fresh salmon more than twice a week!

Canada's Catch of the Day

There is a bounty of seafood available to Canadians, both freshwater and seawater. The better-known species are those such as sole, cod, salmon, trout, halibut, crab and shrimp. If you tend to stick with the fish that are familiar to you, think what others you may be missing out on! Take the plunge and try species that are new to you. There are all kinds of wonderful fish out there, just waiting to be tried. Ask the advice of the person selling the fish and remember that most fish are seasonal. Don't insist on a particular type of fish if it is not at its prime.

Poaching Fish

A wonderful way of poaching fish, as an alternative to using a special poaching pan, is to do it in the oven. Wrap the fish in aluminum foil, to which lemon juice or white wine, butter and seasonings can be added and the fish will cook in its own juices. Use the "Canadian Method" on page 72, but add an extra 5 minutes to give the heat time to penetrate the foil.

Pan-frying Fish

Pan-frying or broiling is the most common way to cook fresh fish, and because it is done quickly with a high heat, none of the precious juices are lost. Give each fillet a squeeze of lemon juice and a grind of pepper, or try one of our ideas on page 75, and it is ready to eat!

For the best results when frying or broiling fish:

- ❒ Use a very high heat, and baste the fish as you go.
- ❒ Use clarified butter - this is important (see the side bar). But equally important is to combine it about half and half with cooking oil. This stops the butter from burning.
- ❒ Only turn the fillet over once while it is cooking or it might fall apart.

Tasty Ideas for Fish

Add a few ingredients to the fish pan, and you suddenly have a delicious sauce to serve with your fish:

- Lemon juice served with lemon wedges and capers as garnishes
- Spicy tomato sauce with a sprinkling of chopped chives and a dollop of sour cream
- Tartar sauce or homemade mustard and lemon wedges
- Parsley, garlic and wine mixed with butter, then heated before drizzling over the fish
- Watercress and cream added to warmed butter

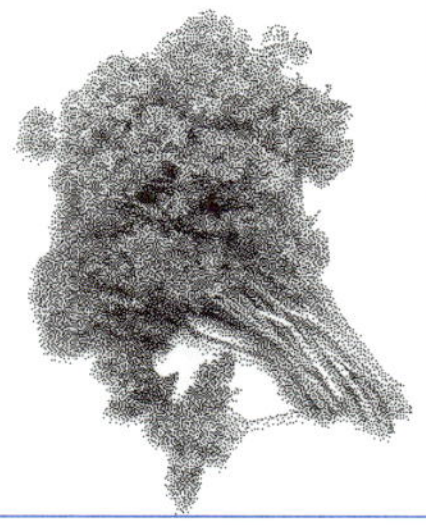

Blackened Fish is not a traditional Cajun dish. The trend was started by a New Orleans restauranteur, Paul Prudhomme, in 1979 after a camping trip. He loved the taste of the smoky fish cooked over an open fire and decided to try for the same effect in the kitchen.

Manhattan Snapper

A delicious uptown sauce that turns the humble snapper into a gastronomic delight. This recipe makes 4 servings.

4	thick pieces of snapper
2 tbsp / *30 ml*	olive oil
1	onion, finely chopped
1	garlic clove, crushed
1 lb / *500 g*	ripe tomatoes, peeled and chopped
	salt and freshly ground black pepper
¼ lb / *110 g*	mushrooms, thinly sliced
1 tbsp / *15 ml*	freshly chopped basil
1 tbsp / *15 ml*	capers, chopped
	juice of ½ lemon
12	black olives, cut in half

PREHEAT your oven to 375°F (190°C).

START BY MAKING the tomato sauce. Heat the olive oil in a saucepan and fry the onion for about 5 minutes.

ADD THE GARLIC AND TOMATOES. Season with salt and pepper, then bring to a simmer and cook gently - uncovered - for 15 minutes, stirring occasionally.

STIR IN THE SLICED MUSHROOMS and simmer for another 10 minutes. Add the basil and chopped capers, and you have your sauce.

NOW PLACE THE SNAPPER in a shallow baking dish or tin. Season with a shake or two of salt and a grind of pepper, then sprinkle a little lemon juice over each fillet. Next, spoon an equal quantity of the sauce onto each piece of fish and arrange a few olives on top. Cover the dish with aluminum foil and bake it on a high shelf for about 20 minutes or so, depending on the thickness of the fish (check the "Canadian Method" on page 72 if you are unsure). You will need to add an extra 5 minutes to allow the heat to penetrate the foil.

SERVE THE FISH WITH NEW POTATOES or brown rice and a tossed green salad.

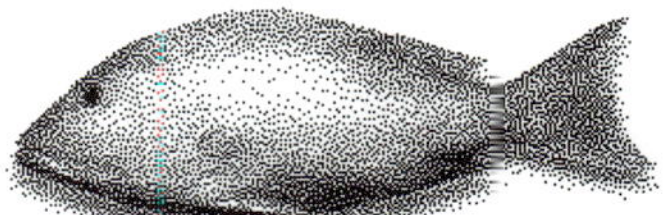

GOT A SALMON? LUCKY YOU!

In Canada, we have some of the best salmon in the world. Luxurious sockeye or inexpensive pink, salmon is a fabulously easy way to feed a table of people.

Before you cook a whole salmon, check its vital statistics. Whether poached, stuffed, barbequed or pan-fried, the fat content will determine how long it needs. The oilier the flesh, the longer it takes

Long before the settlers arrived in Canada, the native people were smoking their salmon draped over poles in cedar tents. They would let the fish cure for at least six days, then the dried salmon "jerky" would last right through the winter.

Salmon tastes equally good served hot, at room temperature or chilled.

"Fish, to taste right, must swim three times - in water, in butter and in wine."

Polish Saying

to cook through. When the salmon is ready, arrange it on a large plate, surrounded by chopped lettuce, watercress or sprigs of parsley.

- **Sockeye**: also known as red salmon. This is a more expensive type of salmon, as it has a higher oil content and a deeper red colour. It is suited to stronger flavourings and is usually marketed for canning.
- **Coho or cohoe**: also called silver salmon, bluebacks and silversides. A popular game fish, coho is valued next to sockeye. It is marketed fresh or frozen, but some is canned.
- **Chinook**: also known as spring, tyee, king or quinnat salmon. It is a very popular sports fish, and the flesh comes in many different colours - everything from bright red and various shades of pink to white. Chinook is sold on the market fresh or frozen.
- **Pink**: pink salmon is nicknamed humpback or humpy because of the grotesque humped back that the male fish develops. Commercially, the delicately coloured pink salmon is used mainly for canning.
- **Chum**: also known as keta, dog, qualla, calico or fall salmon. It is the last of the Pacific salmon to spawn, beginning in the late fall. The flesh of chum is even paler pink than the pink salmon and is canned, dry-salted and frozen.

Bill Brown's Barbequed Salmon

Bill Brown's Barbequed Salmon

½ cup / *125 ml*	oil
2 tbsp / *30 ml*	soy sauce
2	garlic cloves, crushed
1 tsp / *5 ml*	salt
¼ tsp / *1 ml*	ground black pepper
¼ cup / *60 ml*	rye, scotch or bourbon whiskey
2 tsp / *10 ml*	Rogers Demerara Sugar
6 to 8	salmon steaks or one large fillet

Don't let this be the one that got away! It's one of the best marinades we have found, with its unique flavours perfectly enhancing the natural taste of salmon. This recipe serves 6.

COMBINE ALL THE INGREDIENTS to make the marinade. If possible, marinate the fish for at least 2 hours before you use it. Even better is to mix your marinade in the morning and leave the salmon soaking in it, refrigerated, until dinner time.

HEAT THE COALS to medium-hot, about 45 minutes before you want to barbeque the salmon. Place the grill 4 in (10 cm) above the heat. Place the fish on a piece of foil, so you won't lose any of the wonderful juices.

BASTE THE SALMON with the remaining marinade while you barbeque it. Use the "Canadian Method" (page 72) to work out how long to cook the fish. For example: if the salmon is 1 in (2.5 cm) thick, it will need 3 to 4 minutes per side.

Good Sauces to Serve With Salmon

- Spoonfuls of natural plain yogurt with chopped fresh tarragon and a splash of wine vinegar
- Tomato sauce made with chopped tomatoes, olive oil, wine vinegar and fresh herbs
- Parsley and lemon butter
- Mustard sauce: use a blender to mix together fresh parsley, chopped onion, fresh tarragon, garlic, olive oil, wine vinegar and mustard

When you marinate fish, do it in the refrigerator - never at room temperature.

A salmon marinade tastes just as good with other strongly flavoured fish such as swordfish, tuna, mackerel or bluefish. Their natural oils will keep them nice and moist on the barbeque.

Cooking Seafood

Let's face it: there is nothing quite like a dish of fresh, delicately flavoured shellfish. But remember: they are dainty creatures. Treat them gently, and you will be rewarded with delicious flavour. It is breeding season from May through to August and, generally speaking, you should avoid eating shellfish during these summer months. This is not only for conservation reasons, but the shellfish themselves do not taste as good.

For the best tasting seafood dishes, keep these points in mind:

- Recipes for mussels, oysters and clams are fairly interchangeable, and are often seasoned with a good white wine. For every serving, allow about 1 tbsp (15 ml) of wine.
- Raw shellfish such as oysters, clams and scallops should always be served well chilled.
- Crab meat tastes wonderful in salads with mayonnaise and hard-boiled eggs.
- Clam juice is intensely salty, so don't add salt until you have tasted the dish.

"Consider the lobster -
Crustacean mobster;
His manners are frightful,
But, oh, he's delightful..."

Mary Hosford

If you are lucky enough to catch yourself a rainbow trout, try this method of cooking it right on the spot. An angler friend suggests: "Clean the trout, rub it well with salt, wrap it in clean leaves, cover with mud and bury in hot ashes." Apparently, the trout will be cooked to perfection!

Capers, the small, green pickled buds of a Mediterranean plant, are a delicious accompaniment for most fish dishes. Not only do they taste great, they also add a special touch to the presentation.

Delicious Ways to Eat Fresh Oysters

- **Broiled**: broil them in their half shells with cream, black pepper and Parmesan cheese.
- **Fried**: roll them in flour, salt, pepper and a touch of paprika, then fry them in sizzling butter for 2 minutes until golden.

Until the end of the last century, oysters and lobsters were pretty common fare. However, as they became scarce and got more and more expensive, their status increased!

- **Baked**: keep them in their half shells and put them in an ovenproof dish. Add a knob of butter and a tablespoon of white breadcrumbs to each oyster, and bake in a very hot oven (425°F / 220°C) for 5 minutes.
- **Raw**: serve straight out of the shell, with lemon juice or a vinegar dressing and plenty of black pepper.

Light Scallop Fritters

1¼ cups / *310 ml*	flour
2	eggs, separated
¾ cup / *180 ml*	beer
½ tsp / *2 ml*	dried thyme
½ tsp / *2 ml*	basil
½ tsp / *2 ml*	cayenne
	salt and freshly ground black pepper
3 cups / *750 ml*	safflower oil
2¼ lbs / *1 kg*	sea scallops, shelled

The perfect complement for the delicate taste of scallops. Enjoy the crisp shellfish in beer batter with your favourite spicy salsa, tartar sauce or tomato chutney (see our recipe on page 149).

GENTLY COMBINE 1 cup (250 ml) of flour and the egg yolks in a mixing bowl. Pour in enough of the beer to make a smooth batter, then stir in the herbs, spice, salt and pepper.

LET THE BATTER REST for 1 hour, then beat the egg whites until they are stiff. Fold them into the batter.

HEAT THE OIL to 375°F (180°C).

DUST THE SCALLOPS with the rest of the flour. Dip them into the batter, one at a time, and put them straight into the hot oil. Fry a small batch of the fritters until they are golden brown, then keep them hot until you have cooked the rest in batches. Serve immediately.

TEN THINGS TO DO WITH SHELLFISH

There are hundreds of recipes for preparing shellfish, whether steamed, grilled, broiled, deep-fried or baked. As a springboard for your own creative concoctions, take a look at our ten favourite ideas:

- Marinate in lemon juice for an hour and eat raw.
- Marinate in olive oil, garlic, salt and pepper for 25 minutes, then put them under a hot broiler.
- Sprinkle Pernod over prawns then toss them with olive oil, lemon juice and thinly sliced mushrooms.
- Dress with natural yogurt and finely chopped watercress and tarragon.

If you are having trouble opening clams, you can help them to relax their muscles. How? Arrange clams in a single layer in a pan and leave them in the freezer for 15 minutes.

- Marinate in groundnut oil, fresh ginger, lime juice and garlic. Drain and toss briefly in a hot frying pan.
- Scramble with eggs and freshly chopped coriander leaves.
- Use a marinade of lemon juice, turmeric and garlic for oysters. Egg and breadcrumb them and deep-fry for 4 minutes, or until golden.
- Serve scallops with a warm dressing of fried bacon and chilled melon balls. Scatter with fresh chives.
- Marinate in olive oil, vinegar, mustard, garlic and salt. After 30 minutes, stir into mayonnaise with a drop of Tabasco sauce.
- Sandwich between pieces of hot toast spread with mango chutney and crisply fried bacon.

Herbs for Seafood

Fresh herbs and other flavourings taste wonderful in seafood dishes. Try some of these for a difference:

Baked or broiled fish: savory, tarragon, thyme, lime juice, chives

Poached fish: a mixture of white wine and water with a bay leaf, peppercorns, onion and lemon peel

Steamed fish: lemon juice, wine, parsley, thyme, basil

Salmon and other oily fish: dill seed, fennel, rosemary, garlic

Shellfish: garlic, basil, bay, chervil, chives, dill, fennel seed, marjoram, rosemary, tarragon, thyme

Fish soup: bay, sage (very sparingly), savory, tarragon, thyme

Tasty Leftovers

There are plenty of delicious things you can do with fish the next day:

- Mix with mayonnaise and chopped celery for a salad sandwich.
- Add to fish chowder 5 minutes before serving.
- Turn into a main course salad.

At Expo 67 in Montreal, Inuit women demonstrated how they cooked salmon in a dishwasher.

Hypnotism, and Other Ways to Kill a Lobster

As the saying goes, "you gotta do what you gotta do". If you feel a little uneasy about throwing a live lobster into boiling water, try hypnotizing it first (this is no joke, and the Lobster Institute insists that it works 100 percent of the time). Simply rub the lobster up and down its back with your fingertip, nice and easy. It will soon stand stock-still, so you can pop it into the boiling water without getting pinched.

"A man hath no better thing under the sun than to eat, and to drink, and to be merry."

The Bible, Ecclesiastes 8:15

With all the sources for inspiration around, there's no reason to run out of dinnertime ideas. These books all offer great recipes, good ideas and beautiful pictures:

The Canadian Fish Cookbook
by A. Jan Howarth
Vancouver:
Douglas & McIntyre, 1993

This book is complete and thorough, and explains everything from buying, cleaning and preparing fish to cooking it. There are over 170 recipes.

Six O'Clock Solutions
by Eve Johnson
Vancouver:
Pacific Press Books, 1995

Full of contemporary recipes that are deliciously assembled by Eve Johnson and the Vancouver Sun.

Fish
by Shirley King
Vermont:
Chapter Publishing Company, 1996

If you are looking for more inspiration, stop fishing around and go straight to this web site:

http://www.foodservice.ca/cuisine/recipes.htm

The following organizations have booklets of free recipes they are happy to send out:

B.C. Farmed Salmon Institute
506-1200 West Pender Street
Vancouver, British Columbia
V6E 2S9
1-800-661-7256

B.C. Salmon Marketing Council
1100-1200 West 73rd Avenue
Vancouver, British Columbia
V6P 6G5
(604) 267-3030

- Toss chunks of cooked fish and peas in a cream sauce for a magnificent pasta dish.
- Fry some fish cakes. Mix the fish with mashed potatoes seasoned with salt and pepper, shape into small flat patties and fry until golden.

Famous Seafood Dishes of the World

Fresh fish and shellfish are traditional fare in almost every country. Hardly surprising, when you consider that two-thirds of the world is covered by water!

Here are some of the more famous seafood dishes; it is definitely worth finding a good recipe and trying it for yourself:

- **Gravlax**: A Swedish dish of raw salmon, marinated in pepper, dill, sugar and salt.
- **Lobster Newburg**: A concoction of lobster pieces, served with plenty of cream, madeira wine and cayenne pepper.
- **Oysters Rockefeller**: An American dish of oysters in their shells, accompanied by spinach and cheese sauce.
- **Seviche**: A South American favourite and one of the world's greatest marinated raw seafood dishes. Scallops are prepared in peppers, tomatoes, herbs and lime juice, then served with avocado.

"He was a bold man who first swallowed an oyster."

James I, 1566 - 1625

POULTRY

"I want there to be no peasant in my kingdom so poor that he cannot have a chicken in his pot every Sunday."

Henri IV, 1553-1610

Chickens and other birds (geese, turkeys and ducks to name a few) are classic dishes on most of the world's menus. Poultry can be cooked by almost any method, and its mild flavour goes well with a wide variety of sauces and accompaniments. No longer misunderstood and overcooked, chicken is dressed up or down, barbequed, casseroled and curried to create a succulent, tasty meal.

For the best-tasting poultry, remember these points:

- ❐ Buy free-range if you can - the flavour is worth paying extra for.
- ❐ Use herbs to really bring out the best in a bird. Try them with Oriental and Mediterranean flavours.
- ❐ Make sure the heat isn't too high when you cook chicken. A gentle heat will keep it moist and succulent.
- ❐ Avoid turkeys that are described as "self-basting." You can easily baste them yourself, and the flavour is always much nicer.

When you sauté chicken, use a moderate heat. If the fat gets too hot, the chicken won't have as good a flavour.

"We can learn to be cooks,

but we must be born knowing

how to roast."

The Physiology of Taste
Anthelme Brillat-Savarin, 1755-1826

Chicken Through the Ages

The age of a chicken, and how it has been raised, makes a big difference to the flavour. In general, younger birds have less fat - but they also have less taste. Fresh, free-range chickens are definitely the best choice.

- Broilers are young chickens, weighing between 1 and 1½ lbs (450 and 675 g). As mentioned above, broilers are not a good choice in terms of flavour.

- Fryers are from 2½ to 3½ lb (1.1 to 1.5 kg) in weight and are interchangeable with broilers. Look for yellow fat and plump breasts.

- Roasters and pullets weigh between 3½ and 6½ lb (1.5 and 2.7 kg), are very meaty and are good for roasting, baking, barbequing and quick cooking.

- Hens and fowl are older birds, weighing up to 8 lb (3.4 kg). While it takes longer to cook them, they have the best flavour and are great for stock or chicken salad.

At the turn of the century, chicken was considered an expensive treat. Veal was cheap in comparison!

In China, women who have just given birth are fed chicken soup, chicken and eggs. In fact, a customary gift to the family of a newborn baby is a chicken, to feed the mother.

If you rub the skin of a bird with white vermouth before you cook it, it will come out of the oven a glossy brown colour.

Roasting Chicken

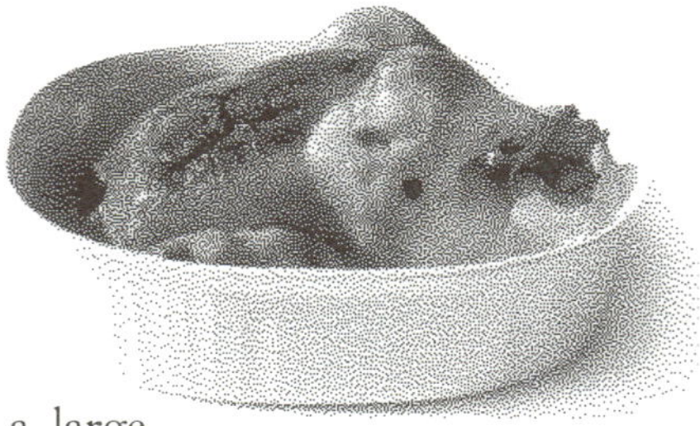

Accompanied by fresh green vegetables, buttered carrots and roasted potatoes, a roasted chicken makes a traditional dinner large enough for six people. Roast a large bird - even if there are only two of you - so you have plenty of leftovers.

- Frozen chicken must be thoroughly defrosted before you cook it.

- Older chickens with more fat in the skin will need less basting.

- To give a chicken more flavour, season it the day before you roast it.

- Roast a chicken breast side down for the first 40 minutes; the legs will be thoroughly cooked, while the breast meat remains juicy.

- Rather than basting a chicken when it is cooking in the oven, try placing six slices of bacon over the breast. They will do the job for you.

Broiled Mustard Chicken Wings

Our wings are crisp and golden, and packed with the delicious flavours of garlic and mustard. They are never greasy, which makes them ideal to serve as hors d'oeuvres - whatever the occasion.

2 tbsp / *30 ml*	plain yogurt
2 tbsp / *30 ml* plus 1½ tsp / *37 ml*	Dijon mustard
1	large garlic clove, minced
1½ lb / *675 g*	chicken wings (about 8)
2 tbsp / *30 ml*	fine breadcrumbs
1 tsp / *5 ml*	mustard seeds
	salt and freshly ground black pepper
4 tsp / *20 ml*	olive oil

IN A LARGE BOWL, stir together the yogurt, 1½ tsp (5 ml) of the mustard and the minced garlic.

CUT OFF THE WING TIPS, but keep them to make soup stock (see page 34 of the Soups section).

ADD THE WINGS TO YOGURT MIXTURE, stirring to coat well, and marinate them for 10 minutes. Meanwhile, preheat your broiler.

IN ANOTHER BOWL, mix together the breadcrumbs, mustard seeds, and salt and pepper to taste.

ARRANGE THE WINGS, skin side down, on an oiled rack of the broiler pan and season with salt and pepper. Broil the wings 3 to 4 in (7.5 to 10 cm) from the heat until golden brown. This will take about 10 minutes. Now turn the wings skin side up and season with salt and pepper. Broil them for another 5 minutes.

SPREAD THE SKIN SIDES with the remaining 2 tbsps (30 ml) of mustard and sprinkle with the breadcrumb mixture. Very lightly drizzle some olive oil over all the wings and broil them until crisp and golden, about 3 to 5 minutes.

YOU CAN SERVE the wings hot, or at room temperature.

ROASTING CHART

To get a crispier skin, preheat your oven to 425°F (215°C). Cook the bird at that temperature for 15 minutes, then reduce the heat to 350°F (180°C).

Different kinds of poultry have different roasting times:

	Unstuffed	Stuffed
Chicken	20 minutes per 1 lb (450 g)	Add an extra 20 minutes to total cooking time.
Turkey	20 - 22 minutes per 1 lb (450 g)	25 minutes per 1 lb (450 g)
Duck	15 - 20 minutes per 1 lb (450 g)	Don't stuff duck.
Goose	20 - 25 minutes per 1 lb (450 g)	Don't stuff goose.

When you roast a chicken, use the leftovers to make a light stock for soup (see page 34 for some pointers).

After handling raw poultry, always wash your hands, utensils and the cutting surface. Poultry can be contaminated with many bacteria, so it is important to be careful.

If you are drinking wine with your meal, add a spoonful of it to the gravy to give it a nice flavour.

For a traditional apple, sage and onion stuffing see page 25.

"Jemima Puddle-duck was a simpleton: not even the mention of sage and onions made her suspicious. She went round the farm garden, nibbling off snippets of all the different sorts of herbs that are used for stuffing roast duck."

The Tale of Jemima Puddle-Duck
Beatrix Potter, 1866-1943

After stuffing a turkey, seal the opening with a small onion.

Take a look at page 50 of the Salads section for a delicious turkey salad recipe.

Sensational Stuffings

A herb stuffing tastes great with any bird and really completes the meal. Stuffings do not always get cooked inside the bird; if you are roasting a duck, for example, the stuffing tends to absorb too much fat. You can still serve it by rolling the mixture into small balls and frying it. Goose is a poor conductor of heat, so cook the stuffing separately in a dish - not inside the bird.

Try one of these ideas for great stuffing:

Chicken

- Minced pork, breadcrumbs, onion and sage
- Wholemeal breadcrumbs, bacon and freshly chopped tarragon
- Grapes, breadcrumbs, garlic and freshly chopped tarragon

Turkey

Use the classic stuffing of breadcrumbs with herbs, onion and celery and add one of the following:

- Chopped raw oysters
- Chopped chicken liver and dried apricots
- Skinned, cooked chestnuts
- Sausage meat
- Chopped apples, prunes and walnuts or almonds
- Cooked rice to replace the breadcrumbs

Duck

- Sauerkraut, dill seeds, duck liver and onion
- Minced pork, breadcrumbs, onion and sage

Goose

- Onions, sausage and mashed potatoes
- Apple, sage, thyme and cider with wholemeal bread and almonds

Things to Do With Leftover Roast Turkey

It is inevitable that once you have roasted a turkey, you will have plenty of leftovers - unless you are cooking for a party of twenty! There are plenty of tasty things to make with turkey meat the next day (and for the next six, no doubt):

- **Turkey, apple and cranberry sandwich**: Grate an apple or two and stir in a dollop of cranberry sauce. Add chopped walnuts and a drizzle of oil. Season with plenty of salt and pepper, and pile onto brown bread with slices of cold roast turkey.

- **Turkey, hot bacon and chutney sandwich**: Butter two slices of hot toast. Cover one with sliced turkey, then spread mango chutney over it. Cover with hot, crisply fried bacon. Slap on the second piece of toast.

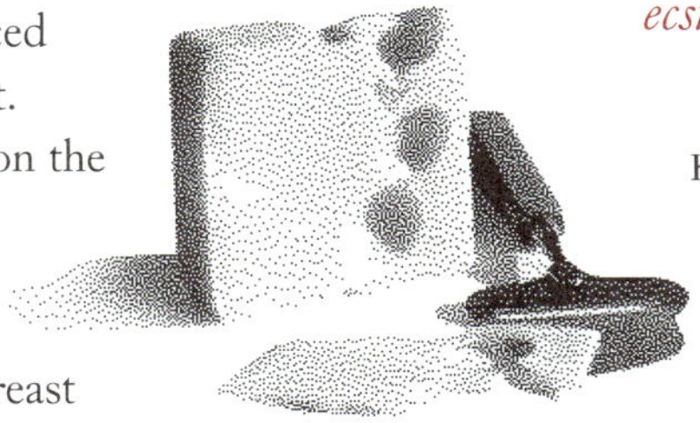

- **Turkey breast with pesto and Gruyère cheese**: Cut the largest, flattest slices of breast you can. Lay them under the broiler and spread with pesto sauce. Cover with thin slices of Gruyère cheese and grill until the cheese starts to melt (the cheese should just be at the melting stage, or it will become rubbery).

"There's cold chicken inside it," replied the Rat briefly; "coldtonguecoldhamcoldbeefpickledgherkinssaladfrenchrollscresssandwidgespottedmeatgingerbeerlemonadesodawater -"

"O stop, stop," cried the Mole in ecstasies: "This is too much!"

The Wind in the Willows
Kenneth Grahame, 1859-1932

Grilled Lime and Yogurt Chicken

This light marinade gives chicken a mystical blend of savoury and spicy flavours. This recipe serves 4.

Make the marinade by mixing all the ingredients plus a dash of salt and pepper in a large baking dish.

Add the chicken breasts in a single layer; coat well on both sides. Let the chicken marinate at room temperature for 30 minutes or, if possible, overnight in the refrigerator.

Heat the broiler. Broil the chicken breasts, about 5 minutes on each side, until cooked through.

Serve with buttered spaghetti squash or tender green beans and your favourite tossed, mixed green salad with mint vinaigrette dressing.

¼ cup / *60 ml*	chopped green onions
3	cloves minced garlic
¾ tsp / *4 ml*	ground cumin
¼ tsp / *1 ml*	caraway seeds
1 tsp / *5 ml*	crushed coriander seeds
1 tsp / *5 ml*	grated lime peel
1 ½ tbsp / *22 ml*	fresh lime juice
½ cup / *125 ml*	plain yogurt
	salt
	ground black pepper
4	boneless, skinless, halved chicken breasts 1 ½ lbs / *675 g*

Roast Turkey

Every Christmas and Thanksgiving millions of Canadian turkeys are roasted. Here is our present to you - a wonderful, succulent method that never ends up dry.

12-14 lb / *5.5-6.5 kg*	oven-ready turkey
6 oz / *170 g*	softened butter
8 oz / *225 g*	bacon slices
	salt and freshly ground black pepper

PREHEAT your oven to 425°F (215°C).

ARRANGE TWO LARGE SHEETS of foil across your roasting pan widthwise, and lengthwise (lightly greased). Lay the turkey on its back in the centre of the pan, then rub it generously all over with the butter, making sure the thigh bones are particularly well covered.

NEXT, SEASON THE BIRD all over with salt and pepper, and lay the bacon slices over the breast.

NOW WRAP the turkey in the foil. The parcel must be firmly sealed but with plenty of room to provide ample air space around most of the upper part of the turkey. To do this, bring the ends of one piece of foil up and fold them over to make a pleat along the length of the breastbone, well above the breast. Then bring the ends of the other piece of foil up and crimp and fold to make a neat parcel.

PLACE THE ROASTING PAN on a low shelf in the oven and cook at 425°F (215°C) for 15 minutes. Then lower the heat to 350°F (180°C) and cook for another 3 hours for a 12 lb (5.5 kg), or 3½ hours for a 14 lb (6.5 kg) bird.

TEAR THE FOIL AWAY from the top and sides of the bird, and remove the bacon slices to allow the skin to brown and crisp. Turn the heat up to 400°F (200°C), and cook the turkey for another 30 minutes. The turkey will need frequent basting during this time, so the whole operation will probably take closer to 40 to 45 minutes.

TO TEST IF THE TURKEY IS COOKED, pierce the thickest part of the leg with a thin skewer: the juices running out of it should be golden and clear. The same applies to any part of the bird you test - there should be no trace of pinkness in the juices. You can also give the leg a little tug to make sure it gives a little.

LEAVE THE TURKEY in a warmish place for 20 minutes to "relax" before carving. Then carve and enjoy!

Grape Stuffing

The perfect stuffing for summer. Light and delicious, it adds a wonderfully fruity flavour to chicken or turkey.

3½ oz / *100 g*	butter
1	medium onion, finely chopped
4 oz / *110 g*	fresh breadcrumbs
4	garlic cloves, crushed
1 tbsp / *15 ml*	freshly chopped parsley
1 tsp / *5 ml*	freshly chopped tarragon
6 oz / *170 g*	seedless grapes, or halved and seeded grapes

MELT ½ oz (14 g) of the butter in a small saucepan and cook the finely chopped onion for about 6 minutes or until soft, then add the remaining butter and allow it to melt.

NOW TRANSFER the onion and the buttery juices to a bowl, add the breadcrumbs, then stir in the crushed garlic, chopped parsley, tarragon and grapes. Taste and season with salt and pepper before stuffing the chicken or turkey.

Barbequing Chicken

A simple baste with olive oil and herbs is enough to make barbequed chicken succulent and full of flavour, or try a marinade for extra zest. But don't limit yourself to chicken when you are grilling. Game hens also grill beautifully, as do marinated duck breasts.

While burgers and steaks are easy to grill, chicken tends to be a little trickier. In order to get that perfect blend of crispy on the outside and tender, juicy meat on the inside, follow these tips:

- ❐ Precook the chicken before it goes on the barbeque.
- ❐ Baste the chicken often as it is grilling.
- ❐ Barbeque your chicken on the bone for moister meat.
- ❐ Test as you grill; chicken is ready when the juices run clear but aren't pink.
- ❐ To get very moist, tender chicken breasts, soak them in buttermilk for 3 to 4 hours in the refrigerator before you grill them.

In the late 1700s, an American called William Ralston hosted a dinner party. The main course? Hummingbirds stuffed with baked almonds, placed inside a linnet. The linnet (a small songbird) was then put inside a snipe, and the snipe in a goose, on top of which two ducks were laid and topped with breast of goose. The whole dish had been soaked for six days in raisin wine and smoked over sandalwood, before being slowly roasted on a spit.

Good Accompaniments for Chicken Curry

- Indian pickles and mango chutney
- Diced cucumber in natural yogurt
- Slices of banana rolled in coconut
- Basmati or wild rice
- Heated flat bread such as *nan* or *paratha* (available in supermarkets and Indian stores)

When you roast a turkey, the secret is to make sure that it doesn't go right from the fridge into the oven. Let your bird reach room temperature before you put it into the oven. That way, cooking times won't be affected.

Four Tasty Ways to Grill Chicken

- ❐ Brush chicken with oil and 2 tbsp (50 ml) of spicy Dijon mustard.
- ❐ Marinate chicken pieces in lemon juice, olive oil, red wine vinegar, honey and plenty of garlic and fresh herbs. Continue brushing the marinade over the chicken as it grills.

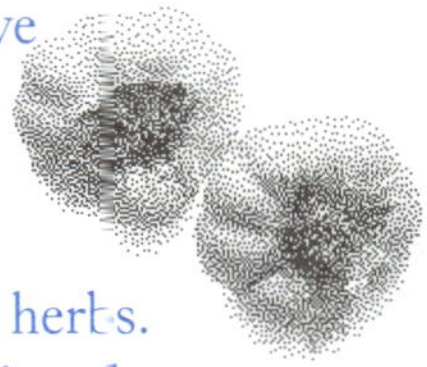

- ❐ Mix together liquid honey, light soy sauce and lemon juice. Sprinkle in some Tabasco sauce and crushed garlic. Brush the chicken with it for a fiery finish.
- ❐ Mix together butter, fresh breadcrumbs, chopped parsley and a minced clove of garlic. Spread the paste over the chicken 5 minutes before it's supposed to finish cooking.

Chicken Curry With Ginger

2 to 2½ lbs / *1 to 1.25 kg*	skinned chicken legs and thighs and boned, skinned chicken breasts
3 tsp / *15 ml*	salt
½ cup / *125 ml*	vegetable oil
1½ cups / *375 ml*	chopped onions
1 tbsp / *15 ml*	chopped garlic
1½ tsp / *7 ml*	scraped, chopped gingerroot
1 tsp / *5 ml*	ground cumin
1 tsp / *5 ml*	turmeric
1 tsp / *5 ml*	dried cilantro
½ tsp / *2 ml*	ground hot red pepper
½ cup / *125 ml*	water
1 cup / *250 ml*	chopped tomatoes
2 tbsp / *30 ml*	freshly chopped coriander
½ cup / *125 ml*	plain yogurt
1 tbsp / *15 ml*	fresh lemon juice

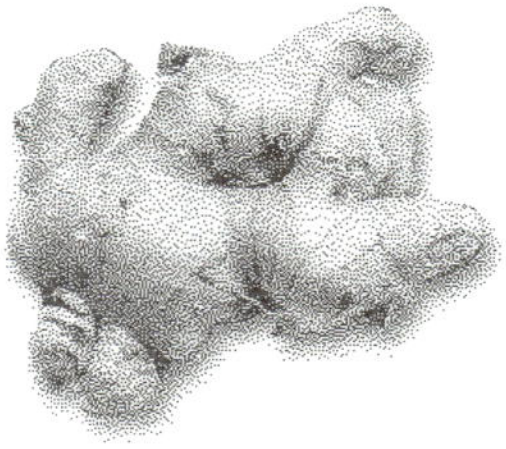

Chicken Curry With Ginger

Ginger is one of the best spices to cook with chicken. It makes a wonderful flavour combination, and this curry is fresh and light enough to please everyone. This recipe makes 4 to 6 servings.

PAT THE CHICKEN PIECES dry with paper towels and cut the chicken breasts into large pieces. Sprinkle all the chicken with 2 tsp (10 ml) of salt.

IN A HEAVY SAUCEPAN, heat the oil over a high heat. Add the chicken pieces and fry them for about 3 or 4 minutes, turning them over so they are white and firm on both sides. You don't need to cook them right through - that comes later. Put the pieces aside on a plate.

ADD THE ONIONS, garlic and ginger to the oil that is left in the pan and fry them until the onions are soft and golden brown. Don't let the oil get too hot or the ingredients will burn.

REDUCE TO A LOW HEAT. Add the cumin, turmeric, dried cilantro, red pepper and 1 tbsp (15 ml) of the water. Fry everything for a minute or two, stirring constantly.

STIR IN THE TOMATOES, 1 tbsp (15 ml) of the fresh coriander, the yogurt and the remaining 1 tsp (5 ml) of salt.

INCREASE THE HEAT AGAIN to medium and add the chicken. Pour in the rest of the water. Bring to a boil, turning the chicken in the sauce so all the pieces are evenly coated.

SPRINKLE THE TOP with the rest of the fresh coriander. Reduce the heat to low, put the lid on the saucepan and leave it to simmer for 20 minutes. The chicken should be tender but not falling apart.

TO SERVE, ARRANGE THE CHICKEN on a heated plate, pour the remaining sauce over and sprinkle with lemon juice. Prepare lots of rice to eat with it.

The word "curry" comes from the Tamil word *kari*, which means sauce.

DUCK

Duck has a wonderful, succulent flavour and very rich meat. The main thing to remember when you are roasting a duck is that it is very fatty meat, and needs to be cooked in a particular way:

- ❒ Before your duck goes in the oven, prick it all over with a sharp, pointed knife.
- ❒ Always stand the duck on a rack when it is roasting to let the fat run off.
- ❒ To stop the fat burning, take the duck out of the oven every 20 minutes and drain the liquid into a large bowl.

- Roast your duck for a long time to get rid of the fat and to leave the flesh moist and crisply skinned (see the roasting chart on page 83 for cooking times).

Herbs for Poultry

All these herbs give a wonderful flavour to birds. Add them to the stuffing, the marinade or the sauce or tuck them under the skin before roasting.

Chicken and turkey: tarragon, chervil, chives, basil, parsley

Duck and goose: sage, rosemary, bay, fennel, thyme

Flavours

Duck and Goose: The rich meat and crisp skin of duck and goose are best partnered with simple, sharp flavours.

- Tart fruit such as cherries and Seville oranges are ideal.
- Try them with fresh green vegetables such as spinach, broccoli, beans or garden peas.
- Oriental spices such as ginger and lemon grass are perfect for cutting the rich fattiness - cook them with rice.

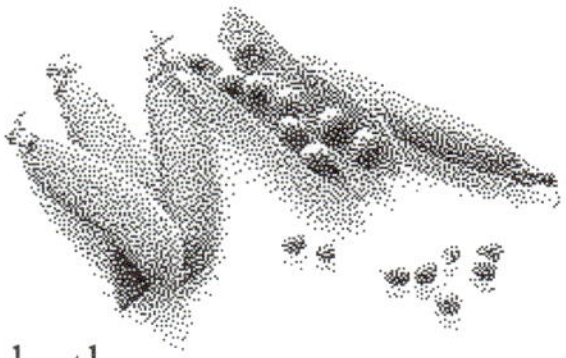

Chicken and turkey: Chicken and turkey both go well with almost anything.

- Cook them with wine, cider or stock for extra taste.
- They are good with all the staples - rice, bread and potatoes.
- You can use any combination of tastemakers, from practically any region: East Indian, Chinese or Middle Eastern.
- How about American style, served with corn, mashed potatoes, biscuits and gravy?

If possible, buy fresh birds rather than frozen or cold-storage ones; they have much more flavour. Fresh birds can be bought at kosher meat markets or butcher shops but not at supermarkets.

The Ancient Egyptians enjoyed eating duck, the Chinese domesticated and bred the bird for food over 2,000 years ago, and the Romans introduced it all over Europe.

"O, duck, though, roast, succulent duck of the Barque and Bite, served with orange sauce, mouth-meltingly delicious! You I salute. Fresh, tender and unbelievable."

Collected Poems
George Macbeth, 1932-92

One of the best herbs to use with chicken is tarragon. Soak 1 tsp (5ml) of dried tarragon in ½ cup (125 ml) of dry white wine for half an hour. Pour the mixture over the chicken and cook it any way you like.

Be adventurous with your cooking! Have a read of these books and you will find there are a million and one delicious poultry dishes still to be discovered:

The New Complete Book of Chicken Wings
by Joie Warner
Toronto:
Little, Brown/Flavour Publications, 1989

Plenty of good recipes for fun-to-eat wings, salads, side dishes and dips. The savoury marinades are delicious with other barbequed meats too.

The New Chatelaine Cookbook
by Monda Rosenberg
Toronto:
Macmillan Canada, 1992

A one-hour Sunday roast? We couldn't believe it either, but it is a truly fast, wonderfully tasty recipe. Another particular favourite from this book is the Elegant Ginger Chicken.

For more exciting chicken dishes, cruise the Internet. Here is a site that has some great recipes:

http://www.yahoo.com/entertainment/food_and_eating/recipes/chicken

Nearly every province has a chicken or turkey marketing board. These ones are happy to send you free recipes and information about cooking poultry:

B.C. Chicken Marketing Board
5752-176th Street
Cloverdale, British Columbia
V3A 4C8
(604) 576-2855

Alberta Chicken Marketing Board
101-11826 100 Avenue
Edmonton, Alberta
T5V 0K3
(403) 488-2125

Famous Poultry Dishes of the World

Poultry dishes have been enjoyed since the beginning of history. A favourite of the Ancient Romans was rich duck served with honey and dates. These days, we tend to eat lighter, healthier meals, but poultry still fits the bill perfectly.

- **Tandoori**: An Indian dish of baked chicken that is marinated in yogurt, chilli powder and tomato purée. Traditionally, Tandoori chicken is cooked in a bed of embers in a special clay oven until the flesh is tender, but the outside is crispy.

- **Mole Poblana**: A festive Mexican dish of turkey with a chocolate sauce, full of herbs, spices and chile peppers. This dish goes back to the 16th century and is still very popular in Mexico today.

- **Coq au Vin**: A French casserole, cooked with plenty of red wine and herbs. Traditionally, Coq au Vin was a good way of cooking a farm-yard cockerel to make it more tender, but these days most people use chicken.

"A good meal makes a man feel more charitable toward the whole world than any sermon."

Arthur Pendenys

MEAT

"Heap high the groaning platter with pink fillets, suckling pig and thick gammon, celestial chef."

Collected Poems
George Macbeth, 1932-1992

We are becoming a more global community. Meat recipes and ideas from other countries and cultures are so plentiful here in Canada that we constantly find fresh new tastes showing up at the dinner table. Today's recipe repertoire has expanded to match the way we live, but roasts and casseroles will always have their place in our hearts and on our tables.

To get the best taste from your meat:

- ❒ Take your time. When making a pot roast or a meat casserole, even a cheap cut will become succulent and delicious if you cook it slowly.
- ❒ Be adventurous and experiment with lots of herbs and spices.
- ❒ Roast your meat on the bone. It stays moister and the flavour will always be better.
- ❒ Cook pork through, unlike beef and lamb, and never serve it rare.
- ❒ Cook outside on a barbeque to make the most of summertime weather. Fresh air and wood smoke make all the difference to the flavour of meat.
- ❒ Cook with plenty of wine, as a general rule. Use red wine for red meats and white wine for the paler meats.

Fresh offal (the livers, kidneys, hearts and brains of animals) is a true delicacy and still one of the cheapest ways to buy meat. Give it a try!

"He tilted up the pot, and a glorious stream of hot rich stew gurgled into the plate. It was, indeed, the most beautiful stew in the world, being made of partridges, and pheasants, and chickens, and hares, and rabbits, and peahens, and guinea-fowls, and one or two other things."

The Wind in the Willows
Kenneth Grahame, 1859-1932

For perfect crackling on roast pork, score the skin in deep, parallel lines, not too far apart, and right down through the fat. A butcher can do this for you.

"Carve a ham as if you were shaving the face of a friend."

Henri Charpentier

Add 1 tsp (5 ml) of Rogers Granulated Sugar to gravy. It won't sweeten it, but it will enhance the flavour.

Roasting Meat

Roasting is based on warm air circulating around the meat, cooking it evenly. The melting fat bastes the meat as it cooks. For the best flavour, buy and cook your meat on the bone and always use good quality cuts.

Beef: rib, loin, sirloin or tenderloin

Lamb: rib, loin or leg

Pork: loin or tenderloin

- For roasts with no fat, coat the meat lightly with oil or mustard.
- Roast the meat on a rack so it doesn't stew in its own fat.
- Mix a spoonful of granulated sugar with water or cranberry juice and brush it over the meat before you roast it. This seals in the juices and keeps the meat moist.
- For a juicier roast with a tasty outside crust, start it in a very hot oven, then reduce the temperature and continue cooking (see our chart below for roasting times).
- Let the roast rest, tented in foil, for at least 20 minutes before carving. The juices settle and make the meat moister.

Roasting Chart

The length of time your meat cooks in the oven will make a big difference to the taste. Don't roast it until it becomes dry and stringy.

	Temperature	Rare	Medium	Well Done
Beef	475°F (250°C), after 15 minutes turn it down to 400°F (200°C)	12 minutes per 1 lb (450 g)	16 minutes per 1 lb (450 g)	18-20 minutes per 1 lb (450 g)
Pork	425°F (220°C), after 15 minutes turn it down to 350°F (180°C)	Pork should always be well done.		20-25 minutes per 1 lb (450 g)
Lamb	475°F (250°C), after 15 minutes turn it down to 400°F (200°C)	12 minutes per 1 lb (450 g)	16 minutes per 1 lb (450 g)	18-20 minutes per 1 lb (450 g)

Accompaniments for Roasted Meat

Gravy has always been the traditional accompaniment for roasted meat. There are other flavours, however, from all around the world that go supremely well with meat and really help to spark up a meal:

- **Beef**: onion or tomato chutney, mustard and herb butter, horseradish sauce, Yorkshire pudding, braised celery, artichokes, parsnips and fennel
- **Pork**: caramelized apples, applesauce, onions and prunes, cranberry jelly, sauerkraut and spiced red cabbage, pickles
- **Lamb**: mint jelly, ratatouille (see page 56 for the recipe), new potatoes with mint and baby carrots, saffron rice

Hogs were often called "mortgage lifters" by early Canadian settlers because, unlike grain crops, they could be depended on for income in any kind of weather.

Baked Festival Ham

Ham needs a little help to enter into the holiday spirit. This recipe both tenderizes the meat and infuses it with character and sophistication. This recipe makes 16 six-ounce (170 g) servings.

12-14 lb / *5.5-6.5 kg*	ham, fully cooked, with bone in
1 cup / *250 ml*	Rogers Best Brown Sugar
1 tsp / *5 ml*	ground cloves
14 oz / *398 ml*	canned crushed pineapple, with juice
1 cup / *250 ml*	bourbon
1 cup / *250 ml*	orange marmalade

PREHEAT your oven to 350°F (180°C).

PEEL THE SKIN from the ham and trim the exterior fat to an even thickness of ¼ in (6 mm).

COMBINE THE SUGAR and cloves and pat this mixture evenly over the top of the ham. Roast the coated ham for 30 minutes.

COMBINE THE PINEAPPLE, bourbon and marmalade in a saucepan over medium heat. Be careful with the bourbon - don't let it flame.

POUR THE SAUCE over the ham and put it back in the oven. Cook until done, basting frequently, for approximately 3 hours.

REMOVE THE HAM from the roasting pan. Keep it warm and let it rest for 30 minutes before carving.

Marinades

Marinades are truly miraculous. If you have some meat that is less than perfect, leave it to marinate for a couple of hours, and it will be transformed. Not only does the flavour improve, but the meat itself becomes so tender it practically falls apart in your mouth. Marinades can be a simple blend of herbs, seasonings and oils, or a more complicated cooked recipe, which usually involves red wine,

In many western countries, lamb is the traditional dish to serve on Easter Sunday. Romans, especially, eat huge platters of roasted lamb accompanied by white wine.

"The pig, if I am not mistaken,

Supplies us sausage, ham, and bacon.

Let others say his heart is big -

I call it stupid of the pig."

Happy Days

Ogden Nash, 1902-1971

If you are at all unsure of the quality of your meat, don't roast it. Make a pot roast instead, and let it cook slowly for a few hours.

fruit and other ingredients. You can always make a marinade from what is in the cupboard, as long as you have some sugar, oil and herbs.

- Wine is the perfect ingredient for marinades, both for its distinctive flavour and its ability to break down the meat's tissues.
- Soya sauce is another good tastemaker for marinades.
- Veal and pork need less time to marinate, while game, beef and lamb require longer.
- If you cut your meat into small pieces, it won't need so long in the marinade.
- Be sure to completely cover the meat with the marinade and keep it refrigerated. Stir it once or twice.

Herbs for Marinades

Some herbs are natural partners with certain meats, so have a look at the list of herbs on page 96 and 97. Any of these herbs will add great flavour to a marinade:

- Garlic
- Basil
- Coriander seeds and leaves
- Mint
- Onion greens and bulbs
- Rosemary
- Tarragon

Miraculous Marinade

3	garlic cloves, finely chopped
½ tsp / *2 ml*	ground black pepper
¼ tsp / *1 ml*	cayenne pepper
¼ cup / *60 ml*	lemon or orange juice
¼ cup / *60 ml*	vegetable oil
¼ cup / *60 ml*	tomato chutney, puréed until smooth
1 tbsp / *15 ml*	Rogers Best Brown Sugar
¼ cup / *60 ml*	red wine

Miraculous Marinade

This is the best marinade we know of. Hot and zesty, sweet and spicy. It tenderizes and flavours all kinds of meat, so try it with your steaks for a tasty change of pace.
This recipe makes enough to marinate 6 servings of meat.

MIX ALL THE INGREDIENTS in a bowl, then leave the meat in it for at least 2 hours. It's that simple! Use it for spareribs, pork chops, chicken wings and chicken thighs.

THIS MARINADE can be stored in the refrigerator for up to two weeks.

Barbequing Meat

Forget what the calendar says. Barbeque season is all year long. Food seldom tastes better than when it is fresh off the grill. Flavour your meat with a marinade, garlic, butter, a hint of lemon, or just olive oil and fresh air.

- When you are barbequing, always use tender cuts of meat.
- If you have not marinated your meat, brush it lightly with oil before putting it on the grill to stop it from sticking.
- Test as you grill. Burgers are perfect when there is no trace of pink in the middle. Steaks are done to individual taste.
- Precook chicken, spareribs and whole roasts before barbequing them.
- Vegetables also taste wonderful barbequed. See page 62 for some tasty suggestions.

Aromatic Meats

For added taste and aroma when you are barbequing, try some of the different wood chips and hardwood charcoals available. Alternatively, soak leaves and branches in water and put them on the coals - they smoke the meat without any flames.

- Mesquite, hickory and oak give food a pleasant, smoky flavour.
- Fruit woods, like peach, apple and cherry impart a mild sweetness.
- Grape vines burn very hot and when combined with herbs give grilled food a wonderfully smoky flavour.
- Try soaking juniper berries, whole sweet spices such as cinnamon, cloves, nutmeg and orange or lemon peel. Put them in the embers for an aromatic infusion.

The Best Burgers

Burgers are the first thing we make to celebrate summer. They also mark the last barbeque of fall and provide a quick and tasty meal any time of year. Burgers are a Canadian classic that you can customize a million different ways.

Marinades and glazes are nothing without Rogers soft sugars:

- They are wonderful flavour boosters.
- They add a mouth-watering sheen to meat.
- They give us that finger-licking stickiness we love on our spareribs and chicken wings.

For safety's sake, use a fresh platter (not the one that held the raw meat) to carry cooked food from the barbeque to the table.

Marinating meat before it is barbequed adds flavour and makes the meat more tender.

The native inhabitants of Quebec are believed to have taught French settlers to cook and eat outdoors when the weather was fine, a custom unheard of at the time in France.

Tourtière, a French Canadian speciality traditionally served on Christmas Eve, is a deliciously spicy meat pie. Originally, it was made from passenger pigeons (*tourtes*), which are now extinct.

"Anyone who doesn't think that the best hamburger place in the world is in his home town is a sissy."

Calvin Trillin

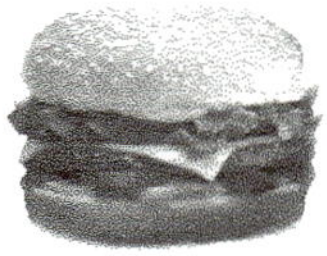

The secret for the best-tasting burgers is to use quality meat. Don't simply buy a tray of ground beef; instead, get a good piece of the tail end of beef fillet, or a piece of rump steak, and mince it at home in a food processor. The difference in flavour is worth any extra expense.

The leaner the beef, the drier the hamburger. Try and find meat with a fair amount of fat - between 10 and 20 percent is perfect. Season it with salt and pepper and shape it into loose patties with your hands.

Here are some more tips for the best-tasting burgers:

- Keep your burgers simple. Herbs are fine but don't add egg or breadcrumbs.
- Handle burgers as little as possible - this keeps them juicy.
- Never flatten patties on the grill with a spatula.
- Cook patties completely until no pink meat remains.

Tasty Burger Additions

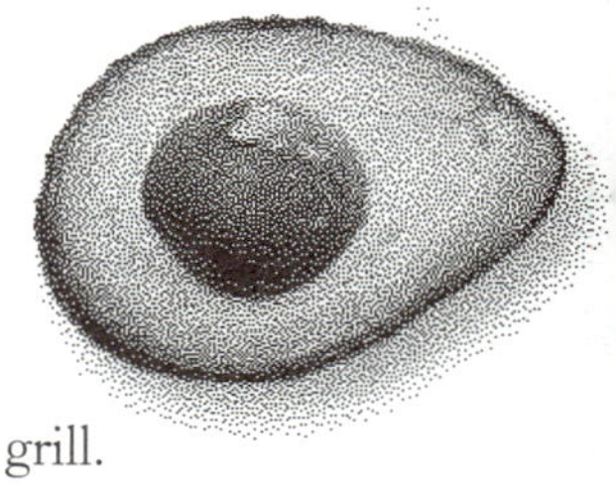

- ❒ Add a slice of tangy Cheddar, Swiss, Mozzarella or Monterey Jack.
- ❒ Sandwich a nugget of Danish blue cheese between two thin patties, seal the edges and grill.
- ❒ Top with avocado slices, bean sprouts and crisp bacon.
- ❒ Smack on a spoonful of freshly made spicy salsa or guacamole (see how to make on page 50).
- ❒ Pan-fry some mushrooms or roast some red peppers.

For something different, combine 2 tbsp (30 ml) Rogers Golden Yellow Sugar; 1/3 cup (85 ml) ketchup, 2 tbsp (30 ml) mustard, then pour it over your favourite meat loaf. Bake as usual.

Herbs for Meat

Herbs add the finishing touch to any meat dish. Here are some of our favourites:

Beef: basil, bay, caraway seeds, chervil, marjoram (for pot roasts), mint, oregano, parsley

Lamb: basil, chervil, cumin, dill, lemon balm, marjoram, mint, parsley, rosemary, savory, thyme

Pork: chervil, coriander, fennel, marjoram, rosemary, sage, savory, thyme

Ham: juniper berries, marjoram, mint, mustard, oregano, parsley, rosemary, savory

This Is Not Your Average Meat Loaf

This version of the classic dish has a pâté-like texture and a complex array of flavours. Rediscover how tasty meat loaf can be. This recipe makes 6 to 8 servings.

PREHEAT YOUR OVEN to 375°F (190°C). Grease a loaf pan.

PUT THE MINCED BEEF into a large mixing bowl with the pork, onions, chopped bell pepper, tomato purée and garlic. Give everything a thorough mixing, seasoning well with salt and freshly ground pepper.

CUT THE CRUSTS OFF the bread and soak the slices in the milk, then squeeze out the excess milk and add the bread to the rest of the ingredients, along with the mixed herbs and parsley. Now give the mixture another thorough mixing and stir in the beaten egg to bind it all together.

PRESS THE MIXTURE into the loaf pan, spreading evenly, and bake it in the oven for 1¼ hours. When the meat loaf is cooked, you will be able to tell because it will have shrunk away from the sides of the pan.

1 lb / *450 g*	good quality lean minced beef
½ lb / *225 g*	minced pork or pork sausage meat
2	medium onions, minced
1	small bell pepper, seeded and finely chopped
2 tsp / *10 ml*	tomato purée
1	garlic clove, crushed
2	white bread slices
3 tbsp / *45 ml*	milk
1 tsp / *5 ml*	dried mixed herbs
2 tbsp / *30 ml*	freshly chopped parsley
1	egg, beaten
	salt and freshly ground pepper

This Is Not Your Average Meat Loaf

CASSEROLES FOR OUR TIME

A casserole makes a wonderful meal any night of the week. Often a complete meal-in-a-pot, casseroles cook slowly and independently without needing much attention from the cook.

Although casseroles are easy to prepare, there are some important points to remember for the best taste:

- ❐ Bring the meat to room temperature and dry well with paper towels before browning it.
- ❐ Fry cubes of meat in small batches at a high temperature.
- ❐ Try to avoid overcrowding the meat - otherwise it will steam, not brown.
- ❐ Never cook with a wine you wouldn't drink.

"Breaths of hot, steaming wholesome things that stew and bubble, and uptilt the pot-lids too."

James Whitcomb Riley, 1849-1916

If you freeze a casserole, it weakens the flavour of herbs and spices. Add a sprinkling of fresh parsley or other herbs after defrosting.

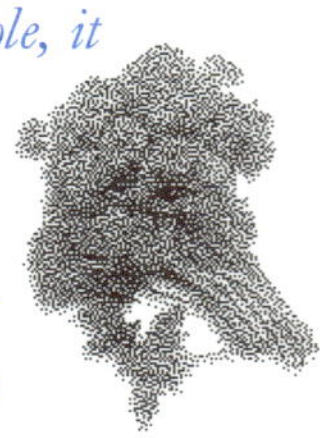

See page 40 for dumplings that are perfect to eat with a casserole.

Cattle have been domesticated for several thousand years. They have only been in North America, however, since 1493, when Christopher Columbus brought them over on his second expedition.

What is the difference between casseroles and pot roasts? Pot roasting is a method of steaming a large piece of meat with a small amount of stock in the bottom of a dish. Casseroles, on the other hand, are like stews. They are made with chunks of browned meat and plenty of wine and herbs.

Cooking With Wine

The custom of using wine in cooking goes back to ancient times. It is a wonderful tastemaker, yet it's often overlooked in Canadian kitchens. Red wine, which should be fairly full-bodied, is perfect for marinades, beef bourguignon, stews, and other red meat dishes. It is also good for cooking some vegetables such as red kidney beans. White wine, on the other hand, should be dry and slightly acidic. Use white wine for white meat dishes, when cooking fish or shellfish and in chicken recipes. Cook only with wine that you would be happy to drink, and use less salt than you normally would as its taste will be intensified.

Beef Bourguignon

2 lb / *900 g*	chuck steak
3 tbsp / *45 ml*	olive oil
1	medium onion, sliced
1 tbsp / *15 ml*	flour
1¾ cups / *410 ml*	good quality red wine (Burgundy is best)
2	garlic cloves, chopped
2	sprigs fresh thyme
1	bay leaf
1½ cups / *375 g*	small onions
1 cup / *250 g*	chopped, uncooked bacon
¼ lb / *110 g*	mushrooms, sliced
	salt and freshly ground pepper

The finest thing you can do with beef. This French classic takes a little extra time but is well worth the effort.
This recipe serves 6.

PREHEAT YOUR OVEN to 275°F (140°C).

HEAT 2 tbsp (30 ml) of the olive oil in a large, flameproof casserole until it is sizzling. Cut the chuck steak into 2 in (5 cm) cubes. Sear the chunks of beef, a few at a time, until they turn a rich dark brown on all sides. As the meat cubes brown, take them out and put them to one side on a plate.

ADD THE SLICED ONION to the casserole and brown that too.

RETURN THE MEAT to the casserole, then sprinkle in the flour stirring it around to soak up all the juices.

GRADUALLY POUR IN THE WINE, stirring constantly.

ADD THE CHOPPED GARLIC and herbs, season to taste with salt and pepper, and cook in the oven with the lid on for 2 hours.

IN A SMALL FRYING PAN, using a bit more oil, fry the small onions and chopped bacon until they're lightly browned. Add them to the casserole with the sliced mushrooms.

PUT THE LID BACK ON and cook for another hour.

Prize-Winning Alamo Chili

This could make you a world champion, so keep it a secret. Spiced up - not down - and with plenty of diced chuck, this is our favourite chili recipe. Once tasted, it will be yours too. Olé!
This recipe serves 4.

½ lb / *225 g*	dried red kidney beans
1 tbsp / *15 ml*	beef drippings or oil
2	medium onions, chopped
1	garlic clove, crushed
1 lb / *450 g*	beef chuck, cut into very small pieces
1 tbsp / *15 ml*	flour
2 tbsp / *30 ml*	tomato purée
1 pint / *565 ml*	hot beef stock (see tips for making stock on page 34)
1 tsp / *5 ml*	crushed dried chile pepper
1	can tomatoes
1 tsp / *5 ml*	cumin seed
1 tsp / *5 ml*	dried basil
1 tsp / *5 ml*	dried oregano
1 tbsp / *15 ml*	freshly chopped dill
1 tbsp / *15 ml*	chopped Italian parsley
1	large green pepper, seeded and chopped
	salt

COVER THE BEANS with cold water, bring them to the boiling point and boil briskly for 10 minutes. Now turn the heat off and let them soak in the hot water for an hour.

TOWARDS THE END of the soaking time, preheat your oven to 300°F (150°C). In a flameproof casserole dish, melt the beef drippings or oil and gently cook the onions and garlic for about 6 minutes.

TURN THE HEAT UP, add the beef and brown it well, stirring it around a bit. Sprinkle in the flour, stir it in to soak up the juices, then mix the tomato purée with the hot stock and add it gradually to the meat and onions.

ADD THE DRIED CHILE PEPPERS, cumin, basil, oregano, dill, parsley, drained tomatoes and red beans. Bring the chili to the simmering point.

NOW COOK THE CASSEROLE in the oven for about 1½ hours with the lid on. When the time's up, stir in the chopped green pepper, cover again and cook for another 30 minutes. Add salt as necessary before serving.

COOKING WITH BACON

Bacon, especially smoked bacon, has a strong flavour that goes a long way. Try using it as a seasoning rather than as an ingredient in your cooking. Crumble cooked bacon over a leafy salad, or toss a handful of bacon bits into a vegetable stir fry.

If you don't use up a package quickly, try freezing individual strips; the bacon stays fresh and you can take out as many slices as you need.

Italian *pancetta* (pronounced pan-cheh-tuh) makes a nice change from bacon and gives a lovely savoury-sweet taste to sauces, pasta dishes and vegetables. *Pancetta* is cured in salt and spices and is not smoked.

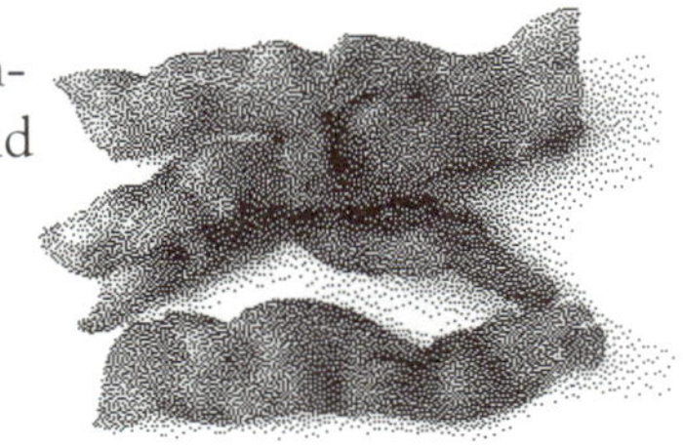

During the War of 1812, the U.S. government sent its soldiers barrels of pork to eat. On the side of the barrels was the name of the meat packer, Sam Wilson. The soldiers referred to the pork as "Uncle Sam's Meat," and thus gave birth to the American government's nickname of Uncle Sam.

With all these sources for inspiration, there is no reason to run out of dinnertime ideas. These books offer good ideas and great recipes:

Dinners at Home
by Lee Bailey
New York:
Random House, 1995

Comes complete with beautiful photos, recipes, schedules and even time plans to help you pull off dinner with style.

Peasant's Choice
by James Barber
New York:
Hastings House, 1994

If you've seen his show on TV, you know chef and author James Barber cooks only dishes that are simple, fast and extremely delicious. We're big-time fans of his Pork Stew Like You've Never Tasted - just one of the unusual, easy and tempting entries in this book.

The Canadian Living Barbeque and Summer Foods Cookbook
by Margaret Fraser and Food Writers of Canadian Living
Mississauga:
Random House of Canada, 1989

Additional Sources:

Winning Tastes of Beef
Canadian Living
Vancouver:
Telemedia Communication, 1996

If you are looking for recipes for tonight's dinner, use the Internet. We particularly like this web site for meat recipes:

http://www.foodservice.ca/cuisine/recipes.htm

Famous Meat Dishes of the World

No matter whether you prefer your meat rare or done to a turn, these dishes are loved the world over. Try them and they will become your favourites too:

- **Char Siu**: A rich red roast pork from the Canton area in China. The pork is marinated in soy sauce, then used for dishes such as fried rice and noodles.

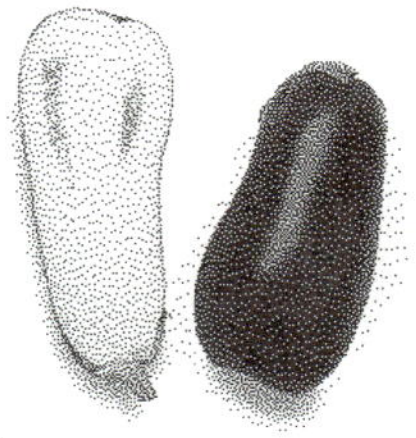

- **Moussaka**: This special Greek dish made from layers of eggplant, ground lamb and tomato should be made with plenty of cinnamon to give it a truly authentic flavour.
- **Carpetbag Steaks**: A traditional Australian way of cooking steaks, with oysters inserted in the middle.

"Bring hither the fatted calf and kill it; and let us eat, and be merry."

The Bible, Luke 15:23

BREAKFAST

"All happiness depends on a leisurely breakfast."

John Gunther, 1901-1970

When it comes to breakfast, Rogers whole-heartedly agrees with John Gunther. Wake up to great taste! Whether it is a fluffy, steaming stack of pancakes, toast and homemade jam, or fresh fruit with your favourite cereal and a glass of orange juice, there is nothing like a tasty breakfast. Get your day off to a delicious - and nutritious - start. Your body will thank you.

Cereals

You can get a good percentage of your daily minerals and vitamins from a bowl of cereal, either hot or cold, served with milk, sugar and a topping. With a little ingenuity, it can taste different every day of the year!

Try these ideas if your taste buds are craving more flavour:

- Sprinkle on some Rogers Best Brown or crunchy Rogers Demerara Sugar, especially over hot cereal - they provide an unexpected and delicious flavour and texture.
- Top a bowl of thick, chilled yogurt with Rogers Golden Syrup and a generous sprinkle of wheat germ.
- Slice fresh fruit over your breakfast. We love bananas, melon (especially sprinkled with ginger), kiwi fruit and fresh berries.
- Try some chopped nuts, raisins or currants.
- Mix equal quantities of plain yogurt and chopped fruit - strawberries, blueberries, blackberries or cranberries are all good. Add enough Rogers Berry Sugar to accentuate the flavours.

When Grape Nut cereal was first produced, it was promoted as a cure for appendicitis, consumption and malaria!

Granola adds crunch to applesauce and makes an instant nutritious topping for ice cream. Try it in cookies and crumbles too.

- Completely cover a bowl of granola with yogurt, then sprinkle Rogers Demerara Sugar over the top.
- Stew some rhubarb and surprise your taste buds one morning.

Pancakes

Based on the simplest of ingredients, pancakes taste equally good sweet or savoury. They are easy to make, and your choice of toppings is only limited by imagination. Why use a store-bought mix when homemade pancakes are tastier and just as quick?

"First, flour and salt together
In a mixing bowl are placed.
Next you break the eggs in
And stir them to a paste.
Add the milk and water
In dribbles, slow and steady;
All the while, keep mixing
Then the batter's ready."

The Rhyming Irish Cookbook
Gordon Snell

Five Steps for Perfect Pancakes

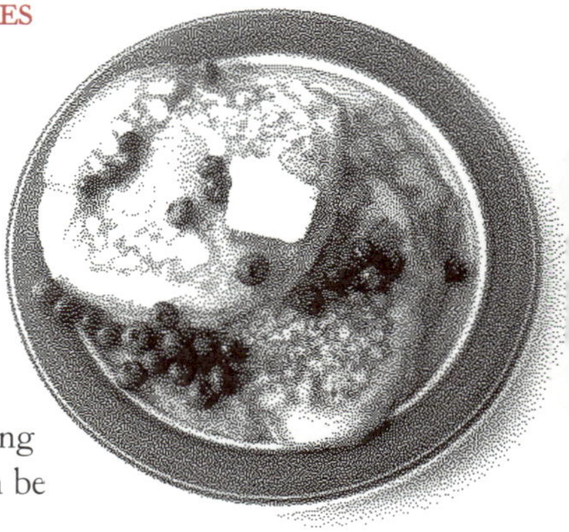

- ❒ Only mix the batter until you have moistened the dry ingredients; a few lumps don't matter. Just a few strokes should do it.
- ❒ Cook your pancakes in a frying pan that has been lightly greased with vegetable oil. Non-stick frying pans are even better, but they can be quite expensive.
- ❒ When the edges start to go brown and bubbles appear on the surface, turn the pancakes over. Allow slightly less cooking time for the second side (it should take a total of about 2 minutes).
- ❒ Don't turn your pancakes over more than once - it will make them tough.
- ❒ Serve your pancakes as soon as they are ready.

Symbolic of good fortune and happiness, pancakes will make your wishes come true in France - but it is no easy feat. You must touch the handle of the frying pan, hold a coin and make your wish just as the pancake is being flipped.

Pour on the Syrup

For the best breakfast toppings, turn to your syrup bottle. There is wonderful maple syrup, of course, and a variety of maple-flavoured syrups such as Rogers Canadian Syrup on the supermarket shelves. Rogers Golden Syrup is also a classic pancake topping. This pure cane sugar syrup brings out the best in your breakfast pancakes and waffles.

Tasty Additions

To add more flavour to your pancakes, experiment with some different ingredients in the mixture:

- Chopped walnuts, pecans or macadamia nuts
- Chopped apples
- A teaspoon (5 ml) of grated lemon rind
- A tablespoon (15 ml) of frozen orange juice concentrate
- Some grated cheese
- Crisp bacon bits or ham
- A handful of fresh or frozen blueberries
- A sliced banana
- Chocolate chips

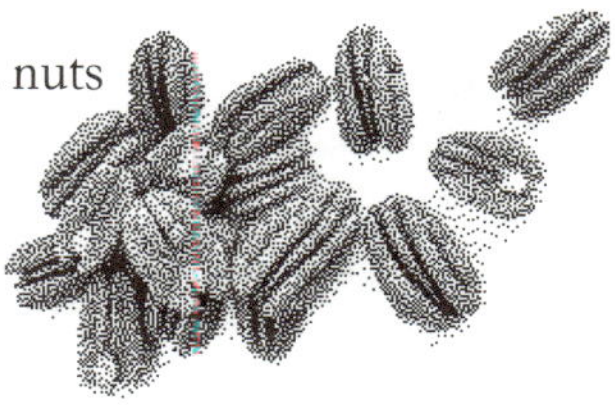

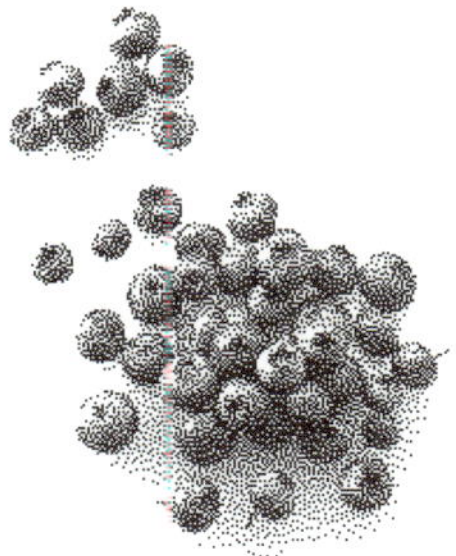

If you have to keep pancakes warm in the oven, separate them with tea towels. Alternatively, arrange them in a single layer on a wire rack set on a cookie sheet (to stop them from going soggy).

Once you have opened a bottle of syrup, keep it in the refrigerator. If it crystallizes, give the bottle a quick bath in warm water to make the syrup liquid again.

Breakfast Butter Pancakes

These pancakes are so easy to prepare from scratch - and so tasty - that you will never be tempted to use a mix again. It's the Rogers Golden Syrup that gives them such a wonderful flavour. This recipe makes about 20 pancakes.

2 cups / *500 ml*	flour
2 tsp / *10 ml*	baking powder
2 tsp / *10 ml*	Rogers Granulated Sugar
2	pinches salt
2	eggs
2 cups / *500 ml*	milk
2 tbsp / *30 ml*	Rogers Golden Syrup
2 tbsp / *30 ml*	melted butter

IN A LARGE BOWL, sift the flour, baking powder, sugar and salt together.

IN ANOTHER BOWL beat the eggs, then mix in the milk and Rogers Golden Syrup. Now pour in the melted butter.

QUICKLY STIR THE MILK mixture into the dry ingredients. Be careful not to over mix the batter. If you need to, thin the batter by adding more milk.

HEAT YOUR FRYING PAN or griddle. Because there is butter in this recipe, you don't need to grease the surface after the first pancake.

POUR ON THE PANCAKE BATTER, a spoonful at a time, using a tablespoon (15 ml) measure or a large serving spoon.

TURN THE PANCAKES OVER when small bubbles appear and the surface begins to set.

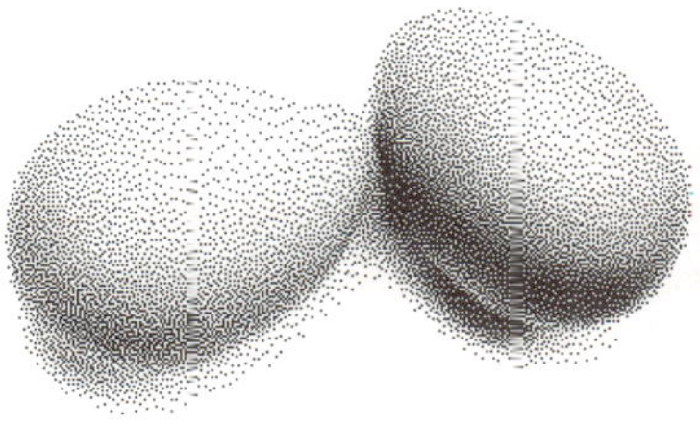

Breakfast Butter Pancakes

"My wife and I tried to breakfast together, but we had to stop or our marriage would have been wrecked."

Winston Churchill, 1874-1965

Don't drop pancake batter from high up. Instead, let it pour from the tip of the spoon.

At the annual stampede in Calgary, chuckwagon breakfasts are a popular event. Hundreds of pancakes with maple syrup are served up alongside eggs, bacon, sausages and hash browns.

To make your pancakes lighter and fluffier, separate the eggs and beat the whites until they form peaks. When the recipe says to add the eggs, mix in the yolks. Gently fold the whites into the mixture at the very end.

Before baking powder was invented, cooks would try all kinds of ways to make their batter lighter. There is a recipe for pancakes from the Middle Ages that recommends making a hole in the middle of the mixture and blowing into it "with a gode blaste of wynde"!

Crêpes and English Pancakes

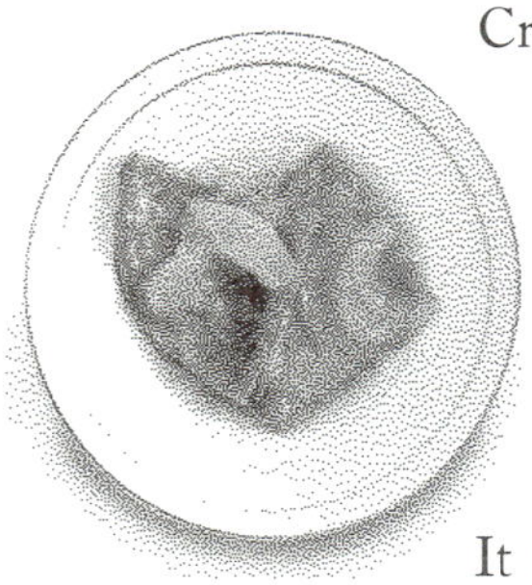

Crêpes and English pancakes are made from a mixture of flour, milk and eggs, and are thinner and more delicate than breakfast pancakes. You can eat them for breakfast, brunch, as a savoury dinner or rolled up with butter, lemon juice and sugar (the traditional "Shrove Tuesday" fare in England).

It is definitely worth finding a good recipe for crêpes. Make them very thin, and try one of these serving ideas:

- Slices of smoked salmon, sour cream and fresh dill
- Sour cream and chives
- Tuna and onion
- Sautéed shrimps and mushrooms
- Asparagus with Hollandaise sauce

Waffles

Waffles are the star attraction at any brunch, and taste delicious when you make them from scratch. They are quick, easy, and you can cook them right at the table if you have an electric waffle iron. They are also foolproof. If the first one doesn't work out, just thicken the batter with more flour, or thin it with milk.

- ❒ Mix the batter between batches to stop it from settling.
- ❒ Never wash an electric waffle iron with water, or grease it. Most waffle batters have enough butter in them to stop them from sticking anyway.
- ❒ To cook bacon with your waffles, just place it directly on the batter and shut the waffle iron. It comes out crisp and brown.

Tasty Additions

To add more flavour to your waffles, experiment with some different ingredients in the mixture:

- Crisply fried bacon bits with cornmeal
- Half a cup (125 ml) of blueberries, cranberries or raisins
- Small chunks of unsweetened chocolate with cinnamon and vanilla

Until the 1950s, when maple syrup was cheap and plentiful, Canadian woodsmen would boil up cups of tea from maple sap instead of water!

Gingerbread Waffles

A touch of ginger and cinnamon, and a little buttermilk, make these waffles wonderful. Remember to fold in the egg whites gently. This recipe makes about 12 waffles.

1/3 cup / *80 ml*	Rogers Best Brown Sugar
2	eggs, separated
2 cups / *500 ml*	buttermilk (or sour milk)
½ cup / *125 ml*	Rogers Golden Syrup
6 tbsp / *90 ml*	melted butter
1 cup / *250 ml*	flour
1 cup / *250 ml*	whole-wheat flour
3 tsp / *15 ml*	baking powder
1 tsp / *5 ml*	baking soda
1 tsp / *5 ml*	each of ground ginger, cinnamon and allspice
½ tsp / *2 ml*	salt
	pinch of cream of tartar

PREHEAT your waffle iron.

BEAT THE SUGAR and egg yolks together, then mix in the buttermilk, Rogers Golden Syrup and butter.

IN A SEPARATE BOWL, combine the flour, baking powder, baking soda, spices and salt, and mix until it is just blended. Don't over beat. Stir in any additional ingredients at this stage (see our suggestions above).

BEAT THE EGG WHITES and cream of tartar together until the egg whites form soft peaks. Gently fold them into the batter.

BAKE THE WAFFLES until they are golden brown and cooked through.

Toppings for Waffles and Pancakes

- Hot blueberry syrup (see our recipe on page 106)
- Rogers Canadian Syrup (regular, maple or butter-flavoured)
- Rogers Golden Syrup
- Fresh fruit
- Sour cream and apple sauce
- Sour cream and raspberries
- Bacon, chives and scrambled egg
- A paste of lemon juice and Rogers Berry Sugar

Cooking With Buttermilk

Buttermilk tastes similar to plain yogurt, but is sweeter and lighter. It adds a nice flavour to baking and makes an excellent substitute for cream and sour cream in soups and salad dressings. If you don't have any buttermilk, you can use regular milk instead. Just add 1 tbsp (5 ml) of lemon juice to a cup (250 ml) of milk, stir, then let it stand for 5 minutes.

Hot Blueberry Syrup

This recipe makes 1 cup of syrup.

1 cup	*/ 250 ml*	blueberries
½ cup	*/ 125 ml*	Rogers Granulated Sugar
½ cup	*/ 125 ml*	water

PUT ALL THE ingredients into a small, heavy saucepan. Bring the mixture to a boil over high heat, stirring occasionally.

REDUCE the heat to medium-low and simmer the syrup for 10 minutes, stirring constantly and crushing the blueberries with the back of a spoon until the berries are soft and the mixture is syrupy. Serve hot.

"There is not a celebrity, a marshal, a composer, or an opera singer who has not given his name to a method of preparing eggs."

James de Coquet

If you are cooking waffles for a crowd at breakfast, it's a good idea to get a head start and make 6 or 7 before everyone arrives. To keep them warm, heat your oven to 200°F (90°C) and put them directly on the oven rack as they cook. Don't cover them.

EGGS

Breakfast just wouldn't be the same without a big dish of scrambled eggs, or a soft-boiled egg and "fingers" of buttered toast. Eggs deserve a soft caress, not brute force.

Be gentle when you cook them and they will reward you well:

- Use the freshest eggs you can find. They not only taste better, they are a lot easier to cook with.
- When you boil eggs, use ones that are at room temperature. Otherwise, they will crack when they go into the hot water.
- Don't over beat your eggs when you make an omelette. They only need a quick stir to mix the yolks and the whites together.
- If you are pan frying with butter, add it to the pan just before you are ready to cook the eggs so the butter doesn't go brown.

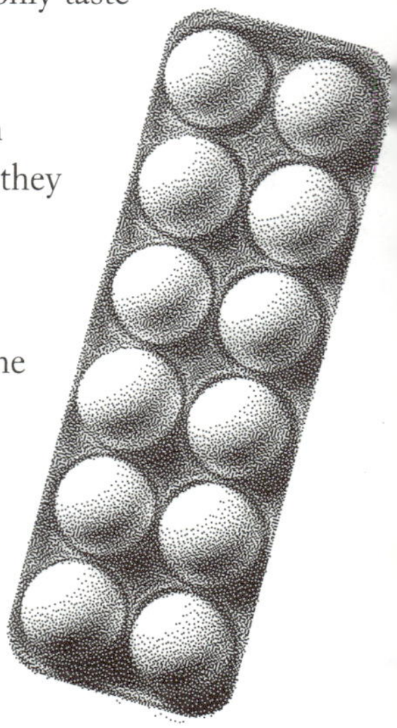

GREAT IDEAS FOR SCRAMBLED EGGS

Next time you scramble some eggs, spark them up with:

- Cottage cheese and chives
- Sautéed sliced mushrooms
- Crisp bacon bits
- Shredded smoked salmon, fresh dill and a grinding of pepper
- Grated Swiss cheese and fresh asparagus tips
- Chopped tomatoes, green onions and a sprinkling of Cheddar cheese
- Cream cheese

- A spoonful of pesto sauce
- Shredded prosciutto
- Fresh coriander and a splash of chilli sauce

When you're scrambling eggs, be careful not to overcook them. Scrambled eggs should be moist - never dry.

Greek-Style Scrambled Eggs

Here is a delicious Greek twist on the breakfast classic. The taste is out of this world! This recipe makes 6 servings.

12	eggs
¼ cup / *60 ml*	half and half cream
	salt and freshly ground black pepper
2 oz / *50 g*	finely chopped onion
3 oz / *75 g*	butter
2 oz / *50 g*	chopped spinach
4 oz / *110 g*	feta cheese, crumbled
3 tbsp / *45 ml*	Greek olives, pitted and chopped

COMBINE THE EGGS, cream, salt and pepper in a mixing bowl. Mix gently until blended together.

SAUTÉ THE ONION in the butter until it's translucent but not brown. Pour the egg mixture into the pan and cook, stirring frequently, until half cooked, which will take about 1 minute.

ADD THE SPINACH to the eggs and continue cooking. Just before the eggs are completely cooked, sprinkle on the cheese.

SPOON THE COOKED EGG MIXTURE onto serving plates and garnish with the olives. Serve immediately.

Greek-Style Scrambled Eggs

The Perfectly Boiled Egg

The next time someone tells you they can't even boil an egg, assure them they are definitely not alone. Boiling eggs properly is a skill, and something that is learned mainly through trial and error. The thing to remember when you are soft-boiling an egg for breakfast is to do it gently so the whites don't become hard. With a tablespoon, lower the egg carefully into gently simmering water. Simmer it for exactly 1 minute, then remove the saucepan from the heat, put a lid on and leave the egg for a further 6 minutes for a large egg, or 5 minutes for a smaller one. This will give you a white that is just set and a soft, creamy yolk, but if you like your egg done more or less than this, add or subtract half a minute.

How to Make an Omelette

Making an omelette is easy, and you have a complete meal that is ready in minutes. You don't need a recipe, but here are a few rules that will ensure you end up with an omelette good enough to frame:

Cinnamon Toast

½ cup / *125 ml*	Rogers Granulated Sugar
2 tsp / *10 ml*	ground cinnamon
6	white bread slices
2 tbsp / *30 ml*	butter

MIX the sugar and cinnamon together.

PREHEAT your broiler and toast one side of the bread slices.

SPREAD the untoasted side with butter, then sprinkle with the cinnamon sugar.

NOW PUT it under the broiler until the sugar melts.

Cinnamon Toast

- Don't over beat the eggs, mix them gently with a dash of salt and pepper.
- When the frying pan is hot, throw in a heaping teaspoon (5 ml) of butter, then turn the heat up to high and swirl the butter round and round so it coats the base and sides of the pan completely.
- As the butter begins to froth, pour in the eggs and shake the pan to spread them out evenly.
- Draw the edges of the omelette toward the centre, letting the pools of egg on the surface run into the channels you have made. Do this until the omelette has set, but the surface is still soft. It should only take about 30 seconds if you have the right heat.

Apple French Toast

Apple French Toast

2	eggs
1/3 cup / *80 ml*	half and half cream
1 tsp / *5 ml*	Rogers Granulated Sugar
½ tsp / *2 ml*	ground cinnamon
	pinch of salt
3	egg bread slices
2 tbsp / *30 ml*	butter

The rich apple syrup, made with Rogers Golden Syrup and rum, transforms our French toast. This recipe serves 2.

WHISK THE EGGS, cream, sugar, cinnamon and salt together in a medium bowl.

ARRANGE THE BREAD SLICES in a 9 in (23 cm) square baking dish.

POUR THE EGG MIXTURE over the bread, turning each slice to coat it properly. If you have time, let the mixture soak into the bread for 20 minutes.

MELT THE BUTTER in a heavy frying pan over medium heat. Add the bread slices and cook them in the butter, one or two at a time. When they are brown, turn them over once (it should take about 12 minutes until they are done).

CUT THE BREAD DIAGONALLY, warm up the apple syrup and spoon it over the toast to serve. A spoonful of sour cream or yogurt is the perfect accompaniment.

Apple Syrup

Apple Syrup

4 tbsp / *60 ml*	unsalted butter
¼ cup / *60 ml*	Rogers Golden Syrup
2	apples peeled, cored and cut into wedges ½ in *(1.5 cm)* thick
¼ cup / *60 ml*	dark rum

MELT THE BUTTER in a large, heavy skillet over medium heat and mix in the Rogers Golden Syrup.

COOK THE APPLES with the butter and syrup very slowly, until the mixture caramelizes and turns a deep, golden brown. Stir the mixture often (it should take about 15 minutes to caramelize properly).

ADD THE RUM and bring the mixture to the boil, scraping up any brown bits.

Toppings for Omelettes

Once you have mastered the art of omelettes, use your imagination to create delicious fillings. Keep in mind that the eggs are the most important part; an omelette should be filled but never overstuffed.

For some filling ideas, try these for taste:

- Sautéed mushrooms with Ricotta cheese, basil and tomato
- Stewed apples and sour cream, with cinnamon and Rogers Best Brown Sugar
- Bacon, Cheddar cheese and baby spinach leaves
- Ratatouille (see our recipe on page 56 of the Vegetables section)
- Red and green peppers, sautéed mushrooms and bean sprouts
- Pan-fried potato chunks, beef strips and salsa
- Ricotta, Mozzarella and Parmesan cheese
- Fresh parsley, basil and chives

Mix chocolate syrup into the egg coating for French toast. When the toast has cooked, drizzle a mixture of maple and chocolate syrup over the top and eat immediately!

Smoothie, Anyone?

For a delicious breakfast drink, grab a yogurt smoothie. They are loaded with calcium, full of flavour and quick to make. Experiment with different smoothie ingredients, depending on what is available. How about these ideas?

- Use fruit juice instead of milk
- Add fresh fruit of the season
- Add frozen berries
- Use flavoured yogurt
- Blend two juices together instead of milk (and leave out the yogurt)

Bananaberry Smoothie

This recipe makes 2 glasses.

½ cup / *125 ml*	strawberries
1	banana
1/3 cup / *80 ml*	plain yogurt
1 cup / *250 ml*	low-fat milk
3	ice cubes

PUT ALL the ingredients in a blender and process until smooth.

If you are looking for more great ways to start the day, get some inspiration from these experts:

At the Tomato
by Diane Clement
Vancouver:
Raincoast Books, 1995

Brunch ideas, eye-opening fresh juices and a whole lot more from Vancouver's Tomato Fresh Food Café.

Pancakes and Waffles
by Elizabeth Alston
New York:
Harper Collins, 1993

We never realized that pancakes can be eaten in so many ways! This treasure trove of recipes has ideas for breakfast, lunch and dinner. There are also plenty of sauces that are just as good on waffles and French toast.

You will flip over this web site - it has some great pancake recipes:

http://www.cs.cmu.edu/~mjw/recipes/bread/pancakes/index.html

Get in touch with these egg marketing boards for some more breakfast recipes:

B.C. Egg Marketing Board
P.O. Box 310
Abbotsford, British Columbia
V2S 4P2
(604) 853-3348

Alberta Egg Producers Board
#15, 1915 - 32nd Avenue N.E.
Calgary, Alberta
T2E 7C8
(403) 250-1197

Saskatchewan Commercial Egg Producers' Marketing Board
P.O. Box 1637
Regina, Saskatchewan
S4P 3C4
(306) 924-1505

Famous Pancakes of the World

When you eat pancakes, you are eating history! Pancakes date back to the Roman Empire, and you can find them in various forms all around the world:

- **Crêpes Suzette**: These are thin, French pancakes, served with a flaming butter and alcohol sauce.
- **Blini**: Russian pancakes, small and raised, traditionally served with caviar and sour cream.
- **Latkes**: Excellent for brunch, or as a side dish, latkes are a Jewish speciality. Serve these large potato and onion pancakes with sour cream and applesauce.

"To eat well in England you should have breakfast three times a day."

W. Somerset Maugham, 1874-1965

MUFFINS & QUICK BREADS

"Give me the luxuries of life and I will willingly do without the necessities."

Frank Lloyd Wright, 1869-1959

Coffee break, lunch or afternoon tea. Muffins and quick breads are anytime treats. When you discover how easy it is to bake your own loaves, muffins and scones, you will turn up your nose at the pale imitations in your grocery store bakery.

These breads are the epitome of fast food. There is no rising time needed, and the basic ingredients are always on hand - flour, milk, baking powder, sugar and eggs - so it's simply a matter of mixing the batter. They are usually ready to bake in less than 10 minutes, just the time you need to heat your oven!

For the best muffins, quick breads and scones:

- ❒ Don't substitute oil in a recipe that calls for butter. It will upset the liquid balance.
- ❒ Choose your sweetener according to your flavour goal. Rogers Golden Syrup, granulated or soft sugars, honey - even maple syrup - will all add their special taste to breads.
- ❒ Don't worry if your batter is not completely combined - it only needs a few strokes to mix everything together.
- ❒ Add fruit, nuts, wheat germ or bran to make high-fibre muffins and quick breads.
- ❒ Mix Rogers Icing Sugar and milk to make a paste you can drizzle over quick breads and muffins.

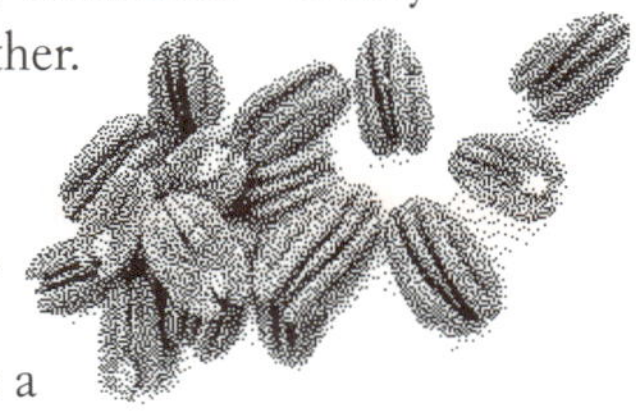

Muffins can be frozen for up to two months. To reheat them, put them in a paper bag. Wet the bag with cold water; then put it in a 350°F (180°C) oven for 15 minutes.

Cooking With Citrus Zest

The zest, or outer rind, of oranges and lemons is a wonderful tastemaker to use when you are baking muffins and quick breads. It provides a strong citrus flavour and contrasts nicely with the sweeter ingredients. One of our favourite muffin flavours is blueberry and lemon, with plenty of zest thrown in. Either grate the zest with a fine grater, or use a vegetable peeler to remove it. Then cut it into small pieces with a knife. Don't use the white inner layer, or pith, as it is bitter and unpleasant.

Muffins

Virtually unknown until two decades ago, muffins have become one of today's most popular breakfast and snack foods. There are muffin shops popping up all over the country, with flavours ranging from fragrant lemon to savoury chick-pea. Fresh and warm, just-baked muffins are a wonderful way to start the day, or to enjoy at lunch or dinner.

The perfect muffin should have a dense, moist interior and be quite crumbly. Here is how to get the best results:

- ❒ Mix the wet and dry muffin ingredients until just moistened.
- ❒ Fill the muffin cups only two-thirds full, so the mixture doesn't overflow.
- ❒ Half fill empty muffin cups with water if you don't have enough mixture to fill all the cups in a pan. This protects the pan and helps the muffins bake more evenly.
- ❒ Bake muffins in the centre of the oven to cook them evenly.

Classic Muffins

Classic Muffins

1¾ cups / *440 ml*	flour
¾ tsp / *4 ml*	salt
2 tsp / *10 ml*	baking powder
2	eggs
4 tbsp / *60 ml*	melted butter
½ cup / *125 ml*	milk
1 tsp / *5 ml*	vanilla extract
¼ cup / *60 ml*	Rogers Golden Syrup

This is the mixture for your muffins. Now pick a flavouring from the list that follows, or get creative and invent your own!
This recipe makes about 12 large muffins.

PREHEAT your oven to 400°F (200°C). Grease the muffin pans.

SIFT THE DRY INGREDIENTS together, then add your chosen flavouring.

BEAT THE EGGS in a separate bowl. Add the melted butter, milk, vanilla and Rogers Golden Syrup.

COMBINE THE LIQUID and the dry ingredients with a few short strokes.

FILL the muffin pans two-thirds full and bake for 20 to 25 minutes.

Tasty Muffin Additions

Your favourite cappuccino bar is the best place to taste the latest muffin flavours. Find a combination you want to try and add the flavourings to our classic muffin recipe above. Make up your own flavours, or try some of our favourites listed here:

- Blueberries, blackberries, raspberries, saskatoons or strawberries
- Chopped apple, apple juice and grated cheese
- Cranberries and lemon zest
- Mashed ripe bananas, semisweet chocolate chips and chopped walnuts
- Chopped pecans, canned pumpkin, orange zest and orange juice

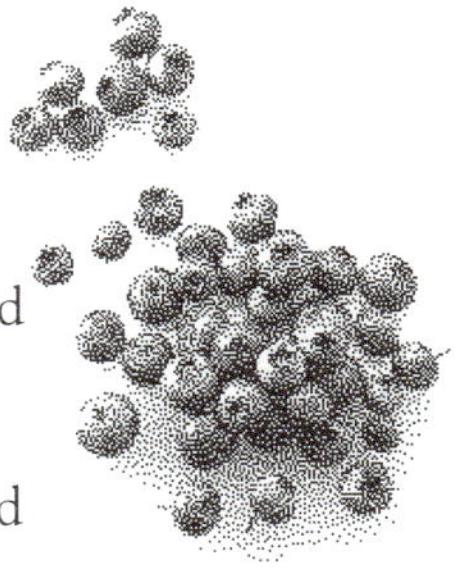

For a tasty surprise, fill the muffin cups halfway, then sprinkle on 1 tsp (5 ml) of Rogers Granulated Sugar mixed with cinnamon. Top with the rest of the batter and finish off with a sprinkle of the sugar mixture.

Rogers Gold Medal Muffins

Packed with fruit and nuts, these are muffins for champions of all ages. This recipe makes 12 large muffins.

PREHEAT the oven to 400°F (200°C). Grease your muffin pans.

COMBINE THE DRY INGREDIENTS in a bowl. In another bowl, combine the liquid ingredients, including the grated orange rind. Now quickly stir the wet and dry ingredients together until just moistened (see our golden rules for mixing muffins).

SPOON THE BATTER into the muffin pans, filling them only two-thirds full. Bake for about 20 minutes or until done.

1 cup / *250 ml*	cooking oats or oatmeal
1 cup / *250 ml*	whole-wheat flour
½ cup / *125 ml*	wheat germ
1 cup / *250 ml*	natural bran
2 tsp / *10 ml*	baking powder
½ tsp / *2 ml*	baking soda
½ tsp / *2 ml*	salt
¼ cup / *60 ml*	chopped nuts
½ cup / *125 ml*	raisins
½ cup / *125 ml*	dried apricots, chopped
1 cup / *250 ml*	orange juice
	grated rind of ½ an orange
½ cup / *125 ml*	plain yogurt
¼ cup / *60 ml*	melted butter
¼ cup / *60 ml*	Rogers Golden Syrup
1	egg

QUICK BREADS

Moist and rich-tasting, these fruit and nut breads use baking powder or baking soda instead of yeast. You don't have to wait for the mixture to rise, and no kneading is required.

Fresh out of the oven, quick breads are crisp and crunchy on the outside and delicately flavoured and textured on the inside. Once wrapped and stored, they get moister and heavier, and the rich flavours blend together.

A great way to make canapés or a sandwich base is to add 1 cup (250 ml) of stuffed green olives, sliced, and 1 cup (250 ml) of chopped nuts to a plain quick bread mixture. When the quick bread has cooked and cooled, cut it up finely. Top the squares with pâté, salmon or anything else that takes your fancy.

"Here is bread, which strengthens man's heart, And therefore is called the staff of life."

Matthew Henry

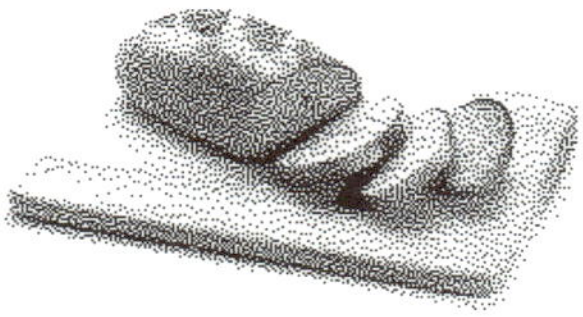

For the best quick breads:

- Bake quick breads in the lower third of the oven, so the bottom gets cooked but the top isn't too brown.
- Treat quick breads like muffins: don't overmix them. About 10 seconds is usually enough.
- Leave them in the refrigerator overnight wrapped in foil. They'll slice better if you do.

Tasty Quick Bread Additions

The best additions to a quick bread recipe are those that add moisture as well as flavour:

- Dates or raisins
- Prunes
- Rogers Golden Syrup, honey or molasses
- Lemon or orange juice, with zest
- Mashed pumpkin
- Crushed pineapple
- Berries (blueberries, blackberries and strawberries all taste great)

Flavoured Butters

Flavoured butter is delicious spread on quick breads, pancakes or crisp waffles (see the Breakfast section, pages 103 and 105, for recipes). The butter will keep for several days in the refrigerator or for weeks in the freezer. If you have homemade jam and marmalade to make flavoured butter with, even better!

- Orange butter: ½ cup (125 ml) butter, 1/3 cup (80 ml) orange marmalade, ½ tsp (2 ml) Rogers Icing Sugar, grated zest of one orange
- Strawberry butter: ½ cup (125 ml) butter, 1/3 cup (80 ml) strawberry jam, ½ tsp (2 ml) fresh lemon juice, ½ tsp (2 ml) Rogers Icing Sugar

- Herb butter: ½ cup (125 ml) butter, 1 tbsp (15 ml) freshly chopped parsley, 1 tbsp (15 ml) freshly chopped dill or tarragon

- Vegetable butter: ½ cup (125 ml) butter, 1 tsp (5 ml) freshly chopped parsley, 1 tsp (5 ml) chopped onion, 1 crushed garlic clove, 1 tbsp (15 ml) chopped sun-dried tomatoes, a sprinkle of salt and pepper

Cream the ingredients together, transfer to a small bowl and chill. Leave the butter to soften before serving.

"I do like a little bit of butter to my bread."

When We Were Very Young
A. A. Milne, 1882-1956

Crunchy Lemon Quick Bread

Easier to make than a pound cake but just as delightful. Light with a crunchy crust, the tangy lemon flavour of this loaf tastes like heaven. This recipe makes 2 loaves.

7 oz / *200 g*	butter, softened
1½ cups / *375 ml*	Rogers Granulated Sugar
4	eggs, separated
2/3 cup / *160 ml*	fresh lemon juice
2 tbsp / *30 ml*	lemon zest
3 cups / *750 ml*	cake flour
4 tsp / *20 ml*	baking powder
1 cup / *250 ml*	milk
	pinch of salt
1 cup / *250 ml*	walnuts, chopped (optional)
¼ cup / *60 ml*	water

PREHEAT YOUR OVEN to 350°F (180°C). Grease two 9 x 5 in (22.5 x 12.5 cm) loaf pans.

CREAM THE BUTTER and 1 cup (250 ml) of sugar together. Beat in the egg yolks, one at a time, then stir in 1/3 cup (80 ml) of the lemon juice. Add the lemon zest.

SIFT TOGETHER THE CAKE FLOUR with the baking powder. Add a third of the flour mixture to the creamed butter and sugar. Then add half the milk, another third of the flour, the remaining milk and the remaining flour. Be careful not to over mix - a few strokes is all the batter needs.

IN ANOTHER BOWL, beat the egg whites with a pinch of salt until they form soft peaks. Stir a quarter of the egg whites thoroughly into the batter with the walnuts (if you want them). Scoop the remaining egg whites onto the top of the batter and gently fold together.

POUR THE BATTER into the prepared loaf pans. Bake on the middle rack of the oven for 45 to 50 minutes. The bread is ready when it pulls away from the sides of the pan and a toothpick inserted into the centre comes out clean. Let each loaf cool in the pan for 5 minutes, then remove it and leave on a wire rack.

IN A SMALL SAUCEPAN, boil the remaining 1/3 cup (80 ml) of the lemon juice, water and the remaining ½ cup (125 ml) of sugar together for 2 minutes. Drizzle the syrup over the loaves while they're still hot.

Brazilian Banana Bread

Brazilian Banana Bread

5	ripe bananas
1 cup / *250 ml*	strong black coffee
1½ cups / *375 ml*	soft butter
1¾ cups / *440 ml*	Rogers Best Brown Sugar
4	eggs
3 tsp / *15 ml*	vanilla extract
¼ cup	lemon juice
1 tsp / *5 ml*	lemon zest
4 cups / *1 L*	flour
1 tsp / *5 ml*	salt
½ tsp / *2 ml*	baking soda
1 tbsp / *15 ml*	baking powder
½ tsp / *2 ml*	ground nutmeg
2 tsp / *10 ml*	ground cinnamon
¾ cup	chopped walnuts

Banana bread should never be bland. This recipe uses bananas soaked in coffee (yes, coffee!) and plenty of spices. This recipe makes 12 to 16 servings.

PREHEAT YOUR OVEN to 350°F (180°C). Generously grease two 9 x 5 in (22.5 x 12.5 cm) loaf pans. In a bowl, leave the bananas to soak in the coffee.

BEAT TOGETHER THE BUTTER and Best Brown Sugar in a large bowl. Add the eggs, one at a time, beating well after each one until the mixture is fluffy.

STIR IN THE VANILLA EXTRACT, lemon juice and lemon zest.

SIFT TOGETHER THE DRY INGREDIENTS. Take the bananas out of the coffee and mash them up. Add the dry ingredients to the butter mixture, a little bit at a time, alternating with the mashed bananas. Leave out a few spoonfuls of the flour mixture. Be careful not to over mix!

NOW STIR IN THE CHOPPED WALNUTS, along with the rest of the flour mixture.

SPREAD THE BATTER EVENLY in the pans and bake for 40 to 50 minutes.

"A good cook is like a sorceress who dispenses happiness."

Shocking Life
Elsa Schiaparelli, 1890-1973

SCONES

Scones are a British tradition, similar to tea biscuits and delicious with jam and cream. Give them a taste and they will quickly become one of your family's traditions too. Fast and simple to make, scones are best when still warm from the oven.

For best results when you make your scones:

- ❒ Handle the dough as little as possible, taking care not to over beat it.
- ❒ Knead the dough five times - that's all it needs.
- ❒ Make sure the dough is at least ¾ in (2 cm) thick. If it is any thinner, the scones will be dry.
- ❒ Bake scones in a hot oven.

Sourdough bread was such an essential part of diets of prospectors around the Cariboo and Klondike goldfields during the gold rush that eventually the prospectors were nicknamed "sourdoughs."

Tasty Scone Additions

Scones can be savoury or sweet, depending on what you add to the dry ingredients:

Savoury

- Freshly grated Parmesan or Cheddar cheese with paprika
- Freshly chopped chives, marjoram, rosemary or parsley
- Cooked, crumbled bacon
- Sautéed chopped onion

Sweet

- Chopped crystallized ginger or dates
- Raisins or currants and cinnamon
- Freshly sliced strawberries, whole raspberries or blueberries

When you add raisins to a scone mixture, soak them first for 5 minutes in milk or juice. Soaking will make them plump and juicy.

Just before you put scones into the oven, sprinkle Rogers Granulated Sugar over the top for a tasty crunch.

Tea Etiquette

- Use a cozy to keep the teapot warm.
- Milk, rather than cream, is best for tea.
- Add the milk and sugar to the cup after pouring in the tea, or you run the risk of scalding the milk.

Cinnamon Raisin Scones

Fluffy, hot from the oven and ready for a dab of homemade jam or a slice of cheese, these raisin scones are ideal for everything from lunch to dessert.

2 cups / *500 ml*	flour
2 tbsp / *30 ml*	Rogers Granulated Sugar
2 tsp / *10 ml*	ground cinnamon
2 tsp / *10 ml*	ground nutmeg
4 tsp / *20 ml*	baking powder
¼ cup / *60 ml*	cold butter
1 cup / *250 ml*	raisins
2/3 cup / *160 ml*	milk

PREHEAT YOUR OVEN to 450°F (230°C).

BLEND THE FLOUR, sugar, spices and baking powder together. With a fork or two small knives cut the butter into the dry ingredients until the mixture is crumbly and looks like small peas. Add the raisins, then mix in the milk.

KNEAD LIGHTLY, folding in half each time. Pat into a round about ¾ in (2 cm) thick. Place on an ungreased baking sheet. Score into eight equal wedges. Brush with milk. Bake near the top of the oven for 12 to 15 minutes, until crisp and golden.

Once you start making quick breads, muffins and scones, you won't want to stop. Here are some books for more ideas:

Company's Coming: Muffins & More
by Jean Pare
Vermillion:
Co's Coming Publications, 1994

A book that's dedicated to quick breads and muffins. It has lots of good recipes and variations.

Simply HeartSmart Cooking
by Bonnie Stern
Toronto:
Random House, c1994

If you like muffins with lots of wholesome ingredients and interesting flavour combinations, there's a section in this book that has some really great suggestions.

All the Best Muffins and Quick Breads
by Joie Warner
Don Mills:
Stoddart, 1994

Additional Sources:

How to Bake
by Nick Malgieri
New York:
Martins Griffin, 1995

Coffeetime Indulgences
by Linda Hageman
New York:
Martins Griffin, 1995

If you are looking for quick bread recipes, try this web site:

http://casper.nmhu.edu/recipes.htm

Fancy a Cup of Tea?

There is nothing nicer than a cup of tea to accompany freshly baked scones or quick bread. Most people use tea bags to brew their tea, but you really do get a better flavour by making it from loose leaves. There are speciality tea stores opening up all over Canada now which offer interesting alternatives to a cup of Earl Grey.

Baking Bread

The best bread is still baked by hand. Bread making can seem a little intimidating if you haven't tried it, but when you get down to it, it is not difficult at all. You don't need a bread machine either; bread dough rises on its own while you are off doing other things, then goes straight into the oven. Fit a few loaves into your day, and you will be rewarded with the special joy of homemade bread, as well as a house filled with the wonderful smell of baking.

To be a successful bread baker, you need a good bread book or two. There have been some wonderful books written; our favourites are listed below:

- **Beard on Breads** *by James Beard*
- **The Way to Cook** *by Julia Child*
- **The Laurel's Kitchen Bread Book** *by Laurel Robertson*

"Without bread, without wine, love is nothing."

French Proverb

CAKES & COOKIES

"C is for Cookie,
that's good enough for me."

The cookie monster
Seasame Street

Baking from scratch is one of the nicest things you can do for friends and family. Especially today, when our palates have become so used to store-bought versions, homebaked cakes and cookies are a much appreciated luxury.

Cookies often only take 30 minutes from start to finish. They are so easy, anyone can make moist, delicious cookies, and there is nothing nicer than a kitchen filled with the aroma of fresh baking.

Cakes

When baking, it's important to be precise and orderly. To get the best taste possible, the way you make a cake is as important as the ingredients you use:

- ❒ Start with all your ingredients at room temperature, especially the eggs.
- ❒ Soften the butter for an hour. And *use* butter because margarine doesn't come close in flavour.
- ❒ Measure ingredients carefully, using the dull edge of a knife to even off your measuring spoons.
- ❒ Bake a cake as soon as you mix it, so you don't lose any of the air in the batter. This keeps the cake nice and light.
- ❒ Always use good quality ingredients in your baking. Never jeopardize taste by using old eggs or stale flour, baking soda and spices.

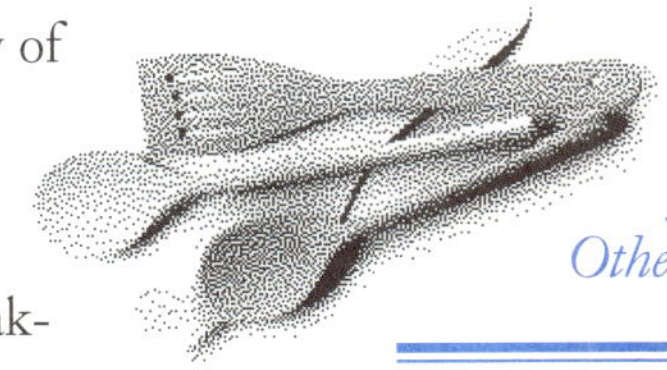

If you want a cake to have crispy edges, flour the cake pan. Otherwise, don't bother.

1 cup / *250 ml*	boiling water
3	squares *(1 oz / 28 g)* of semi-sweet chocolate
½ cup / *125 ml*	butter
1 tsp / *5 ml*	vanilla extract
2 cups / *500 ml*	Rogers Berry Sugar
1 tbsp / *15 ml*	Rogers Golden Syrup
2	eggs, separated
1 tsp / *5 ml*	baking soda
½ cup / *125 ml*	sour cream
2 cups / *500 ml*	flour
2 tbsp / *30 ml*	cocoa powder
1 tsp / *5 ml*	baking powder

Chocolate Frosting

2 tbsp / *30 ml*	butter
¾ cup / *180 ml*	semisweet chocolate chips
6 tbsp / *90 ml*	half and half cream
1¼ cups / *310 ml*	Rogers Icing Sugar, sifted
1 tsp / *5 ml*	vanilla extract

PUT EVERYTHING in a heavy saucepan over low heat and whisk it until smooth. Leave the frosting to cool slightly, then spread it on the cake.

Rogers Chocolate Cake

Sour cream and Rogers Golden Syrup combine to make this a spectacular chocolate cake. Moist and dark, yet never overpowering.

PREHEAT YOUR OVEN to 350°F (180°C). Grease and flour a 10 in (25.5 cm) tube pan.

POUR THE BOILING WATER into a bowl with the chocolate pieces and the butter, then let them stand until everything has melted.

STIR IN THE VANILLA, Rogers Berry Sugar and Rogers Golden Syrup. Whisk in the egg yolks, one at a time, blending well after each one.

MIX THE BAKING SODA and sour cream together and whisk them into the mixture. Sift the flour, cocoa powder and baking powder and add them to the batter, mixing thoroughly.

BEAT THE EGG WHITES until they're stiff and form peaks, then stir a quarter of the egg whites thoroughly into the batter. Scoop the remaining egg whites onto the top of the batter and gently fold together.

POUR THE BATTER into the prepared pan. Place the cake in the middle of the oven and bake for 40 to 50 minutes. Cool the cake in the pan for 10 minutes, remove it and wait until it's completely cool before frosting.

To get lots of air into your cake, always sift your dry ingredients. Hold the sifter or sieve up high to allow in air as you sift, and use a large, roomy mixing bowl.

In certain parts of Africa, sugar cubes used to be a form of currency. Two cubes would be a down payment on a goat, five on a new wife and ten on a share in a second-hand bicycle!

COOKING WITH CHOCOLATE

Chocolate comes in lots of varieties. For cooking, the best kind is called baking chocolate, which is unsweetened and dark and sold in bars. Dark, imported chocolate has 75 percent cocoa butter solids, which gives your cake a concentrated, "chocolatey" taste. Avoid using artificial chocolate in your baking. Grades and ingredients are clearly marked on chocolate packaging, so check them carefully.

Fresh Is Best

Eggs are a vital ingredient when it comes to cakes, and the freshness of your eggs is extremely important.

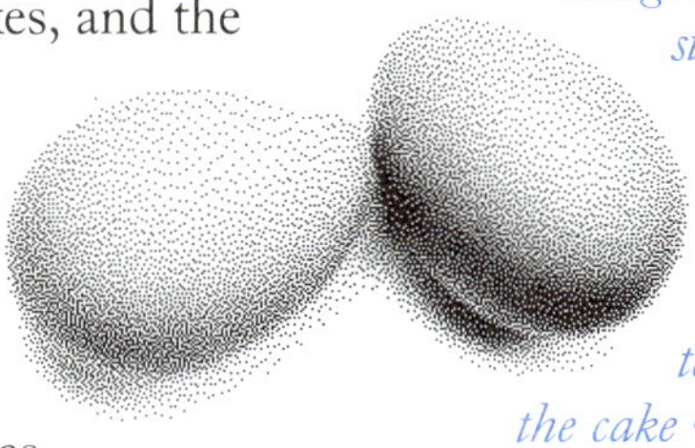

- ❐ Always buy Canada Grade A eggs, which have usually been packed for less than seven days.
- ❐ Store eggs in the refrigerator. They lose as much freshness in one day at room temperature as they do in a week in the refrigerator.
- ❐ If you are not sure how fresh an egg is, a reliable way of telling is to put it in a bowl of cold water. The less fresh the egg is, the more likely it is to float.

Large or extra-large eggs are the standard size when it comes to baking.

Never store cakes and cookies in the same container. The moisture from the cake will make the cookies soggy.

Kids love cupcakes, and you can use practically any cake recipe to make them. Line a muffin or cupcake tin with decorative paper liners and half fill them with cake batter. They will take about 20 to 25 minutes to bake at 375°F (190°C).

Sponge, Chiffon and Angel Food Cakes

These are the glamour cakes. They are light and elegant, yet surprisingly simple to make. What is the secret? It's all in the eggs. Stiffly beaten egg whites and Rogers Berry Sugar give these cakes their volume. Ideally, the egg whites should be beaten in a copper bowl, as they react with the copper and produce a lighter, higher mixture, but a stainless-steel bowl will give you nearly the same effect.

- ❐ Separate the whites just before you are going to use them (it's usually easier to do this when the eggs are cold).
- ❐ Make sure that the bowl and beaters are completely grease free.
- ❐ Beat a little bit of Berry Sugar into the egg whites for elasticity and stability.
- ❐ Sift the ingredients to add more air to the mixture.
- ❐ Only grease the bottom of your cake pan. Ungreased sides help the batter to get a grip and climb higher.
- ❐ After pouring the batter into the pan, draw a knife gently through it to eliminate any large air pockets.

Use Rogers Berry Sugar rather than Rogers Granulated Sugar in your sponge cakes, as it dissolves more easily.

For great flavour, make a sugar syrup from Rogers Berry Sugar dissolved in water. Mix it with liqueur or lemon juice, then dab it over a cake before icing.

The Original Rogers Christmas Cake

The marinating of whole fruits and pecans in Rogers Golden Syrup and rum is the key to this recipe's well-deserved fame. Get the whole family involved and make it one of your Christmas traditions! This recipe makes 2 cakes.

1 lb / *450 g*	pecans
1 lb / *450 g*	pitted dates
½ lb / *225 g*	citron, slivered
½ lb / *225 g*	candied pineapple, cut into bite-sized chunks
1 lb / *450 g*	candied cherries, halved
3 lb / *1.35 kg*	seedless raisins
1 cup / *250 ml*	dark rum
½ cup / *125 ml*	Rogers Golden Syrup
½ lb / *225 g*	butter
1½ cups / *375 ml*	Rogers Granulated Sugar
1 tsp / *5 ml*	vanilla extract
6	eggs, separated
3 cups / *750 ml*	flour
2 tsp / *10 ml*	ground cinnamon
2 tsp / *10 ml*	ground nutmeg
½ tsp / *2 ml*	ground cloves
2 tsp / *10 ml*	cream of tartar
1 tsp / *5 ml*	salt
½ tsp / *2 ml*	baking soda

PUT THE FIRST SIX INGREDIENTS in a bowl with ½ cup (125 ml) of rum and the Rogers Golden Syrup. Tightly cover the mixture and leave it at room temperature for at least 24 hours.

THE NEXT DAY, preheat your oven to 275°F (140°C). Line two 9 in (23 cm) tube pans with two thicknesses of brown paper and grease the paper well with butter.

CREAM THE BUTTER with the Rogers Granulated Sugar and vanilla.

BEAT IN THE EGG YOLKS. Beat the egg whites separately until they're stiff, then fold them gently into the creamed mixture.

STIR IN THE DRY INGREDIENTS, add the fruit and nuts that have been soaking and mix everything together.

DIVIDE THE BATTER evenly between the two prepared pans. Bake both cakes for about 3 hours. When the cakes start to go brown on top, cover them up with more greased brown paper.

LET THE CAKES COOL in their pans on wire racks. Once they have cooled, remove the cakes from the pans and sprinkle the rest of the rum over them.

If you can, make your Christmas cakes about eight weeks before the big day. They taste better if they are given some time to mature.

If you garnish your cake with thickened fillings such as fruit or custard, it can be kept for 24 hours but no longer. Flavoured creams, gelatins or ice creams should be added just before the cake is served so it doesn't become soggy.

Fillings and Decorations

Now that you have made your cake, it's worth taking the extra time to decorate it nicely. There is so much personal pleasure in creating an edible work of art. It's important to remember, however, that some fillings and decorations will decrease the storage time of a cake.

Go ahead and give some of these ideas a try:

Decorations

- Icing or frosting
- Shaved chocolate (use a vegetable peeler for professional looking shavings)

- Fresh fruit such as halved strawberries, grapes or thinly sliced kiwi
- Fresh mint leaves
- A "bouquet" of small flowers such as pansies or nasturtiums
- Melted chocolate drizzled over a lighter-coloured icing
- Sugared flowers
- Icing sugar sprinkled on with a stencil

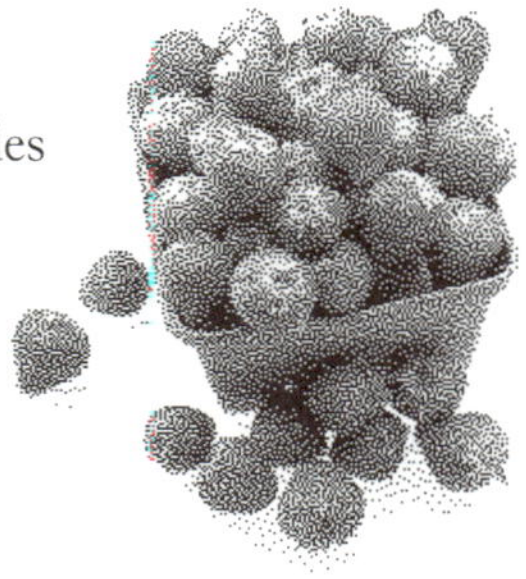

Fillings

- Sweetened, whipped cream
- Homemade preserves (see the Jams, Jellies & Chutneys section on page 141 for some great recipes)
- Vanilla, chocolate, butterscotch or mocha cream

Orange Cream-Cheese Frosting

½ cup	Rogers Icing Sugar
3 oz / *85 g*	cream cheese
1½ tbsp / *22 ml*	cream or milk
1½ tsp / *7 ml*	orange zest
½ tsp / *2 ml*	ground cinnamon
	dash of orange liqueur

COMBINE the cream cheese and milk in a bowl. Beat the icing sugar gradually into the mixture until soft and fluffy.

MIX IN the rest of the ingredients.

Zesty Orange Carrot Cake

Zesty by name, zesty by nature! Orange juice and spices and the cream-cheese frosting are the ingredients that really make this carrot cake. This recipe makes 2 cakes.

2½ cups / *625 ml*	packed finely grated carrots
¼ cup / *60 ml*	orange juice
1½ cups / *375 ml*	soft butter
1¾ cups / *440 ml*	Rogers Best Brown Sugar
4	eggs
3 tsp / *15 ml*	vanilla extract
1 tsp / *5 ml*	orange zest
4 cups / *1 L*	flour
1 tsp / *5 ml*	salt
½ tsp / *2 ml*	baking soda
1 tbsp / *15 ml*	baking powder
1 tsp / *5 ml*	ground allspice
2 tsp / *10 ml*	ground cinnamon
¾ cup / *180 ml*	raisins
¾ cup / *180 ml*	chopped walnuts or pecans

PREHEAT YOUR OVEN to 350°F (180°C). Grease two 9 x 5 in (22.5 x 12.5 cm) loaf pans. In a bowl, soak the grated carrot in the orange juice.

BEAT TOGETHER the butter and the Rogers Best Brown Sugar in a large bowl. Add the eggs, one at a time, beating well after each one until the mixture is fluffy.

STIR IN THE VANILLA and orange zest.

SIFT THE DRY INGREDIENTS TOGETHER. Add them to the butter mixture, a little at a time, alternating with the grated carrot and orange juice mixture. Now stir in the raisins and the chopped walnuts.

SPREAD THE BATTER evenly in the pans and bake for 40 to 50 minutes. Cool for 10 minutes, then take the cakes out of the pans and put them on a rack. While still slightly warm, ice the carrot cakes with Orange Cream-Cheese Frosting (see the recipe above).

If you are filling or frosting a layer cake, sprinkle Rogers Icing Sugar on top of each layer first to keep the liquid from soaking in.

If you need to cream soft sugar and butter together, run the sugar in a blender for awhile. It will break up any lumps and make it easier to cream.

Freezing Your Dough

It's just as easy to stir up a double batch of cookie dough as it is to make a single recipe; you can then freeze the second half to use later. When you are ready to use the frozen cookie dough, take it out of the freezer and let it thaw for about 30 minutes before shaping and baking. Cookie dough should not be frozen for more than six months, while baked cookies can be left in the freezer for up to twelve months.

Coffee and Cake

A special cup of coffee is the perfect after-dinner treat with a slice of cake. For the best coffee, always buy freshly roasted beans, then grind them at home as you need them. If you keep your beans in the freezer, they will stay fresh for up to two months.

Cookies

Nobody knows for sure who invented cookies. Possibly they were a trial by a cake baker who was testing to see if the oven was hot enough before putting a cake in. But since then, cookies have earned their rightful place in our hearts and in our cookie jars.

When you make cookies and bars, the main thing to remember is to mix the batter as little as possible. The less it is handled, the better the cookies will taste.

Some things to remember when you are making cookies:

- ❐ Cream the butter and sugar thoroughly.
- ❐ Mix in the dry ingredients gently. If you are too hard on the dough, you will end up with tough cookies. It's always better to stir the mixture by hand rather than to overdo it with a mixer.
- ❐ Start with all your ingredients at room temperature - especially the eggs.
- ❐ Always measure ingredients carefully.
- ❐ Turn the baking sheet around during baking so your cookies get evenly browned.
- ❐ Don't overcook your cookies. You can usually tell when they are ready to come out of the oven. Most lose their glossy look, and the lighter-coloured ones turn golden around the edges.
- ❐ Don't regrease a hot baking sheet. Let it cool, wipe it, then start again with your next batch.

Oat Cookies

Oats have long been used in Scotland for making cookies; they give a lovely crunch and a characteristic nutty flavour. Some recipes call for "quick-cooking oats," but these oats have been commercially treated and aren't much good for baking. Use rolled oats, which are simply the husked grains that have been mechanically rolled into flakes.

Apricot and Nut Oaties

We have combined the sharp and sweet flavour of apricots with chocolate to create a truly wonderful oatmeal cookie.
This recipe makes 25 large cookies.

2 cups / *500 ml*	flour
½ cup / *125 ml*	Rogers Granulated Sugar
½ cup / *125 ml*	Rogers Golden Yellow Sugar
1 tsp / *5 ml*	baking soda
1 tsp / *5 ml*	ground cinnamon
½ tsp / *2 ml*	salt
1 cup / *250 ml*	butter
1 cup / *250 ml*	chopped walnuts
2½ cups / *625 ml*	uncooked rolled oats
½ tsp / *2 ml*	lemon zest
1 cup / *250 ml*	white chocolate chips
½ cup / *125 ml*	dried apricots, chopped
3	eggs, well beaten
1 tsp / *5 ml*	vanilla extract
½ cup / *125 ml*	milk

Preheat your oven to 350°F (180°C). Grease two cookie sheets.

Sift the flour, Rogers sugars, baking soda, cinnamon and salt into a large mixing bowl. Cut in the butter with a pastry blender or two knives until the pieces are the size of peas.

Mix in the nuts, oats, zest, chocolate chips and chopped apricots. Beat the eggs well, then gradually add them along with the vanilla extract, stirring thoroughly. Now add the milk and gently mix until you are left with a sticky batter.

With an average-sized ice cream scoop, drop a ball of the dough onto one of the cookie sheets. Wet your hand with water and "splat" the dough ball out into a 5 in (12.5 cm) round. These are big cookies!

Repeat with the rest of the dough, then bake for 15 minutes. The cookies are ready when their edges are done but their centres are still soft. Slide the cookies onto a rack to cool.

Crispy or Chewy?

Recipes don't always explain whether cookies will have a crispy or chewy texture. Here's how to tell. If there is a liquid other than oil and eggs in the ingredients, cookies will be chewy. Crispy cookies will have more fat.

To make cookies chewier:

- ❒ Add a bit more liquid, about 1 tbsp (15 ml) per ½ cup (125 ml) of flour.
- ❒ Make the cookies bigger.
- ❒ Bake them for a shorter time until they are lightly coloured.

For extra crunch, roll cookies in Rogers Granulated Sugar or sprinkle a little on top before you bake them.

To make cookies crispier:

- ❒ Use shortening instead of butter.
- ❒ Make the cookies smaller.
- ❒ Bake them for a longer time until they are golden brown.

Experiment with different types of sugar - Rogers makes the whole range. Sugars such as Granulated and Berry make a clean, sweet-tasting cookie. Golden Yellow will give your dough a butterscotch flavour. Best Brown and Demerara make cookies with rich taste and colour.

Oasis Date Cookies

1½ cups / *375 ml*	Rogers Best Brown Sugar
1 cup / *250 ml*	sour cream
2	eggs
1 tsp / *5 ml*	baking soda
2 cups / *500 ml*	flour
1 tsp / *5 ml*	ground cinnamon
½ tsp / *2 ml*	ground cloves
¼ tsp / *1 ml*	ground nutmeg
½ lb / *225 g*	dates, chopped
¾ cup / *180 ml*	crystallized ginger, chopped

Oasis Date Cookies

The sour cream and Rogers Best Brown Sugar give these chewy cookies a refreshingly moist texture. Full of flavour, they are better than finding an oasis in the desert. This recipe makes about 24 cookies.

PREHEAT your oven to 350°F (180°C) and grease two cookie sheets.

WHIP THE ROGERS BEST BROWN SUGAR, sour cream and eggs together until the mixture is light and fluffy.

SIFT TOGETHER the baking soda, flour and spices. Add the dates and ginger, then lightly fold in the creamed mixture until it is all combined.

DROP LARGE SPOONFULS onto the cookie sheets and bake for 10 to 12 minutes.

Keep a piece of vanilla bean in your sugar jar. The gases given off by the bean will add wonderful flavour to Rogers Granulated or Berry Sugar.

To soften cookies, place them in a tightly closed container with a piece of fresh bread. Replace the bread every couple of days.

BAR COOKIES

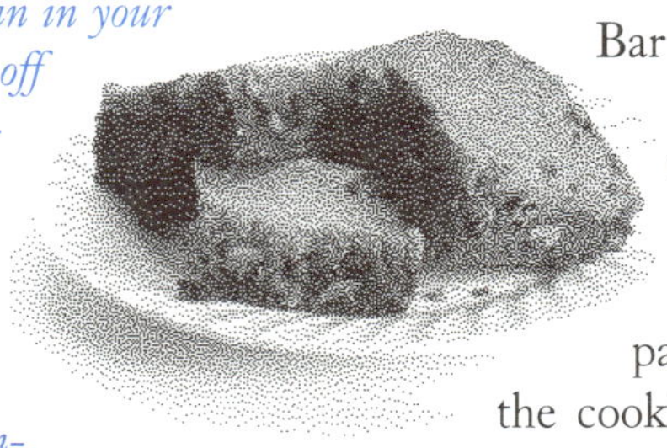

Bar cookies are the same as other cookies, except that they are not baked individually on a cookie sheet, but are pressed altogether in a pan. The most important thing to remember when you are making bar cookies is to use the pan size specified in the recipe. The texture of the cookie will be completely different if you use the wrong size. A pan that is too large will give a dry, brittle result and a pan that is too small will make the cookie taste like cake.

Chocolate Chip Cookies - Without the Chips

Chocolate chip cookies are one of the most-loved cookies in Canada, and everyone has their favourite recipe for them. Always make chocolate chip cookies with butter (never margarine), pure vanilla extract and real chocolate. Use anything less and your cookies will be a pale imitation of the real thing.

You really should use butter for shortbread, but if you find the taste too rich, you can use a combination of half butter and half margarine.

If you feel like experimenting, forget the chocolate chips and try out some of these ideas:

- Chunks of gourmet chocolate
- White chocolate and Macadamia nuts
- One chocolate kiss right in the centre
- Butterscotch chips
- Crushed peppermint candy

During the 14th and 15th centuries, it was not uncommon for European banquets to end with a gingerbread course. Often built to resemble small houses, the gingerbread would be gilded with real gold and studded with gold-dipped cloves.

Highland Butter Shortbread

The secret is in the butter and Rogers Berry Sugar, which combine to give our recipe the real buttery crispness best loved in Scotland. Even Bonny Prince Charlie would have been proud of this shortbread! This recipe makes 12 wedges.

½ cup / *125 ml*	butter, at room temperature
¼ cup / *60 ml*	Rogers Berry Sugar
¾ cup / *180 ml*	flour, sifted
	extra Berry Sugar to dust on top

PREHEAT YOUR OVEN to 325°F (160°C). Use a 9 in square (23 x 23 cm) pan but don't grease it.

IN A LARGE MIXING BOWL, beat the butter with a wooden spoon to soften it. Add the Rogers Berry Sugar, then the flour, a little at a time. The heat from your hands will make the mixture oily, so work the ingredients with a wooden spoon most of the time. Quickly finish off mixing with your hands until you have a dough that doesn't leave any bits in the bowl.

PACK THE MIXTURE into the pan, smoothing the top with a rubber spatula. Mark the top with a knife to show 12 wedges, then prick each wedge several times with a fork. You must do this so the shortbread doesn't rise in the centre when it's baking. Dust with Rogers Berry Sugar before putting the pan into the oven.

BE VERY CAREFUL not to overcook your shortbread. Bake for 20 to 30 minutes, or until it just starts to look pale golden. Leave the shortbread to cool for 10 minutes in the pan, then turn it onto a rack.

Are you inspired to learn more about cake baking? Classic cookbooks like *The Joy of Cooking* will keep you going for years, but for more ideas check out this trio:

Angels in the Kitchen
by Patricia Corrigan
Richmond Hill, Ontario: Distican Inc.,1994

This sweet little book of "divine desserts for any occasion" includes four different Angel Food Cake recipes: chocolate, chocolate filled, raspberry and peppermint.

Ultimate Cake
by Barbara Maher
Reader's Digest, 1996

This book contains over 100 recipes with many helpful photos.

The Wooden Spoon Dessert Cookbook
by Marilyn M. Moore
New York: Atlantic Monthly Press, 1994

A book you will turn to repeatedly for down-home style desserts and plenty of cookie recipes.

Additional Sources:

All the Best Cookies
by Joie Warner
Stoddart, 1994

Luscious Afternoon Teas
by Rosemary Wadey
Vancouver: Raincoast Books, 1996

The Silver Palate Cookbook
by Julee Rosso & Sheila Lukins
New York: Workman Publishing, 1982

There is also a great web site for cake recipes:
http://www.cs.cmu.edu/~mjw/recipes/cake/cake.html

Famous Cakes and Cookies of the World

The expression "sweet tooth" is known all over the world and probably applies to well over half the population. Here are some special cakes and cookies from various countries that have become well loved:

- **Linzer Torte**: A delicious German cake served when there is company. It looks like an open jam pie and is usually cut in thin wedges, as it is very rich.
- **Macaroons**: Small, chewy cookies, crunchy outside and soft inside. Although traditionally made in Italy with ground almonds, egg whites and sugar, these days macaroons are more likely to have coconut in them.
- **Langue-de-Chat**: Finger-shaped cookies from France, usually served with desserts such as ice cream and fruit salad.
- **Black Forest Cake**: A decadently rich chocolate cake, made with many layers and decorated with cherries soaked in alcohol.
- **Sacher Torte**: A famous Viennese Cake, which was created in the last century. Sacher Torte is a heavy chocolate cake, filled with apricot jam and covered with chocolate frosting.

"Cooking and making love are the same. They both stem from the desire to give pleasure."

Madame Lea, famous cook of Lyons, France

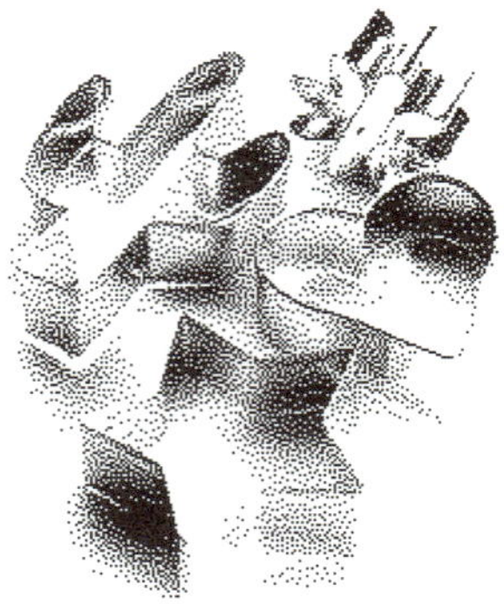

DESSERTS

"But I, when I undress me
Each night, upon my knees
Will ask the lord to bless me
With apple pie and cheese."

Eugene Field, "Apple Pie & Cheese"

Many people would say that dessert is the best part of a meal. We all have a particular sweet favourite, so make sure you leave enough room to enjoy a slice of blueberry pie, a scoop of apple crisp or an elegant mousse. There are hundreds of wonderful desserts, but for the sake of space we have concentrated on the traditional favourites. Take a look at some of the cookbooks we recommend on page 140 for more great dessert ideas.

- ❐ When you are choosing a dessert, consider the rest of the meal. After a heavy meal, fresh fruit or a cool sorbet is perfect.
- ❐ Whether it is a pie or a sundae, take the time to make your dessert an edible work of art.
- ❐ Sugars and spices add extra taste to nearly any kind of dessert, so experiment with different flavours.
- ❐ Don't forget the ice cream!

Let's Hear It for Fruit

Whether it's bubbling in the baking dish as it comes to the table or steaming with the delicious smells of fruit juice, Rogers Best Brown Sugar and cinnamon, a good fruit dessert deserves applause. Food trends come and go, but hot fruit desserts are classics that never fail to please. Serve them with lightly whipped and sweetened cream, or your favourite ice cream.

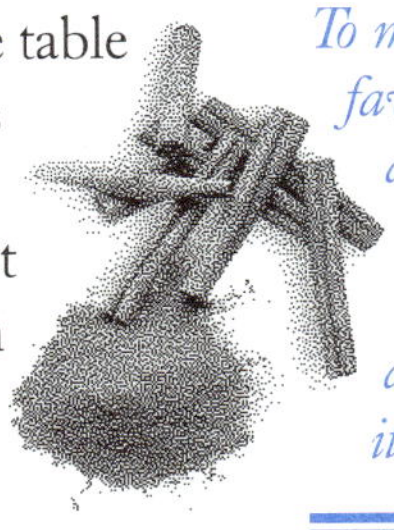

To make whipped cream for your favourite pie or fruit dessert, add a spoonful or two of Rogers Berry Sugar. Alternatively, serve your cream with Rogers Icing Sugar and a drop of vanilla extract - it tastes amazing.

Apple-Berry Cobbler

½ cup / *125 ml*	butter
1 cup / *250 ml*	water
1 cup / *250 ml*	Rogers Granulated Sugar
2 tbsp / *30 ml*	Rogers Golden Yellow Sugar
1½ cups / *625 ml*	self-raising flour
1/3 cup / *80 ml*	milk
½ tsp / *2 ml*	ground cinnamon
1 lb / *450 g*	fresh blackberries
3	apples, peeled and chopped small

Whether you call it a cobbler, crumble, crisp or betty, if you do it our way it will look as good as it tastes. Loaded with berries, apples and spices, this traditional favourite has a real twist to it! This recipe serves 6.

PREHEAT your oven to 350°F (180°C).

MELT HALF OF THE BUTTER in a 10 in (25 x 25 cm) glass baking dish in the oven.

IN A SMALL SAUCEPAN, make a sugar syrup by combining the water and Rogers Granulated Sugar. Heat it over medium heat, stirring occasionally, until the sugar is completely dissolved.

IN A FOOD PROCESSOR, pulse together the flour and remaining butter until the mixture looks like small crumbs. Add the milk and continue pulsing until a dough forms. Don't overdo it! If you don't have a food processor you can make the dough by hand in the same way you make pastry (see pages 132-133).

TURN THE DOUGH OUT onto a lightly floured surface and, with a floured rolling pin, roll it into a rectangle, roughly 9 x 11 in (23 x 28 cm). Sprinkle the dough with cinnamon and scatter the blackberries and chopped apple evenly over the top.

BEGINNING WITH ONE of the long sides, roll up the dough like a jellyroll. Cut it into 1½ in (4 cm) thick slices. Don't worry if the slices fall apart a bit and get messy.

ARRANGE THE SLICES, cut sides up, on the melted butter in the baking dish. Pour the warm sugar syrup over the slices so they are well soaked and bake the apple-berry cobbler in the middle of the oven for 45 minutes.

SPRINKLE THE ROGERS GOLDEN YELLOW SUGAR over the cobbler and put it back in the oven for another 15 minutes, or until it turns a lovely golden colour.

SERVE THE APPLE-BERRY COBBLER warm, with plenty of ice cream or whipped cream.

Fruit bettys, crisps, crunches and crumbles are all basically the same thing. It's the toppings that differ: some use different sugars, while others add oatmeal or toast the crumbs. The secret to success, however, is the fruit - it should be perfectly ripe with no bruises or blemishes.

❐ If the fruit is tart, or not quite ripe, toss it gently with Rogers Granulated Sugar.

❐ Add a little water, cinnamon, lemon zest and unsalted butter for extra flavour.

❐ Bake fruit crisps in a lightly buttered dish, 9 x 9 in (23 x 23 cm).

❐ Let the fruit sit for at least 30 minutes before you add the topping.

"The friendly cow all
red and white,
I love with all my heart:
She gives me cream with
all her might,
To eat with apple tart."

Robert Louis Stevenson, 1850-1894

Variations on the Theme

You can make a fruit crisp out of nearly any kind of berry or fruit. It's worth tracking down the less common berries such as saskatoons, loganberries and gooseberries, which all have sprightly flavours and make excellent desserts.

For other great flavour combinations, check these out:

- Peach, red currant and ginger
- Apple and cranberry
- Blackberry and rhubarb or apple
- Strawberry, blueberry and raspberry
- Pear, ginger and lemon zest
- Apple and raisin

The loganberry, grown commercially in British Columbia, is a hybrid of the blackberry and raspberry. It is a very large, deep red berry with small seeds and a tart flavour that is excellent in pies and other berry desserts.

Our Favourite Fruit Salads

Need a quick and tasty dessert idea? Cut up your favourite fruit and sprinkle it with 1 tsp (5ml) of Rogers Berry Sugar or Rogers Best Brown Sugar to help release the natural juices. Lightly dust the bowl of fruit with cinnamon or grated nutmeg and let it stand for 30 minutes. And there you have it - a delicious fruit salad!

We particularly love these partnerships of fruit and flavour:

- Melon balls (cantaloupe, watermelon, honeydew) in their own juices, with chopped crystallized ginger

Blueberries are native to many regions of Canada, including Lac St. Jean, north of Quebec City, which is reputed to have the finest. In early August, just as the blueberry fields are turning blue, the community has a week-long blueberry party. One of the special treats of the festival is a pie that serves more than 500 people!

- Sliced pears drizzled with maple syrup
- Pineapple chunks, kiwi slices and strawberries splashed with Rogers Golden Syrup and candied lemon zest
- Berries of the season dressed with orange juice and fresh mint
- Sliced peaches spritzed with lemon juice and a sprinkling of Rogers Icing Sugar
- Whole blueberries, dark cherries and halved black grapes

Making Pastry

Anyone can make beautiful pies and pastry. It's easy: just remember that a generous hand with the filling - and the lightest of hands with the pastry - is the key to a successful pie.

- Keep everything as cold as possible the whole way through the recipe.
- Sift the flour, as air is a vital ingredient.
- Use a combination of half butter and half shortening.
- Only use enough ice water to hold the dough together.
- Cut in the fat gently and keep lifting your hands high above the bowl to let in the air.

Add some flavour to your pastry to make it more interesting:

- Cinnamon or nutmeg or both!
- Lemon zest
- Cocoa
- Grated Cheddar cheese (especially for apple pies)
- Finely chopped nuts

Troubleshooting

Is your pastry:

HARD AND TOUGH?

- To prevent the same thing from happening next time, use less water.

TEARING WHEN YOU LIFT IT?

- Either you have used too much fat, the shortening is soft or there is not enough water in the pastry.

DO YOUR PIES BOIL OVER IN THE OVEN?

- Push a few pieces of raw macaroni through the top crust and remove them when the pie has finished baking. The macaroni allows the steam to escape, and stops the juice rising.

Not so long ago, certain cultures regarded a woman's pastry-making skills as her "passport to matrimony." In Hungarian villages, a young woman couldn't think of getting married until her streusel dough was so translucent that her beau could read the newspaper through it!

Perfect Every Time Pastry

This is the best kind of pastry: crisp as you bite it, tender and flaky. Carefully measure the ingredients. All you have to decide now is how to fill it. This recipe makes one 9 in (23 cm) pie crust.

2 cups / *500 ml*	flour
½ tsp / *2 ml*	salt
½ cup / *125 ml*	butter
½ cup / *125 ml*	shortening
¼ cup / *60 ml*	ice water

PREHEAT your oven to 375°F (190°C).

SIFT FLOUR AND SALT into a bowl. Cut in the butter and shortening using two knives, a pastry blender or a fork (leave bits of fat the size of a pea). It's not a good idea to use your fingers, as they'll soften the fat.

SPRINKLE VERY COLD WATER over the mixture, a little bit at a time. Use just enough for the pastry to stay together.

GATHER UP THE PASTRY with your hands and gently pat it together so it forms a smooth ball of dough. The more you handle the dough, the tougher it becomes, so work quickly.

LET YOUR PASTRY REST (wrapped and in the refrigerator) for at least 30 minutes. This makes it easier to roll out and stops it from shrinking in the pie dish.

ON A LIGHTLY FLOURED PIECE of waxed paper on a flat surface, flatten the dough into a disk. Roll it out gently to 1/6-1/8 inch (5 mm) thick.

GENTLY INVERT THE FINISHED PASTRY into the pie dish and remove the waxed paper. Ease any overlapping bits back into the pie plate so you have less to trim off. Try not to stretch the dough at this point, or it'll shrink when you bake it.

POKE HOLES IN THE SIDES and the bottom of the pastry to prevent it from bubbling.

BAKE for 20 to 25 minutes.

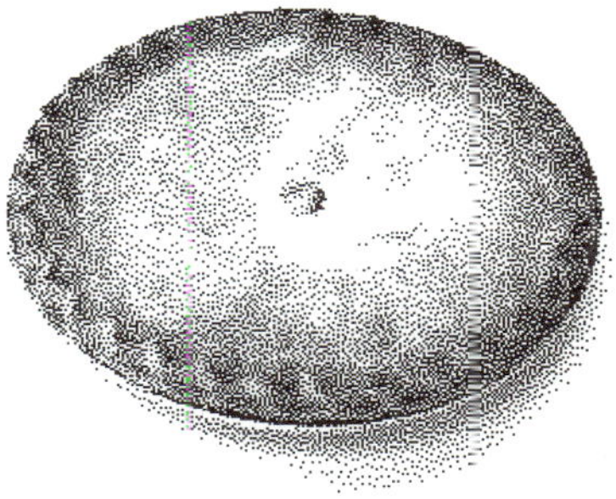

PREPARING YOUR PASTRY

- ❒ Dust your rolling pin with flour - never dust the pastry.
- ❒ Always roll pastry from the centre out.
- ❒ Don't turn the pastry over while you are rolling.
- ❒ Roll it about 2 in (5 cm) larger than the pie plate's dimensions.

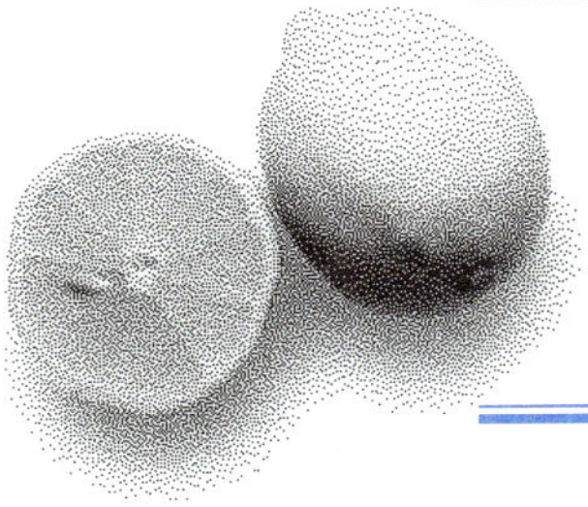

To add more flavour to your lemon pies and tarts, rub a sugar cube over the skin of the lemon before you grate it. This works for oranges too.

Orange Pumpkin Pie

1	uncooked pie shell
2	eggs
14 oz / *398 ml*	cooked or canned plain pumpkin
¾ cup / *180 ml*	Rogers Golden Syrup
½ tsp / *2 ml*	salt
½ tsp / *2 ml*	ground cinnamon
½ tsp / *2 ml*	ground ginger
½ tsp / *2 ml*	ground cloves
½ tsp / *2 ml*	ground allspice
¼ tsp / *1 ml*	ground cardamon
½ cup / *125 ml*	canned evaporated milk
¼ cup / *60 ml*	freshly squeezed orange juice
1 tsp / *5 ml*	finely grated orange zest

We are stepping on hallowed ground by improving the classic pumpkin pie, but are sure you will approve. It's the tang of orange that brings out the sweet, spicy flavour of the pumpkin perfectly. This recipe makes 8 servings.

PREHEAT YOUR OVEN to 450°F (230°C).

BEAT THE EGGS SLIGHTLY, then add the rest of the ingredients and beat everything together well.

POUR THE FILLING into the pastry shell. Bake the pie for 8 minutes, then turn the heat down to 325°F (160°C) and bake it for another 40 to 45 minutes. The pie is ready when a knife inserted near its centre comes out clean.

LET THE PIE cool completely before you cut it. Serve warm with a swirl of whipped cream.

Butter tarts are unique to Canada, but no one is exactly sure where they originated. They may have been adapted from Louisiana's pecan pie, or possibly are a variation on Quebec's famous sugar pie.

SECRETS FOR MARVELLOUS MERINGUE

- ❒ Make sure your bowl and beaters are grease free.
- ❒ If any yolk falls into the egg white, don't use it.
- ❒ Warm the egg whites to room temperature.
- ❒ Beat the egg whites until the peaks hold their shape. If they start to droop, keep beating.

"What moistens the lips and what brightens the eye? What calls back the past, like the rich pumpkin pie?"

James Whittier, 1807-1892

FRUIT PIES

Once you have mastered the basic recipe for pastry, the magic comes from deciding what to put in your pies. Do some experimenting with various tastemakers and fruit. Don't just bake an apple pie, create a work of art instead, oozing with cinnamon and cloves and covered with a golden brown crust. Or how about freshly picked berries in an open-topped pie, with lattice work over the top?

Spiced Cranapple Pie With Lemon Crust

A fruit pie with a difference. The delicious filling is surrounded by tart lemon pastry, providing a wonderful contrast of flavours. This recipe makes 14 to16 slices.

Crust:

1 cup / *250 ml*	flour
1½ tsp	baking powder
	pinch of salt
2 tbsp / *30 ml*	custard powder
½ tsp / *2 ml*	ground cinnamon
½ tsp / *2 ml*	ground allspice
1/3 cup / *80 ml*	butter
	zest from 1 lemon
¼ cup / *60 ml*	Rogers Berry Sugar
1	egg yolk
	chilled milk

Filling:

1¼ lb / *550 g*	apples, peeled and sliced
½ cup / *130 ml*	cranberries
2 tbsp / *30 ml*	water
2 tbsp / *30 ml*	liquid honey
¼ cup / *60 ml*	Rogers Golden Yellow Sugar

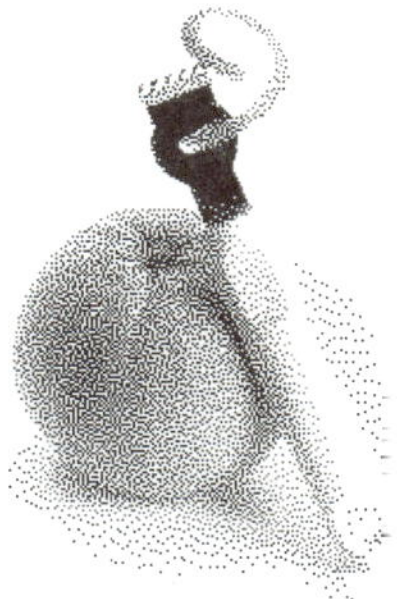

Sift the flour with the salt, baking powder, custard powder and spice into a bowl. Cut in the butter using two knives, a fork or a pastry blender (leave bits of fat the size of a pea). Don't use your fingers, as they'll soften the fat. Now mix the lemon zest and Berry Sugar evenly through the pastry.

Mix in the egg yolk and just enough cold milk to make a pliable dough and knead lightly until smooth. Then wrap the dough with wax paper and chill for an hour or two, while you make the filling.

Place the apple slices into a saucepan with the cranberries and water and cook very gently until just tender. Remove from the heat, stir in the honey and Rogers Golden Yellow Sugar until melted and then leave until cold.

Preheat your oven to 425°F (220°C). Grease an 11 x 7 in (28 x 18 cm) rectangular pan.

Roll out two-thirds of the pastry dough and use it to line the pan. Fill with the apple and cranberry mixture. Roll out the remaining pastry and cut into strips about 1/3 in (1 cm) wide. Make a lattice over the apple filling, attaching the ends to the pastry with a dab of water.

Cook at 425°F (220°C) for 10 minutes, then reduce the temperature to 375°F (190°C) and continue baking for about 20 minutes or until the pastry is golden brown and cooked through.

When the pie is cool, cut it into slices and serve with a dollop of whipped cream.

Sugar and Spice

Any of these tastemakers, when added with butter and Rogers Berry Sugar, will help make a wonderful fruit pie. Here are some of our favourite combinations:

- **Plum**: nutmeg, vanilla
- **Apple**: cinnamon, lemon - no sugar
- **Apricot**: just butter and sugar

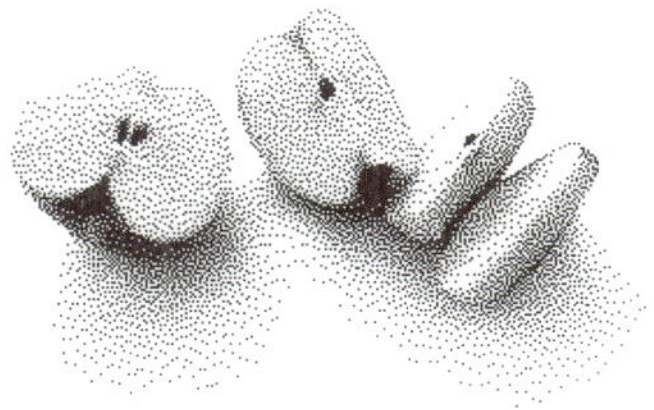

"There is no love sincerer than the love of food."

George Bernard Shaw, 1856-1950

The best pie plates are lightweight aluminum and deep, like the ones cooks used to use. However, use a ceramic or glass pie plate for acidic fruit pies such as apple and cherry or the pies will turn grey.

"I want another slice of rhubarb tart
I want another lovely slice
I'm not disparaging the blueberry pie
But rhubarb tart is, oh, so very nice
A rhubarb what? A rhubarb tart!
A what-barb tart? A rhubarb tart!
I want another slice of rhubarb tart!."

Monty Python's
Flying Circus

Make sure you take out apple seeds, plum pits and apricot pits before you put the fruit in a pie. They're toxic.

Pie is an important part of our Canadian heritage. Early settlers made pies from squash, pumpkin, homemade mincemeat and all sorts of wild berries, which grew everywhere in great numbers.

- **Pear**: mace
- **Nectarine**: grated lemon zest
- **Peach**: lime juice

An Apple a Day...

The type of apples used in your pie can make all the difference to the outcome. Nine times out of ten, if your pie is too sweet or too tart or too watery, it is because of the apples you used.

We have some favourites that always turn out well in pies:

- **Red Rome**: This variety is famous as the finest baking apple available. Sweet yet sufficiently tart to be tasty when it's cooked. Red Rome cooks firm, with less shrinkage than most apples. It's available from late October to February.
- **Macintosh**: Macintosh is excellent for baking. It has a distinctive aroma and a deliciously tangy flavour. The pulp is firm and crisp. It cooks soft and smooth and is available in September.
- **Newton**: The pulp is hard and crisp and excellent for fresh eating and cooking. Newton has a rich, tangy and tart flavour.

Variations on Fillings

Experiment with nature's flavours in your pie fillings - it's hard to go wrong! Just make sure you always use the freshest fruit you can find:

- Apples, raisins, nutmeg, cinnamon and cloves
- Fresh cherries and lemon
- Rhubarb and ginger
- Strawberry and rhubarb
- Blackberry and rhubarb
- Pear and ginger
- Apples and raisins, with a splash of brandy
- Peaches, almonds and cranberry glaze

Cheesecakes

Is it a cake? Or is it a pie? Whatever cheesecakes are, they are delicious! There are endless variations on the cheesecake theme, so try some different versions and see what you come up with.

"The dainties last,

to make the end most sweet."

William Shakespeare, 1564-1616

Create Your Own Cheesecake

This cheesecake alone makes our book worth reading. The lightly textured and tart filling is offset perfectly by the unusual shortbread crust. We have left the topping to your imagination, so create your own, or use one of our ideas on page 138.
This recipe makes 16 servings.

PREHEAT YOUR OVEN to 350°F (180°C).

GENTLY MELT THE BUTTER in a small saucepan, but don't let it brown. Stir the crushed shortbread and hazelnuts into the butter.

TRANSFER THE BISCUIT MIXTURE into a 12 in (30 cm) spring-form pan and press it down evenly to form a base. Place in the refrigerator to chill.

BEAT THE EGGS until light and thick. Sift the sugar and add it very gradually, beating all the time (we use an electric mixer for this, as the mixture needs a lot of beating).

KEEP THE MIXER GOING and add a pinch of salt, the lemon zest, the lemon juice and the vanilla.

IN A SEPARATE BOWL, blend together the sifted flour and the cottage cheese. If you can't buy smooth cottage cheese, put it through a seive or use a blender to get rid of the lumps. Add the blended flour and cottage cheese to the egg mixture.

WHIP THE CREAM and fold it into the filling mixture very gently. Pour the filling over the biscuit base, smoothing it out evenly.

BAKE FOR ABOUT 1 HOUR, then turn off the heat and leave the cheesecake in the oven with the door open. When the cake has completely cooled, chill it in the refrigerator before decorating and serving.

Base:

½ cup / *125 ml*	butter
½ cup / *125 ml*	crushed shortbread biscuits
½ cup / *125 ml*	crushed hazelnuts

Filling:

6	eggs
1½ cups / *375 ml*	Rogers Berry Sugar
	pinch salt
2 tsp / *10 ml*	lemon zest
1 tsp / *15 ml*	lemon juice
1 tsp / *5 ml*	vanilla extract
½ cup / *125 ml*	flour, sifted
2¼ lb / *1 kg*	smooth cottage cheese
2 cups / *500 ml*	whipped cream

Create Your Own Cheesecake

❒ Watch the temperature. Cheesecakes are egg-based, which means they are not happy at a high heat.

❒ Turn the oven off and leave your cheesecake in for a while after it has finished baking. It will shrink slightly as it cools.

❒ Chill your cheesecake well and add the fruit just before serving, so it doesn't soak into the filling.

❒ To store cheesecakes, keep them in the refrigerator.

Cheesecake Toppings

Clusters of frosted grapes are an attractive decoration for cheesecake. To make them, whisk up an egg white. Break the grapes into little clusters of two or three grapes each and dip the bunches into the egg. Roll them around in a saucer of Rogers Berry Sugar until they are well covered, then spread them out on waxed paper for a couple of hours.

Here are some more great ideas:

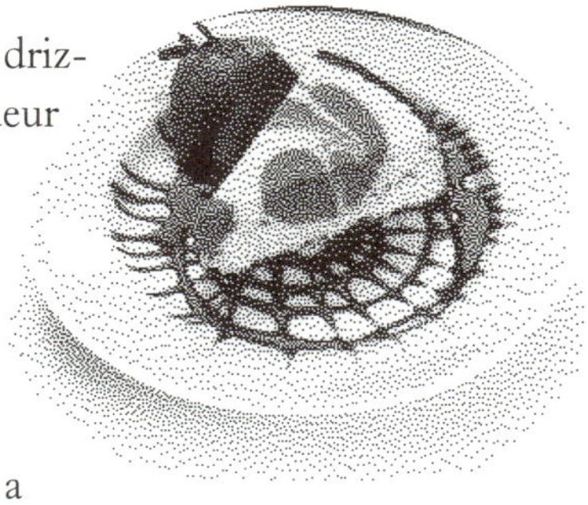

- A sprinkle of roasted almonds and a drizzle of chocolate sauce and coffee liqueur make a great topping.
- Bananas with Rogers Berry Sugar, lemon juice and a drizzle of rum are especially tasty.
- Preserved peaches and brandy make a syrupy, sweet topping.
- Fresh fruit such as strawberries and raspberries always make an attractive topping.

To keep a baked pie shell from becoming soggy, sprinkle it with equal parts of Rogers Granulated Sugar and flour before adding the filling. Alternatively, spread a thin layer of butter on the bottom of the pie plate before putting in the pastry.

If you are making a deep-dish fruit pie, the pastry filling goes over the top of the pie filling rather than underneath it.

Custards and Mousses

It's not always the sweetness of dessert that makes it so irresistible. Often it's the luscious smoothness and luxurious feeling in your mouth of a silky-smooth custard or mousse.

Mousses rely on eggs as a thickener and they are simple to make. There is nothing more elegant than a dessert glass of creamy, chilled mousse. When making chocolate mousse, remember to use chocolate that has a high percentage of cocoa solids (see "Cooking With Chocolate" in the Cakes & Cookies section on page 120 for more information).

Use our brandy snaps recipe on page16 to make crunchy toffee baskets. This is a truly elegant dessert when filled with fruit salad and dusted with Rogers Icing Sugar.

Custards also contain beaten eggs. Custard ingredients are similar to those in mousses, but because custards are baked, their texture is a little less creamy and a little more solid. There are two custards that make spectacular desserts: Crème Brulée and Crème Caramel. Both are basically the same, except that in Crème Brulée the sugar is on top of the custard, while in Crème Caramel it is underneath.

Crème Caramel

What a great classic dessert this is. Delicious and very light, no one is ever too full for Crème Caramel.
This recipe makes 8 servings.

3 tbsp / *45 ml*	Rogers Golden Syrup
4	whole eggs
2	egg yolks
½ cup / *125 ml*	Rogers Granulated Sugar
1 tsp / *5 ml*	vanilla extract
1½ cup / *375 ml*	evaporated milk
	water

PREHEAT YOUR OVEN to 325°F (160°C).

BUTTER a 1 quart (1 L) glass mould and spoon the Rogers Golden Syrup into it.

BEAT THE EGGS, egg yolks and sugar lightly with a fork. Add the vanilla and evaporated milk. Use the milk can as a measure and pour in one can of water. Beat everything together lightly and pour into the mould.

STAND THE MOULD in a baking pan containing 2 in (5 cm) of water. Bake for about 1½ hours or until the custard is set.

TO CHECK DONENESS, insert a knife into the centre of the custard. It should come out clean. Leave the custard overnight in the refrigerator so it is thoroughly chilled. Remove the mould to serve.

Little Things to Wake up a Bowl of Strawberries

- A very light grinding of black pepper with a dash of vodka
- A squeeze of lemon
- Shredded fresh mint
- The juice and seeds from a passion fruit
- A spoonful of orange-flower or rose water

Famous Desserts of the World

Most people have a soft spot for desserts, and Rogers believes there is nothing wrong with indulging your palate every now and then! Desserts are eaten in every corner of the world and are equally delicious - whether you happen to live in Vancouver or Venice.

Nero, emperor of Rome in A.D. 54–68, had a real fondness for sherbets made from fruit, honey and snow. Unfortunately, in the middle of summer there is not a lot of snow around in Italy. According to legend, Nero would command a slave to run to the mountains, gather up snow, and rush it back to the palace!

Once you get hooked on desserts and pie making you will want to find out how everyone else does it. Here are some books to get you started:

Pies and Tarts
by Martha Stewart
New York:
C.N. Potter, 1985

Martha Stewart does a thorough job on pies and tarts. Her recipes include both sweet and savoury, and she always has lots of good advice.

Chocolate Desserts
by Anne Willan
New York:
Dorling Kindersly, 1992

This book, in the popular *Look and Cook* series, makes cooking simple. With plenty of instructional photos and explanations, and some great recipes, this book is simple and straightforward.

We have found an incredible web site on the Internet that is guaranteed to get your stomach rumbling:

http://www.godiva.com/recipes/chocolatier/surprises/index.htm

This egg marketing board has free dessert recipes to send out:

B.C. Egg Marketing Board
P.O. Box 310
Abbotsford, British Columbia
V2S 4P2
(604) 853-3348

Here are some of our favourite desserts that you will find in any good recipe book:

- **Pavlova**: These huge meringue cakes, topped with cream and fresh fruit, are so popular in New Zealand that they have been given the honourary title of "national dessert."
- **Tiramisu**: Lovers of strong coffee, dark chocolate and rich Mascarpone cream cheese will be swept off their feet by this Italian delight.
- **Trifle**: Very popular with the British, trifle is best made with proper custard and fresh sponge cake. The cake is broken into pieces and layered with the custard and plenty of fruit and jam, then it's given a good soaking in sherry.
- **Baklava**: This one is deliciously rich! A syrupy, sweet Greek concoction of filo pastry, almonds, pistachios and walnuts.

"The dessert crowns the dinner. To create a fine dessert, one has to combine the skills of a confectioner, a decorator, a painter, an architect, an icecream manufacturer, a sculptor, and a florist."

Eugène Briffault

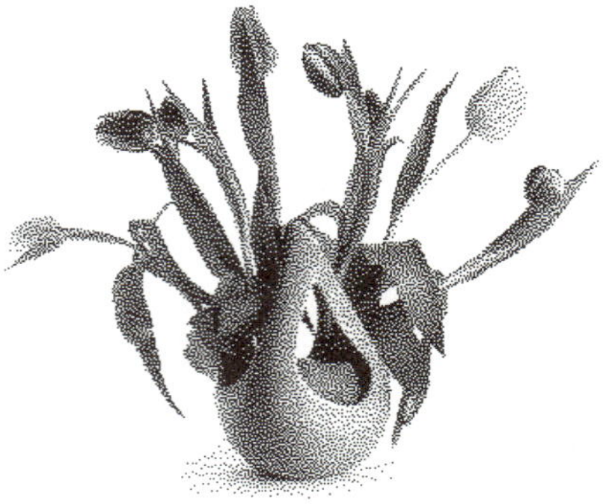

JAMS, JELLIES & CHUTNEYS

"The rule is, jam tomorrow and jam yesterday - but never jam today."

Alice in Wonderland
Lewis Carroll, 1832-1898

These days, we mostly rely on the store for our jam, marmalade and chutney. It's a shame because making your own is so simple and economical - and it always tastes better. There is really nothing to it. Gather up some fruit, vegetables and Rogers Granulated Sugar. Assemble some jars and a pan, and set aside an hour or two.

It is simple to make your own condiments, but keep these points in mind:

- ❐ Have all your jars, spoons, saucers, etc. ready before you begin (see our checklist on page 143).
- ❐ Don't go out and buy special jars; save them from store-bought condiments and ask friends to save theirs as well.
- ❐ Work with small quantities. Don't use more than 6 cups (1.5 L) of fruit or juice at a time.
- ❐ Include some underripe fruit to help your jam or jelly set.
- ❐ Make sure you use the right amount of Rogers Granulated Sugar (check out page 142-143 for the ratio of sugar to fruit, or follow a recipe).

It's that simple!

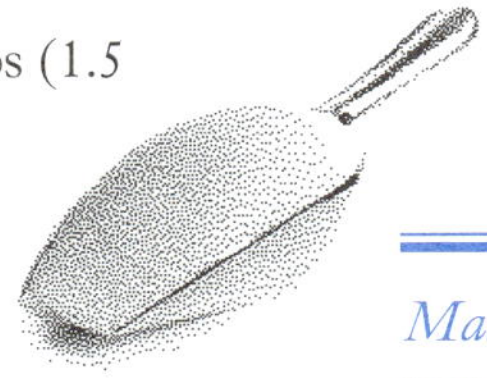

Make sure the fruit is dry before you begin, or the pectin and acid will be diluted. Dusty fruit can be wiped clean, although the boiling process will effectively purify it.

Before you put the lids on your jars, cover the jam with a circle of waxed paper dipped in brandy, or use liquid paraffin. This stops mould from forming on top.

The idea of using sugar to preserve fruit is an old one. One of the first references to it is in records of the marriage feast of King Henry IV and Joan of Navarre (1403), which included "perys in syrippe."

The Magic of Sugar

Granulated sugar is a fundamental part of making jams and chutneys. It not only adds sweetness, it also preserves the fruit and makes the mixture gel. Thanks to sugar, you can control the sweetness of your jelly and the sharpness of your marmalade. When you make your own condiments, you can create new flavour combinations that can't be found in the store, and the taste is divine.

- The sugar controls the setting process, so make sure you have the right amount.
- Warm the sugar before you add it to the pan - this makes it dissolve faster, which improves the flavour. Spread the sugar out in a large dish and leave it in the oven at 250°F (125°C) for 10 minutes.
- Make sure the sugar is completely dissolved before you boil the mixture, otherwise it will crystallize and the finished jam will be sugary.
- When you make chutney, use Rogers Best Brown Sugar for a darker colour and richer flavour.

Making it Gel

The natural setting agent found in fruit is called pectin. This, along with the natural acids, is released when fruit is boiled with granulated sugar. If the fruit's in good condition and some of it is slightly underripe, it will have enough pectin to set properly. It's simple to set your own jams and jellies, so don't be tempted to use commercial pectin. You'll never get the true homemade flavour if you do.

Some kinds of fruit are naturally high in pectin, and some are low. When using fruit that doesn't contain a lot, combine it with fruit that does:

Low pectin fruit

Use 1½ cups (375 ml) Rogers Granulated Sugar to 2 cups (500 ml) fruit.

- strawberries
- peaches
- figs
- blackberries
- blueberries
- cherries
- pears
- grapes

Medium pectin fruit

Use 2 cups (500 ml) granulated sugar to 2 cups (500 ml) fruit.

- raspberries
- apricots
- loganberries

If you use any fruit with bruises or blemishes, it will spoil the flavour of the mixture.

Don't put the labels on until the jam has cooled. The heat will prevent them from sticking properly and they will peel off.

High pectin fruit

Use 2½ cups (625 ml) granulated sugar to 2 cups (500 ml) fruit.

- apples
- gooseberries
- cranberries
- red currants
- plums

How can you tell if your fruit has enough pectin? Gently shake 1 tbsp (15 ml) of the cooled juice with 1 tbsp (15 ml) of rubbing alcohol in a glass. If the fruit juice turns into a transparent "glob," it has enough pectin to set your jam or jelly.

Checklist: Got Everything?

Get your equipment ready before you begin. There is nothing worse than realizing you don't have enough jars halfway through a recipe...

- ✓ Jars (we find the ½ pint (250 ml) size most convenient): the ones with a two-piece metal screw-top lid work well. Wash them in soap and hot water, then rinse them out well. Put the jars in the oven at 250°F (125°C) for 15 minutes to sterilize them.
- ✓ Something to seal the jars with. Waxed paper soaked in brandy or melted paraffin wax both work well.
- ✓ A large heavy pan, big enough so that the contents won't boil over.
- ✓ A teaspoon and four saucers for testing if the mixture is ready. Pop them in the freezer to chill.
- ✓ Labels (the self-sticking kinds are the easiest to use).

Saskatoon berries are small, sweet, purplish berries that grow wild in the Prairie Provinces. Like blueberries, they taste wonderful in pies, preserves and jams.

Is it a jam, jelly or preserve? All three are made with the same basic ingredients of fresh fruit and granulated sugar. The difference is all in the consistency:

- Jam is a purée of fruit.
- Jelly is clear (it is made from the juice, not the fruit pulp).
- Preserves are chunks of fruit cooked in a syrup.

"All over the land there's a
savoury smell,
You meet abroad or at home;
The days of your childhood
come back for a spell,
No matter how far
you may roam.
Tis the scent of preserving..."

Anonymous

Picking Your Own

To make the best jams and jellies, fruit needs to be at its peak. That means ripe and full of natural pectin, but never overripe. Pears, peaches, apricots, strawberries, blackberries and raspberries should all be slightly underripe. Plums and cherries should be just ripe, but still full of flavour. If you are harvesting your own, wait until the early morning dew has dried so the fruit won't go mouldy in your buckets.

Making Jam

Long after summer has gone, berry jam spread on freshly baked bread brings back wonderful memories. Homemade jam not only tastes wonderful, it is also very economical. Pick the fruit yourself, or buy it in season at a local market or roadside stand.

- Really sharp-tasting fruit is great to use for jam because of the tangy concentration of flavour.
- Let soft-skinned fruits (like strawberries and raspberries) sit overnight in the sugar. This will harden them so they don't disintegrate when made into jam.
- When you are boiling the mixture, dissolve the sugar as quickly as possible so you don't lose any of the fruit's flavour.

Seven Simple Steps

When blackberries (or any other fruit) are in season, seize the opportunity to make jars of your very own spreadable sunshine.

For fail-proof jam, follow these seven simple steps:

- Measure your fruit out. For each cup, warm the corresponding amount of granulated sugar (see "Making it Gel" in this section). If the fruit has tough skin, simmer it first.
- If you have more than 6 cups (1.5 L) of fruit, divide the mixture into two batches.
- Add the sugar, but make sure it has completely dissolved before bringing the mixture to a rolling boil.

- When the mixture has boiled, lower the heat and simmer it gently. Keep stirring it with a wooden spoon so it doesn't stick and burn. Start timing.
- After about 15 minutes, dab some jam on a chilled saucer. If the jam gets a wrinkly skin, it is set. If there is no skin, boil the jam for another 3 or 4 minutes and then try again.

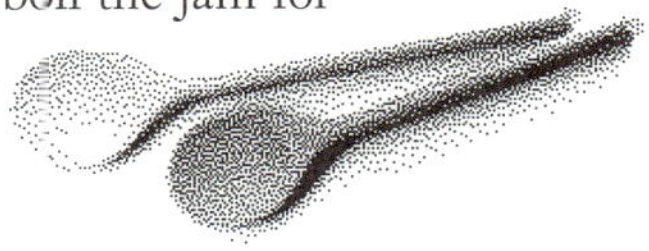

- Stir 1 tsp (5 ml) of butter into the jam to get rid of any sediment floating on the surface.
- After the jam has set, leave it to rest for 15 minutes before putting it into the jars. That way, the fruit won't rise to the surface. Put the labels on when the jars are cold.

The art of jam making began in the Middle East; it was the Crusaders who introduced it to Europe.

Tasty Jam Ideas

- **Apple** and almond; pear; blackberry; chopped ginger
- **Apricot** and passion fruit
- **Cherry** and ground cloves and cinnamon

Spiced Peach and Apple Jam

The unique combination of sweet, spicy and tart makes this a wonderful alternative to the traditional berry jams.
This recipe makes 10 cups of jam.

1	cooking apple
	rind of 2 lemons
4 lb / *2 kg*	peaches
½ cup / *125 ml*	water
1 tsp / *5 ml*	ground allspice
6 cups / *1.5 L*	Rogers Granulated Sugar
1 tsp / *5 ml*	butter

PEEL AND CHOP the apple, but keep the core and seeds. Tie up the apple, core, seeds and lemon rind in a square of cheesecloth and put them into a preserving pan.

REMOVE THE STONES (pits) and slice the peaches. Add the sliced peaches and water to the preserving pan.

BRING SLOWLY to the boil and simmer for 15 minutes, or until the peaches are soft. Remove the cheesecloth bag, squeezing the juice into the pan. Now add the allspice and sugar, stirring to dissolve the sugar.

WHEN THE SUGAR has completely dissolved, bring the jam to a boil. Keep it boiling, stirring all the time, until the setting point is reached (if you are unsure, see our seven simple steps, above).

STIR IN THE BUTTER. Let the jam stand for 15 minutes before pouring into the jars. Seal and label.

Spiced Peach and Apple Jam

Troubleshooting

If your jam doesn't set:

- ❒ If your jam is cooled and potted and still has not set, tip it all back into the pan and boil it again, adding the juice of a small lemon. You either under boiled it the first time, used too much sugar or did not have enough pectin-rich fruit.

If your jam is mouldy:

- ❒ Remove the top 1 in (2.5 cm) of the jam. The rest of it won't be affected, but you should use it straight away.

If your jam is crystallized:

- ❒ Reheat it and add the juice of a small lemon. This tends to happen if the sugar didn't completely dissolve the first time.

If your jam is fermented:

- ❒ This happens if the fruit wasn't good quality, if you didn't add enough granulated sugar or if the jam didn't boil long enough when you made it. There is nothing you can do, except quickly make another batch!

Not Just for Spreading!

Don't stop at toast and jam; you can always find lots of other excuses for dipping into the jar.

- Warm some apricot jam and you have an instant topping that turns sponge cake or gingerbread into dessert.
- Mix plum jam with lemon juice for a tasty Chinese dipping sauce.
- Cookie jar empty? Blend strawberry jam with cream cheese and use it to sandwich graham crackers together.
- Glaze ham or pork chops with your favourite jam to add flavour and make them picture-perfect.

Making Jelly

After you have done battle with the bramble patch, turn your berries into glowing, translucent jelly. Making jelly is just as easy as making jam; the only difference is that you strain the juice first.

- ❒ To make jelly, high pectin fruit is vitally important (have a look at the list on page 143 to check).
- ❒ When you strain the juice, don't squeeze the bag or push the pulp through.
- ❒ Use a damp bag. A dry bag absorbs too much juice.
- ❒ Don't stop at sweet jellies; savoury and herb jellies are delicious too.

Four Easy Steps

There is something magical about making jelly. Almost before your eyes, a mixture of fruit juice and sugar becomes a jelly that drops like a jewel from your spoon.

- ❒ Simmer your fruit until all the juice has come out of it, then let it drain through a jelly bag, an old clean pillowcase or a colander lined with a cloth. Leave the fruit to drain for at least 12 hours.
- ❒ When the fruit has finished draining, measure the juice and warm the right quantity of granulated sugar (see "The Magic of Sugar" on page 142).

- ❐ If you have more than 6 cups (1.5 L) of juice, divide the mixture into two batches.
- ❐ From here on, making jelly is exactly like making jam (see page 144 for the rest of the steps).

Tasty Jelly Ideas

- **Apple** and pineapple; cranberry
- **Grape** and cinnamon; red wine, brandy and cardamon seeds
- **Raspberry** and gooseberry; red, white or black currant
- **Orange** and port wine; grapefruit

In 1775, the French government offered a prize of 12,000 francs to anyone who could invent a way to preserve food so it could travel with the army. In 1810, François Appert patented a method of boiling the food in the container to set up a vacuum seal. This method evolved into the one we use today.

Herb Jelly

A plain apple jelly makes a wonderful base for herbs, savoury or sweet. Try adding a handful of one of the following herbs as you simmer the mixture:

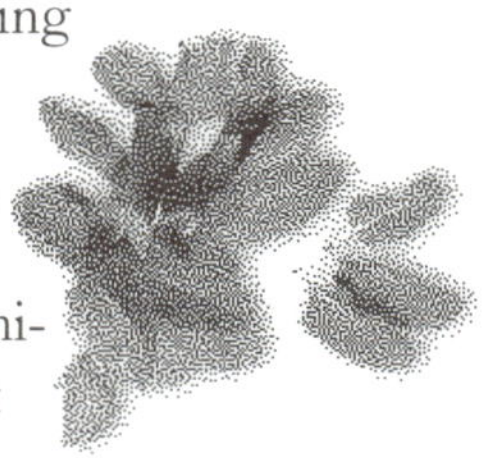

- **Savoury Jellies**: mint, basil, rosemary, sage, thyme
- **Sweet Jellies**: lavender flower petals, scented geranium leaves (rose, apple, peppermint, lemon), sweet violet

Cook's Tip

Is the weather so warm you can't bear to be in the kitchen, let alone stand over a hot stove making jam? Wash and dry the fruit, and store it in plastic containers in the freezer. Now jam making can wait until November!

Marmalade

Zippy, tangy, crystal-clear and loaded with peel, nothing beats homemade marmalade for its cheerful taste and glowing, golden colour. If you prefer your marmalade on the sweeter side, use the full amount of sugar. If you like a little sharpness to wake up your day, use less.

- ❐ Chop the fruit on a plate rather than on a board so you don't lose any of the juices.

Jamaican Red Pepper Jelly

A tropical treat, sweet and hot, that makes a perfect accompaniment for meat, fish, salads - even egg dishes.

9	red peppers
1	banana chile (yellow wax pepper)
1½ cups / *375 ml*	Rogers Granulated Sugar
½ cup / *125 ml*	cider vinegar

Take out the stem and seeds from the red peppers and banana chili. Put them into a food processor and mince together.

Now put the mixture into a large saucepan and bring slowly to a boil, stirring to dissolve the sugar.

Simmer until the mixture thickens, about 20 - 30 minutes. Pour into jars and seal

The word marmalade comes from the Portuguese *marmelada*, meaning "quinces cooked with sugar or honey." It was actually a Scot from Dundee, in about 1790, who came up with the idea of making marmalade from citrus fruit.

The name "grapefruit" comes from the way the fruit hangs in clusters.

- The pith contains a lot of natural pectin, but be sure it goes into a cheesecloth bag and not straight into the mixture or it will make the marmalade bitter.
- It's important to leave marmalade standing for 10 minutes before pouring it into the jars. There are a lot of fruit chunks in it, and this will stop them from rising to the top.

Marmalade Sauce

Marmalade sauce is delicious served hot with dessert, or cold with ice cream. It is also easy to make: simply boil together 1 cup (250 ml) of your homemade marmalade and ½ cup (125 ml) of wine, brandy or whisky. When the mixture reaches the boiling point, strain it through a sieve.

Seville Orange Marmalade

Seville Orange Marmalade

1 quart / *2.25 L*	water
1	lemon
2 lbs / *900 g*	Seville oranges
4 lbs / *1.8 kg*	Rogers Granulated Sugar
1 tsp / *5 ml*	butter

One of the great classic preserves that is easy to make at home. Buy the bittersweet Seville oranges in January when they are available, and celebrate breakfast right through the year.

MEASURE THE WATER into a large preserving pan. Cut the lemon and oranges in half, squeeze and add the juice to the water.

SCOOP THE FLESH, pips and excess pith from the orange peel with a large spoon.

LOOSELY TIE THIS MATERIAL in a square of doubled cheesecloth with some string to make a little bag. Tie the string to the pan's handle. Cut the peel halves into quarters then into strips of your preferred size. We like them chunky. Add the peel to the water and immerse the cheesecloth bag in the liquid.

BRING THE UNCOVERED LIQUID to the simmering point and simmer gently for about 2 hours. Remove the cheesecloth bag, let it cool and then squeeze out the pectin juice into the liquid. Leave to soak overnight.

TRANSFER THE MIXTURE to another container. Return 6 cups (1.5 L) of the stirred mixture to the pan and bring to a simmer. Add 6 cups (1.5 L) of warmed granulated sugar to the pan and stir the mixture occasionally over low heat until the sugar crystals have completely dissolved. Now increase the heat and keep to a rolling boil for at least 30 minutes, stirring frequently until the setting point is reached (if you are unsure, see the seven simple steps for jam on page 144).

STIR IN THE BUTTER. Let the marmalade stand for 15 minutes before pouring it into the jars. Seal and label.

Tasty Marmalade Ideas

- **Orange** with molasses; preserved ginger; brandy
- **Lemon** with mint; mandarins; rhubarb
- **Lime** with rum
- **Grapefruit** with pineapple

Take a look at page 85 for a tasty turkey, bacon and chutney sandwich.

Add spice to baked chicken or pork chops with a spoonful of chutney.

Chutneys

Chutneys, thick and savoury with fruit and spices, are easy to make and delicious to eat. Keep a few jars in the pantry - or in any other cool, dry, dark place - and you will be ready to add instant spicy interest to any meal.

- White vinegar gives a lighter colour and less intense flavour.
- Use jars with clip-on glass lids or plastic coated screw-tops - the vinegar will corrode metal lids.
- Leave chutney to mature for at least two months before you eat it (if you can wait that long!).

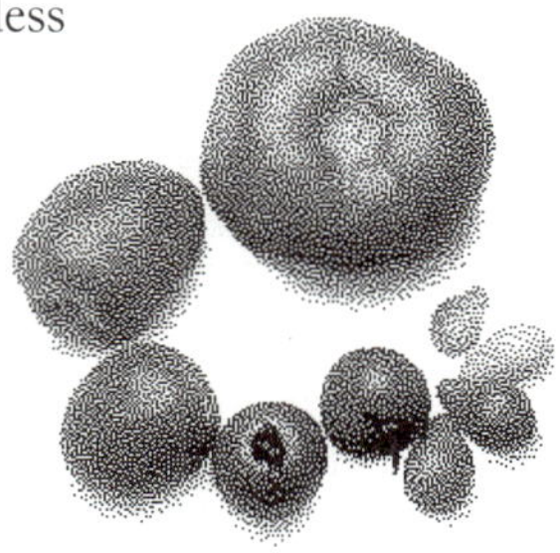

Who are the most enthusiastic home preservers? According to research, people in Saskatchewan are the leaders, with Manitobans in second place.

Chunky Tomato Chutney

Chutney enhances so many dishes! Cook lots of this recipe, made from green tomatoes, currants and spices, so you have some to give away. This recipe makes 6, ½ pint (250 ml) jars of chutney.

12 cups / *3 L*	cubed green tomatoes
3 cups / *750 ml*	currants
2¼ cups / *550 ml*	Rogers Best Brown Sugar
2 cups / *500 ml*	cider vinegar
1 tbsp / *15 ml*	salt
1	large onion, chopped
1	garlic clove, chopped
2 tsp / *10 ml*	ground allspice
1 tsp / *5 ml*	ground ginger
1 tsp / *5 ml*	crushed black pepper
½ tsp / *2.5 ml*	dried chile peppers

Prepare your jars and warm the sugar as you would for jam.

Mix the tomatoes, currants, sugar and vinegar in a large pan and cook over low heat, stirring frequently, until the sugar has dissolved.

Add the remaining ingredients and mix well.

Increase the heat and simmer until it becomes thick, approximately 1½ to 2 hours. Stir the mixture often. To test if the chutney's ready, draw a wooden spoon across the bottom of the pan. If it leaves a clean line, the chutney's ready to bottle.

Spoon into hot, sterilized jars and seal.

Chunky Tomato Chutney

When you've gathered your fruit but need some inspiration for the next stage, these books will have what you're looking for:

Clearly Delicious
by Elisabeth Lambert Ortiz
Toronto:
Macmillan Canada, 1994

Glorious photographs and clear directions make this one a winner. Banana Chutney, Grapefruit and Ginger Marmalade, Pear and Cashew Conserve... there's enough in this book to keep you busy all through the year.

The Encyclopaedia of Homemade Preserves
by Myra Street
Toronto:
Elan Press, 1996

There's something for everyone here. Contains recipes for 150 different jams, jellies and other condiments - including conserves, chutneys, curds and pickles.

Preserving
by Oded Schwartz
The Reader's Digest Association (Canada) Ltd., 1996

The ultimate illustrated guide to every type of preserve. Beautiful colour illustrations, clear instructions and wide-ranging recipes make this book essential for the serious preserver.

It is best to use ground spices when making chutney. If you want to use whole spices, tie them in a cheesecloth bag and float it in the mixture.

Tasty Chutney Ideas

- Apple and pineapple; walnuts; dried apricots
- Mango and dates; preserved ginger and raisins; dry chiles
- Tomato and chiles, molasses and fresh ginger; sultanas; dates

*"September blow soft,
till the fruit's in the loft."*

16th-Century Proverb

I N D E X

D

E

L

M

N

O

P

Q

R

S

T

V

W

Y

"Some men live to eat, while I eat to live."

Socrates